W9-AXH-343

More Praise for *Theodore Roosevelt on Leadership*

"James Strock has written the book that Theodore Roosevelt's admirers have been waiting for—a clear, concise, and compelling account of TR's philosophy of living and working. This is a book that you will want to read and re-read."

—John Allen Gable, Ph.D.,
executive director, Theodore Roosevelt Association

"As rousing and inspirational as its protean subject, *Theodore Roosevelt on Leadership* is ideally timed—not only to coincide with the centennial of America's first modern president, but to combat the cynicism and artifice that beset our culture. In mining TR's life for the gold of individual character and national purpose, James Strock gives us a memorable portrait of an unforgettable American."

—Richard Norton Smith,
presidential historian

"This captivating volume is a must-read for people in business, the nonprofit sector, and government who cannot achieve their goals without inspiring others."

—Carla A. Hills,
chair and CEO of Hills & Company,
International Consultants; former U.S. Trade Ambassador
and U.S. Secretary of Housing and Urban Development

"James Strock's incredible account of Theodore Roosevelt's inspirational and strategic leadership of our country will become a primer for today's business and governmental executive in sustaining our global economy. His knowledge and interpretation of TR's strength, courage, and vision is unsurpassed. I thoroughly recommend this as required reading for both the aspiring manager and the seasoned executive."

—Carl D. Perry,
president and CEO, Enova Systems Inc.

"I highly recommend this insightful account of the leadership philosophies that defined a truly extraordinary leader and one of our most dynamic (and sometimes controversial) presidents. An exhilarating read for every executive and aspiring top executive—made particularly interesting by illustrative, fascinating vignettes from TR's life."

—Malcolm R. Currie,
chairman and CEO (ret.), Hughes Aircraft Co.

"In a time when perception is regarded as reality, it is nice to be reminded of the real thing. TR didn't know about spin or use phrases like 'maximizing goals.' Common sense and tenacity, combined with the leadership principles illustrated in this inspiring book, are timeless and irresistible."

—John Milius,
Hollywood writer and director

"No one exemplified management ability more than Theodore Roosevelt, the greatest executive of his era, whose extraordinary leadership talents are so well documented in James Strock's book. *Theodore Roosevelt on Leadership* is an outstanding reference manual for rising leaders."

—Putney Westerfield,
chairman emeritus, Boyden International;
former publisher, *Fortune*

"The values and principles that made Theodore Roosevelt such a great leader are as relevant today as they were during his lifetime. In this very readable book, James Strock shows readers how they can apply TR's remarkable leadership qualities to their own lives and careers."

—George Montgomery,
investment banker and trustee of Environmental Defense

"James Strock has done a masterful job of drawing strategic leadership lessons from the life of TR and serving them up to readers for productive application in their businesses and their lives. TR's leadership has never been more relevant than in today's 'white-knuckle' business arena. The timing for this work is perfect!"

—Dave Anderson,
president, LearntoLead.com

THEODORE ROOSEVELT ON LEADERSHIP

Executive Lessons from the Bully Pulpit

JAMES M. STROCK

FORUM
An Imprint of Prima Publishing

FORUM
An Imprint of Prima Publishing
3000 Lava Ridge Court
Roseville, CA 95661

Strock, James M.
Theodore Roosevelt on leadership : executive lessons from the bully pulpit / James M. Strock.
p. cm. — (On leadership series)
Includes bibliographical references (p.) and index.
ISBN 0-7615-2661-7
1. Roosevelt, Theodore, 1858–1919. 2. Political leadership—United States—History—20th century. 3. United States—Politics and government—1901–1909. 4. Management—United States—Case studies. I. Title. II. Series.
E757.S93 2001
973.91'1—dc21 00-066242

01 02 03 HH 10 9 8 7 6 5 4 3 2 1
Printed in the United States of America

To the newest Americans

There is always a tendency to believe that a hundred small men can furnish leadership equal to that of one big man. That is not so. . . . Nothing can fully take the place of the indispensable work of leadership.

—THEODORE ROOSEVELT

If I have anything at all resembling genius, it is in the gift for leadership. . . . To tell the truth, I like to believe that, by what I have accomplished without *great gifts, I may be a source of encouragement to American[s].*

—THEODORE ROOSEVELT

CONTENTS

PROLOGUE: SEPTEMBER 1901

THE DAWN OF the twentieth century was a time for the United States to take stock.

The American Experiment was remarkably new. The national government, which was the boldest attempt to establish a republican democracy in history, had been established just over a hundred years before. The bloody Civil War that roiled the nation between 1861 and 1865 left lingering legacies, still felt keenly in American life at the turn of the twentieth century.

The nineteenth century had been a time of unmatched change. The United States—Lincoln's calculated use of the singular was becoming more comfortably customary with the passage of time—was hurtling headlong toward its destiny. In 1800 the nation encompassed 13 states and 5 million Americans; by 1900 it had expanded inexorably westward, with 45 states and 76 million people.

It is not surprising that the *New York Times* declared, on January 1, 1900, that the twentieth century would bring "a brighter dawn of civilization."

Perhaps no group was more keenly aware of the progress than those older Americans whose lives spanned virtually the entirety of American history. In Philadelphia, Elizabeth Cooper McIntyre was ninety-nine years old in 1900, having been born in the year that President John Adams led the move of the capital from Philadelphia to Washington, D.C. In the words of Judy Crichton:

> [Mrs. McIntyre] could remember when there were no fireboxes or friction matches, no postage stamps or envelopes, when communication was as slow as it was uncertain and signaling was done from town to town by means of fires on mountaintops or waving flags. In her youth it had taken six weeks to get news from Europe; now it took six seconds. Mrs. McIntyre had seen the coming of the cable, the telegraph and telephone, trolleys and high-speed trains. . . . Many Americans now had ice in the summer and heat in the winter and artificial light—kerosene, gas, or electric—which could be summoned any time of night or day. There were modern coal stoves and bathtubs with running water and water closets that flushed waste away.

The *Indianapolis Journal* noted on January 7, 1900: "No single feature of nineteenth-century progress has been more remarkable or more significant of advancing civilization than the improvement in the condition of the working classes." The writer added that in 1800, slavery existed not only in the United States but also in the West Indies and South America. Readers likely needed no reminder that this evil institution had been eradicated a mere generation before in the United States, only in 1888 in Brazil, and that it functioned in full force in other parts of the world of 1900.

As everyday Americans celebrated the dramatic progress in their midst, from a distance other nations watched the United States unmistakably emerging onto the world stage. Only Russia and Canada swept across larger land areas.

Among Western nations, only Russia had a larger population. At the time of Queen Victoria's death in January 1901 the British Empire was at its zenith, asserting jurisdiction over approximately one-quarter of the earth's population (400 million people out of 1.6 billion estimated total) and land mass. London was the world's most important city. The incomparable British naval fleet implicitly stood watch over its rambunctious offspring, giving America time in which to grow, largely unmolested amidst the machinations of great power politics.

By 1900 the U.S. economy was the most productive in the history of the world. Historian John Milton Cooper presents some indicators:

> American commerce, transportation, industry, and agriculture were wonders of the world. By almost any measure of economic performance, the United States excelled. Steel production in 1900 amounted to over ten million tons, more than a third higher than Germany's, the closest competitor. Railroad trackage stretched to 167,000 miles, or one-third of the world's total. Per-capita income was estimated at $569, far above the nearest rival, Britain. Literacy rates stood at nearly 90 percent of the populace. The country had over 2,200 newspapers and nearly one thousand colleges and universities, with a combined student body of nearly 240,000. School enrollment amounted to over sixteen million pupils—the world's largest in both numbers and percentage of the population. Of those students, nearly one hundred thousand would graduate from secondary schools in 1900, also ahead of every other nation in numbers and percentages, and nearly double the total in 1890.

The new economy required new industrial and financial institutions. On March 3, 1901, the legendary financier J. P. Morgan announced the organization of the largest corporation in the world, to be called United States Steel. It would be capitalized at $1.4 billion. In contrast, the annual budget of the entire federal government was approximately $350 million.

EMBLEMATIC OF the optimism of the new century was the Pan-American Exposition, open from May to November 1901, in Buffalo, New York.

The Buffalo exposition was the latest in a series of international fairs built on the spectacular success of the Crystal Palace Exposition held in London in 1851. Historians Thomas Leary and Elizabeth Sholes write of the experience of the 8 million visitors to the 1901 exposition:

> They were dazzled by an array of monumental buildings housing hundreds of exhibits of their time and place. If overwhelmed by this array, they could take refuge in the Midway with its funhouses, its amusements, and exotic curiosities. At night, the weary visitor could enjoy an electrical spectacle. *Harper's Weekly* said the best part of the Pan-Am was the summer night sky, the people, the beauty of the illuminated lagoons, and the electric lights everywhere.

Eight million visitors. The visitors made up a group larger than ten percent of the entire U.S. population. A comparable percentage today would mean nearly 30 million visitors—which is all but unimaginable, if only because our lives provide so many alternative avenues of entertainment and diversion. From the perspective of our time, Leary and Sholes find the Buffalo exposition to have been "a tribute to the rampant materialism and imperialism," but they also recognize that it "was also probably the most incredible experience an ordinary person ever had."

Indeed it was. Commonplaces of our time, such as electric lighting piercing the evening sky, were far from commonplace in the America of 1901. Most Americans' lives were much harder, much more circumscribed than today. Electric power was beginning to be used in homes but was limited to a relative handful of the wealthy in major cities. Lighting was largely from oil lamps and lanterns of various types. There was no home refrigeration as we now know it. Stoves were heated by coal or wood, replenished constantly. Food was not available at neighborhood grocery stores, prepared and wrapped in the protective packaging to which we have become accustomed. Household work was unmitigated drudgery, from heating "sad irons" on the stove to handscrubbing of laundry. In many places, especially rural areas, water was hand-pumped out of doors. The outhouse was a familiar appurtenance. Even for those with money, there were no chain stores or convenience stores or shopping centers to which to turn spontaneously for assistance.

Personal mobility had yet to be transformed by the internal combustion engine; a mere 8,000 automobiles were registered in the United States in 1900. Cooper reports that there was only one mile of smooth paved road in the entire nation. Airplanes were still in the future. Neither was the isolation broken by telephones. There were only 1,356 telephones in the entire nation at the turn of the century, and they were limited to the government, the rich, and some businesses.

Though Americans had achieved the highest per capita income in the world—and a small elite accumulated epic fortunes—the hourly manufacturing wage in 1900, in today's dollars, was $3.43. Workplace regulation, beginning with child labor and industrial safety, was all but nonexistent. Buffers against privation—such as public and private health insurance, unemployment insurance, pension plans, and Social Security—did not exist in forms we would recognize.

The six-day workweek—often built on ten-hour days—was the norm for many Americans. The options for applying any remaining leisure time were quite limited by twenty-first-century standards.

There were no televisions or radios, much less computers. Cinema was not an option. Ordinary people were of necessity rather self-sufficient in entertaining themselves, their families, and friends. They might derive pleasure from walking, from telling stories, from reading books and plays and poetry aloud, from various participatory games, and from church services and associated social events.

Perhaps the most expressive indicators are those of life expectancy: At the turn of the century, it was forty-seven for males, fifty-one for females. These numbers—almost thirty years below what Americans of the early twenty-first century can assume—reflect not only the difficulties of daily life, but also the limitations of health and hygiene of the time.

Childbirth remained hazardous: Perhaps 1 in 200 women died in childbirth in America in 1900, compared to 1 in 10,000 today. Infant mortality was staggering; by some estimates as many as 1 in 10 children died before their first birthday, and in some regions the number rose to as many as 1 in 4. Among the general population, deaths were common from typhoid, diphtheria, influenza, polio, meningitis, pneumonia, and tuberculosis.

The bright lights of the Pan-American Exposition must have looked very bright indeed to the Americans of 1901.

INEVITABLY, THE POLITICAL leaders of the day were drawn to Buffalo.

The most important was the president of the United States, William McKinley, who had postponed his visit from the May opening to September in deference to the delicate health of his beloved wife, Ida, an epileptic.

McKinley was at the summit of his career. Affectionately called "the Major," a socially acceptable allusion to his commendable military service in the Civil War, the often-underestimated Ohio politician swept into a second term on

November 6, 1900. His opponent, Democrat William Jennings Bryan of Nebraska, managed to carry only the "Solid South" and four sparsely populated western states—even losing, in journalist Mark Sullivan's succinct rendition, "his own state, his own city and his own precinct."

Today presidential polls occasionally distinguish "white males" as one of several categories of voters; in 1900 white males were the predominant category. Fewer than half of the adult population were legally eligible to vote. Only about five percent of American women—located in desolate Wyoming, Idaho, Colorado, and Utah—had been granted the franchise. African-Americans and many economically disadvantaged whites were barred by various devices from voting in the South, as were numerous new immigrants in the North.

The federal government's role in daily life was limited, almost beyond our imagination a century later. An observer at the time explained:

> We have been free from any great catastrophe; and, as a nation, have been largely engaged in getting and spending. Until the national income tax was imposed [by a constitutional amendment ratified in 1913], a man might go from the cradle to the grave without realizing that he had any relation with the National Government, much less that he owed it any duty. The national taxes were for the most part . . . indirect. There was no compulsory military service and our citizens came naturally to think of the nation as a benevolent institution from which much was to be expected and to which nothing should be given in terms of treasure or service.

This state of affairs should not be read as diminishing the achievement of the McKinley ticket in 1900, which included the young governor of New York, Theodore Roosevelt, for vice president. Their hard-fought campaign earned the approval of the electorate as it then stood—remarkably inclusive by the standards of their time. Though bolshevism and fascism were yet to arise from the bloody puddles of the First World War, the swiftness of socioeconomic change and a widespread fear of anarchism were prompting many thoughtful people to take politics increasingly seriously.

McKinley's visit was scheduled for Thursday, September 5, and Friday, September 6. He toured the exposition and nearby attractions, delivering several speeches. Methodically taking hold of the moment, McKinley gingerly hinted at reform of the most controversial economic policy of the day: the tariff schedule that limited imports and was the main source of federal government revenue and power in the post–Civil War years.

On Friday afternoon Mrs. McKinley became ill and withdrew from further events. At 4:30 P.M., President McKinley arrived at the Temple of Music. Dismissing the security concerns expressed by one of his aides, he insisted on greeting the public, who respectfully moved past, one by one, to shake his hand.

A boyish-looking twenty-five-year-old named Leon Czolgosz progressed unobtrusively through the extended receiving line, like a bacillus in a bloodstream. As Czolgosz reached the front, McKinley turned his gaze toward him, extending his hand. Czolgosz's outstretched right hand, shrouded by a handkerchief, fired a concealed pistol twice into McKinley's abdomen at point-blank range. The preternaturally dignified president, often compared in life to a statue, managed to "straighten up, and pressing his lips together, give Czolgosz the most scornful and contemptuous look possible to imagine." Then his stout body gave way.

At that moment Vice President Roosevelt was the guest of the Vermont Fish and Game League on Isle la Motte in Lake Champlain. As the afternoon came to a close, he was at a lawn reception outside the home of his host, former governor

Nelson Fisk. Fisk was called into the house to take a long-distance telephone call; Roosevelt was soon summoned. As the vice president disappeared inside, the locks tumbled shut in his wake, unmistakably breaking the informality of the occasion. Some in the crowd, sensing the somber undercurrent, likely recalled that McKinley himself had been the guest at a similar occasion, at the same place, with many of the same people, four years earlier.

Informed of the McKinley shooting, as yet unsure of the severity of his wounds, Roosevelt departed at once for Buffalo.

Over the next several days McKinley rallied. On Tuesday, September 10, Roosevelt, believing him to be "practically out of danger," departed Buffalo for the Adirondacks, also in his home state of New York. The distant, isolated destination was selected, at least in part, to reassure the nation of the president's recovery.

On Friday, September 13, after climbing Mount Tahawus, Roosevelt paused with his small party for an early afternoon lunch near a lake. Looking up, he later recalled, "I saw a guide coming out of the woods on our trail from below. I felt at once that he had bad news, and, sure enough, he handed me a telegram saying that the President's condition was much worse and that I must come to Buffalo immediately." The vice president was fully fifty miles from the nearest railroad station, ten miles from the nearest telephone. Walking and then riding on wilderness trails and roads into and through the night, Roosevelt constantly urged his drivers to press the limits of their relayed horses into the darkness, on treacherous, sometimes boarded, roads: "Push along! Hurry up! Go faster!" Finally reaching the train station at dawn on Saturday, Roosevelt learned that McKinley had died. He boarded a special train for the final leg of his fateful journey.

On the afternoon of Saturday, September 14, having undertaken the 440-mile trip from his Adirondack lunch at breakneck speed, he reached Buffalo. Shortly thereafter, standing before a local judge in a private home, surrounded by members of McKinley's cabinet, Theodore Roosevelt took the oath confirming his accession to the presidency of the United States.

IN SEPTEMBER 1901, for only the fifth time in American history, a vice president succeeded to the presidency following the death of the incumbent. In the midst of widespread and heartfelt grief at the loss of McKinley, people sensed that executive power would henceforth be wielded by a very different, rather unconventional leader. Years before he was a national candidate, Roosevelt wrote with unconscious prescience of presidential tickets: "It has . . . frequently happened that the two candidates have been totally dissimilar in character and even in party principle. Very odd results have followed in more than one instance."

Certainly the results were striking in this instance. At forty-two, just weeks from his next birthday on October 27, Theodore Roosevelt became and remains the youngest person to assume the presidency. In little more than four years he had vaulted from a subcabinet post in the executive bureaucracy into the White House. The personality of the man was every bit as extraordinary as his rise.

McKinley was a traditional figure of calculated reserve, representing the burden of the past of the Civil War generation, indelibly marked by the turbulence of the 1860s. Roosevelt represented the rising generation. Born in 1858, he shared many traits of America itself at the dawn of the twentieth century: Each was improbable, uninhibited, and unruly—with an endearing touch of the unexpected.

Like the nation itself, Roosevelt was many-sided and impossible to ignore. He was "a steam engine in trousers," "pure act," "the child," "a child of seven," a "violent and spasmodic mind," "the typical American." A distinguished foreign visitor to the Roosevelt White House exclaimed, "My dear fellow, do you know the two most extraordinary things I have seen in your country? Niagara Falls and the President of the United States—both great wonders of nature!" Author Richard Washburn Child said, "His personality so crowds the room that the walls are worn thin and threaten to burst outward. You go to the White House, you shake hands with Roosevelt and hear him talk—and then go home to wring the personality out of your clothes." The charge of his physical presence led to frequent comparisons to those new, exciting, as yet largely mysterious forces, electricity and radioactivity.

TR—he was the first president publicly referred to by his initials—stood at five feet nine inches, likely weighing at the time a shade under 200 pounds. He was physically powerful, distinguished by an immense, disproportionate chest, the result of years of disciplined exercise and ceaseless exertion. His hands and feet were tapered, delicate by comparison. They were mute, unmistakable reminders that his body—described in the far away past as a "pitiful specimen"—was the product more of will than nature.

Roosevelt's will had brought him a long way. A diffident boy, wobbly on pipe-stem legs, too weak to offer more than feeble resistance to adolescent bullies, he became a deputy sheriff in the Dakota Territory and the heroic leader of the Rough Riders fighting in Cuba during the Spanish-American War. Schooled at home by tutors for reasons of health, he graduated Phi Beta Kappa from Harvard. Raised in the "Silk Stocking" district of Manhattan, he transformed himself from "tenderfoot" to respected rancher in the "Wild West," and explorer of parts unknown in the Amazon. A devoted outdoorsman with knowledge and love for nature rivaling that of specialists, he was an avid sportsman tending at times toward blood lust. Far from gifted as an athlete, he relentlessly pushed himself and others toward what he called "the strenuous life" and was a founder of the National Collegiate Athletic Association. The epitome of the man of action, he was also a man of thought who became president of the American Historical Association. Eager to assert the opinions gleaned from his manifold experiences and voracious reading, Roosevelt was astonishingly prolific, writing more than thirty volumes—estimated at 2.5 million words, reaching perhaps 18 million if his thousands of letters are included. While achieving what one contemporary called "the most interesting career ever vouchsafed to any American," he was an unabashedly devoted husband and father; even the most malicious among his legion of critics would not suggest otherwise.

As soon as this force of nature charged into the Executive Mansion (which he would soon officially rename the White House), he would bend and ultimately break the previous bounds of his new office, as he had done throughout his career. If much of Roosevelt's presidential legacy appears commonplace today, that is arguably the greatest tribute to its ongoing significance.

Roosevelt created the modern presidency. He labeled it—"the bully pulpit"—and gave it life. TR followed the advice of his friend and confidant Massachusetts senator Henry Cabot Lodge, making customs by breaking them. He was the first president to describe the domestic programs of his administration in a single phrase to convey his vision: the "Square Deal." Bringing the curtain down on an era when government was viewed as the handmaiden, if not the courtesan, of regnant financial and industrial combinations, Roosevelt declared that the federal government had a transcendent, incontrovertible role as the representative and guardian of the public interest. He was the first president to apply federal government authority on behalf of organized labor in a dispute with management. His leadership was indispensable in securing significant national regulation of railroads. In the wake of public outrage following the publication of Upton Sinclair's *The Jungle,* TR effectuated enactment of the Meat Inspection Act. His administration fathered the Pure Food and Drug Act and the Federal Employer's Liability Act.

His eye for the future sharpened by his familiarity with the past, Roosevelt undertook an unprecedented agenda of natural resources conservation—embracing 150 million acres of land into federal protection—presaging future generations' environmental consciousness. Understanding that sustained progress would depend at least as much on the states as the federal government, TR brought the nation's governors together in Washington, for the first time, for a conference on conservation. As his presidency wound down, recognizing that nature heeds no national boundaries, he laid the groundwork for the first international environmental conference.

Roosevelt incarnated America's entrance onto the world stage of the twentieth century. The nation itself, like a strong individual, should "speak softly and carry a big stick; you will go far." He "took" the Panama Canal while Congress debated, making the United States the symbolic and strategic link between the Atlantic and Pacific Oceans. He led Americans into reluctant assumption of great power status, building a world-class naval fleet. His conspicuous zest in brandishing the "Big Stick" enabled critics to credibly deplore him as a dangerous warmonger; he definitively countered that during his nearly eight years as president, "not one shot had been fired against a foreign foe." This most combative of men would be the first American to receive the Nobel Peace Prize. (In January 2001, more than a century after his celebrated heroism in the Spanish-American War, Roosevelt posthumously was accorded the Medal of Honor. TR now stands as the sole president awarded the Medal of Honor, the only person to achieve America's highest military decoration *and* the Nobel Peace Prize, and, along with General Douglas MacArthur's father, Arthur, one of two Medal of Honor winners whose sons who would earn the same military recognition.)

While expanding the federal government's role at home and abroad, Roosevelt paid close attention to the bottom line. As in other settings, his approach was to keep his eyes on the stars—but his feet on the ground. His appointments were lauded by independent experts as being the best in memory; some of his departments were seen as at least as efficient as any private sector enterprises. TR established the now-familiar approach of tasking outside commissions with the review and reform of government spending. He proudly claimed that his administration reduced the national debt by $90 million.

ROOSEVELT, APTLY DESCRIBED as a "preacher militant," recast the presidency as a seat of moral leadership. If presidents had such a role in the past, it was at best episodic and altogether absent in the post–Civil War years. Roosevelt believed that the more a leader's actions might affect the lives of others, the more that others must demand that a leader's values reflect what he called "character." In a democracy, where the people are sovereign, the leaders necessarily reflect the character of the people. Roosevelt declared: "Sometimes I hear our countrymen . . . abroad saying: 'Oh, you mustn't judge us by our politicians.' I always want to interrupt and answer: 'You *must* judge us by our politicians.'"

Today few Americans would wish to be judged by their politicians—or, for that matter, by leaders in the corporate or nonprofit sector. That sense, as much as deficient historical teaching, may underlie a 1993 poll finding that nearly sixty percent of American high school seniors had never heard of Theodore Roosevelt. At the turn of the twenty-first century interest in TR appears to be on the rise. A 2000 survey of historians for the C-SPAN cable television network ranked the presidency of Theodore Roosevelt fourth in overall accomplishment, below only those of Washington, Lincoln, and Franklin Roosevelt. Intriguingly, a simultaneous poll of C-SPAN viewers ranked TR third, perhaps reflecting fascination with his leadership style and recognition of similarities between his time and our own.

Parts of Roosevelt's political legacy are being rediscovered today. In our eyes, the Grand Canyon he saved may be an even more significant monument to his leadership than his visage on Mount Rushmore. In another era of record levels of immigration we understand his sense of urgency in redefining "Americanism" to ensure that the newest Americans not only bolster the economy but also strengthen the fabric of the national tapestry. His declamations against "special interest" domination of politics sound uncannily current. His commitment to preserve national values by reforming institutions in the midst of unprecedented change strikes a chord. Against the backdrop of today's Information Age abundance and bustle Roosevelt's distant warning brings us up short: "The things that will destroy America are prosperity-at-any-price, safety-first instead of duty-first, the love of soft living, and the get-rich-quick theory of life."

Roosevelt, who routinely turned to history for guidance, nonetheless cautioned: "There is nothing cheaper than to sneer at and belittle the great men and great deeds and great thoughts of a bygone time—unless it is to magnify them and to ascribe preposterous and impossible virtues to the period." Times change, and a key to useful learning is to isolate what he called the "essentials."

Theodore Roosevelt was born to the top echelon of economic and social privilege, yet he regarded himself as a self-made figure. Given that most of the qualities of leadership with which he is identified were developed by him in an act of will, the characterization is apt. As such, Roosevelt intended that his life offer lessons of leadership from which others might learn. Gifford Pinchot, an energetic if erratic conservationist and politician who played a key supporting role through much of Roosevelt's career, explained: "The people loved Roosevelt because he was like them. In him the common qualities were lifted to a higher tension and a greater power, but they were still the same. . . . He was like the rest of us, except that there was so much more of him."

Peter Drucker, perhaps the most respected management theorist of our time, frequently educates executives by turning to exemplars from politics or the military—including Lincoln, Franklin Roosevelt, Generals Grant and Patton, and others. The breadth of the stages on which they acted, the turbulent times they mastered, and the great consequences—for good or for ill—of their leadership provide lessons applicable to executives in various settings.

Theodore Roosevelt unquestionably offers lessons as a leader. Pinchot's verdict—"The gift of leadership belonged to him in supreme degree"—has been echoed by others then and since. There are advantages in studying TR: He consciously developed his leadership skills, performed on a public stage, and recorded many of his thoughts and practices in writing. He believed the power of his example to be one of his most important services as a leader. As Roosevelt wrote of General Grant, "It is part of the man's greatness that now we can use his career purely for illustration."

ENTREPRENEURS ARE MARKED by the ability to paint a vision and move others toward its actualization. The greater the vision, the more radical the departure, and the more skill is required in persuasion. Some of their most significant abilities may not lend themselves to quantitative measurement.

Managers tend to be more "down to earth." Their work translates the visions of the entrepreneur into quantifiable inputs and outputs, affixing individual accountability for performance. Entrepreneurial and managerial talents must be brought within a single harness if an organization is to succeed over time in a rapidly changing environment.

Effective leaders must have the ability to work in both realms. They must be capable of understanding and communicating effectively with outside groups affecting the enterprise. They must make certain that their internal and external communications are in sync. Leaders, like others, tend to have greater or lesser abilities in some areas than others. Successful leaders assemble and motivate teams eliciting the best from each person, with the group's effort representing far more than the sum of the parts.

Roosevelt was striking in his abilities to perform in all areas necessary for leadership at the highest level.

The trajectory of TR's career, unconventional in its time, is less unfamiliar to us today. In our time an individual no longer has the realistic expectation of maintaining one job, for the same organization, over the entirety of a working life. Roosevelt, a century ago, took an entrepreneur's approach to living; in today's parlance, he followed Tom Peters's philosophy of being the CEO of "yourself.com."

Roosevelt holds our attention, because in addition to being an effective leader, he strove to be a moral one. He was a spectacular exception to Lord Acton's timeless injunction: "Power tends to corrupt, and absolute power corrupts absolutely." TR arguably served most unselfishly when he held the greatest power. The preponderance of his actions that critics can credibly characterize as self-serving occurred when he held little or no direct power. His greatest act of self-abnegation was at his moment of supreme power—prospectively declining a third presidential term (then not barred by the Constitution) on the evening he decisively won the 1904 election.

Roosevelt equally was an exception to Acton's succeeding observation, "Great men are almost always bad men." Today there is much uncertainty as to how far we should demand that our leaders be held to account on a moral plane. One thing is clear: The greater the extent that a leader may affect the lives of others, the more we expect adherence to shared moral standards.

Roosevelt's achievements as an individual are breathtaking but something we can comprehend. Much less familiar, from our remove, is a leader who credibly, publicly attempts to frame his program as consistent with the Ten Commandments and the Golden Rule. In a new Gilded Age, when corporate and political leaders from the Oval Office on down routinely turn to lawyers and propagandists to justify activities that schoolchildren would recognize as violating one or more of the Decalogue, Roosevelt's example may be especially apt.

TR lived by a demanding if conventional moral code; he believed his example to be central to his capacity to define and apply his leadership along moral lines. Where lesser souls might hide behind oak-paneled doors to cover timidity, Roosevelt never hesitated to thrust himself squarely in harm's way if his personal intervention or example would serve his leadership—whether on the battlefield in Cuba, fighting corporate or union or congressional power, or as an eager passenger in those dangerous but exciting new technological marvels, the airplane and the submarine.

Roosevelt recognized that his robust advocacy of moral leadership threw his shortcomings and failures into sharp relief. At times his pursuit of "realizable ideals" emphasized the realizable to the detriment of the ideals. His clarion calls for "righteousness" could verge on self-righteousness; his penchant for action could metamorphose into ruthlessness. TR acknowledged, referring to one of his less defensible appointments, "In politics we have to do a great many things we ought not to do." His outraged, sometimes disproportionate reactions to critics who questioned the moral basis of his significant actions—such as the construction of the Panama Canal—inadvertently shed light on his own unresolved doubts.

Such defects are placed in appropriate perspective when one takes into account the boldness of his projects, his boyish enthusiasm, his willingness to learn and grow and forgive himself and others, and his unconquerable capacity to overcome tragedy and defeat. TR strove to transform himself into a leader worthy of the causes and people he would serve. He understood that the shared humanity revealed in his limitations and failures made his example all the more applicable and compelling.

In a speech at Santa Barbara, California, on May 9, 1903, Roosevelt declared: "The problems differ from generation to generation, but the qualities needed to solve them remain unchanged from world's end to world's end." In 1908, as he prepared to leave the presidency, he offered a valedictory: "[M]ost of all, I believe whatever value my service may have, comes even more from what I am than from what I do."

The overriding lesson of Theodore Roosevelt is that leadership is a way of life.

Part One

IN THE ARENA

It is not the critic who counts; not the man who points out how the strong man stumbles, or where the doer of deeds could have done better. The credit belongs to the man who is actually in the arena, whose face is marred by dust and sweat and blood; who strives valiantly; who errs, and comes short again and again, because there is no effort without error or shortcoming; who knows the great enthusiasms, the great devotions; who spends himself in a worthy cause; who at the best knows in the end the triumph of high achievement, and who at the worst, if he fails, at least fails while daring greatly, so that his place shall never be with those cold and timid souls who know neither victory nor defeat.

—Theodore Roosevelt

Chapter One

LEADING—WHEREVER YOU ARE

Do what you can, with what you have, where you are.

—Theodore Roosevelt

Whatsoever thy hand findeth to do, do it with thy might.

—Ecclesiastes, quoted by Owen Wister, describing Roosevelt

So many things appear inevitable in retrospect.

At first glance few phenomena appear more inevitable than the singular career of Theodore Roosevelt. Looking back on his ascent to the presidency, the path seems seamless, predestined. People seeking to learn from Roosevelt's example might be forgiven for initially imputing a high degree of calculation—if not cunning—to the protagonist himself.

To be sure, Roosevelt, like anyone ambitious for achievement, studiously examined the careers of others and weighed his own options thoughtfully. Nonetheless, one of the most striking aspects of his career is the absence of design.

A fundamental lesson of Roosevelt's leadership is his example of relentless attention to the job at hand, undisturbed by vain attempts to divine the consequences of his actions on his future prospects. Many of TR's critics, from his time through our own, have dismissed his declarations in this regard as naïve, trivial—nothing more than a shopworn, transparent cloak unconvincingly tossed across unbridled ambition, deceiving none but the credulous, perhaps including Roosevelt himself. In fact, however, as with other aspects of his approach to leadership, much of its power arises from its simplicity and transparency.

IN 1895, at the age of thirty-six, Roosevelt was appointed one of four members of the New York City Police Board. Granted the title of president on his first day, TR blew into the musty, comfortably corrupt bureaucracy with the force of a hurricane. While some (generally on the outside) found his influence refreshing, others (generally on the inside) found it unsettling.

Two noted journalists, Lincoln Steffens and Jacob Riis, worked at Roosevelt's side at the time. Seeking to understand TR's apparently inexhaustible activity at the Board (perhaps assuming the effort was disproportionate to the task), they wondered aloud whether it was an indicator of ambition—perhaps reaching all the way from the Mulberry Street police offices to the White House. They put the question to Roosevelt directly: was he working toward the presidency? Steffens recalled the robust reaction:

> TR leaped to his feet, ran around his desk, and fists clenched, teeth bared, he seemed about to strike or throttle Riis, who cowered away, amazed.
>
> "Don't you dare ask me that," TR yelled at Riis. "Don't you put such ideas into my head. No friend of mine would ever say a thing like that, you—you—"
>
> Riis's shocked face or TR's recollection that he had few friends as devoted as Jake Riis halted him. He backed away, came up again to Riis, and put his arm around his shoulder.

Then he beckoned me close and in an awed tone of voice explained.

"Never, never, you must never either of you ever remind a man at work on a political job that he may be president. It almost always kills him politically. He loses his nerve; he can't do his work; he gives up the very traits that are making him a possibility. I, for instance, I am going to do great things here, hard things that require all the courage, ability, work that I am capable of, and I can do them if I think of them alone. But if I get to thinking of what it might lead to— . . .

"I must be wanting to be president. Every young man does. But I won't let myself think about it. I'll be careful, calculating, cautious in word and act, and so—I'll beat myself. See?"

Roosevelt had not always followed this approach. Later in life, looking back on his precocious service in the New York Assembly (to which he was elected to three one-year terms, the first when he was twenty-three years old), he wrote:

> [A]t one period [I] began to believe that I had a future before me, and that it behooved me to be very far-sighted and scan each action carefully with a view to its possible effect on that future. This speedily made me useless to the public and an object of aversion to myself; and I then made up my mind that I would try not to think of the future at all, but would proceed on the assumption that each office I held would be the last I ever should hold, and I would confine myself to trying to do my work as well as possible while I held that office. I found that for me personally this was the only way in which I could either enjoy myself or render good service to the country, and I never afterwards deviated from this plan.

This approach requires, as a practical matter, that an individual be willfully self-contained, able to walk away without hesitation after putting one's position on the line for principle. Roosevelt wrote to a British journalist during his presidency:

> Although I have been pretty steadily in politics since I left college, I have always steadfastly refused to regard politics as a career, for save under exceptional circumstances I do not believe that any American can afford to try to make this his definite career in life. With us politics are of a distinctly kaleidoscopic nature. Nobody can tell when he will be upset; and if a man is to be of real use he ought to be able at times to philosophically accept defeat and to go on about some other kind of useful work, either permanently or at least temporarily until his chances again permit him to turn to political affairs. *Every office I have held I have quite sincerely believed would be the last I should hold.*

Roosevelt's maxim has application for leaders in every realm. His planning related not so much to his career as to his approach to life. Early on he recognized that the vagaries of fate are beyond the capacity of anyone to foresee, much less manage. TR understood that though the most brilliant cannot reliably calculate their own interest, those possessing commonplace gifts can discern their duty. In so doing they might have to act against their apparent path to advancement. Nonetheless they would be of better service in the present and more worthy of leadership roles in the future.

TR's approach assumes that the motivating purpose of leadership is service to others. Those aspiring to leadership should cultivate the characteristics he called "character": "decency" (including "morality . . . clean living, the faculty of treating fairly those round about, the qualities that make a man a decent husband, a decent father, a good neighbor, a good man to deal with or work beside"), "courage," and "common sense." A determined focus on the moral aspects of leadership is not only the right thing to do; it continuously strengthens and informs the practical aspects of the leader's work, keeping him attuned to the needs and wishes of others.

Roosevelt was not a naif—far from it. He knew that an individual might achieve a position of power following a series of self-interested career calculations. He believed that such means of advancement would likely mean that the "leader" would not be able to act on his own terms. Without such latitude an individual likely would not achieve the "disinterestedness" required to serve others unreservedly. In the spring of 1884 he expressed a view that would recur through the remainder of his life: "I will not stay in public life unless I can do so *on my own terms*; and my ideal—whether lived up to or not—is rather a high one."

A congressman of the era, Charles G. Washburn, explored Roosevelt's course of action in his book, *Theodore Roosevelt: The Logic of His Career.* Washburn, an admirer of TR who had known him since college days, presented his career as highly unconventional. He concluded that Roosevelt, whose name and career became synonymous with leadership, was not a "politician" in the pejorative sense suggesting self-interested opportunism.

The implications of Roosevelt's approach become evident when one views his career from his standpoint as he was going forward, rather than from our time looking back.

AS A "WHIPPERSNAPPER" assemblyman from the Silk Stocking district of Manhattan, TR, in his own words, "rose like a rocket." He publicly challenged corruption not only among the Democrats of Tammany Hall, but also within his own Republican Party. His verbal fusillades against the "wealthy criminal class" hit close to home, straining relations with patrons understood to be indispensable to advancement in the political system of the time.

In 1884, his third year in office, Roosevelt plunged headfirst into national politics. He assumed a conspicuous role in the intra-party challenge to the presumptive Republican presidential nominee, James G. Blaine of Maine. The "Plumed Knight" was the paradigm nonpareil of the corruption as well as roguish charm of Gilded Age politics. Win or lose, Roosevelt was placing himself in a political quandary. Blaine was nominated. TR returned to the fold, supporting him in the general election. Having previously offended the party leadership, he now disappointed his natural supporters among colleagues and friends (and some of his family) from the convention fight. The Republican national ticket was defeated in the November election.

As 1884 drew to a close, TR was politically marooned. He was exhausted from a series of personal tribulations. He declined renomination for his Assembly seat and offers of nomination for Congress. He withdrew from the East and from politics, living much of the time in the Dakota Badlands. With no clear prospects, concerned that he was politically "dead," he did his best in an entirely new venue. Immersing himself in the life of the frontier that was visibly vanishing by the year, Roosevelt built himself into the man we now recognize. Banishing the remnants of his childhood timidity and physical weakness, he emerged bronzed, muscular, hardened. Having begun as an East Coast "tenderfoot" whose Western wardrobe was furnished in part by Tiffany's, he held his own among the cowboys. TR roped and herded cattle, hunted large game, captured outlaws, and knocked out a ruffian in a bar with a well-placed sucker punch. He poured a sizable portion of his inheritance into a ranching business that was destined to fail. He read and wrote books and articles and carried on a continual correspondence.

Where more "practical" types might have regarded this period as an unproductive cul-de-sac in Roosevelt's career, he later concluded that he would not have become president were it not for the personal growth resulting from his experiences in the Badlands.

At the time, though, his prospects remained uncertain. By 1886 he knew it was time to resume his life in New York.

Roosevelt considered the possibility of the presidency of the New York City Board of Health. Setting a pattern that would recur over the rest of his life, he also declared his availability for military service should border skirmishes with Mexico ignite into war (they did not).

Offered the Republican nomination for mayor of New York for the November 1886 election, he seized it. He ran hard but finished third in a three-way race. Stingingly disappointed, TR feared his political life was finished. Looking back a generation later, a shrewd student of New York City politics observed: "I have always thought that one of the most important things that happened to him was that defeat. Perhaps if he had been elected mayor he would have suffered the fate of all men who have been mayors of New York, namely official extinction."

TR persevered in his literary labors, all the while keeping an eye on the political scene. The national election of 1888 presented another opportunity for Roosevelt to make his way into public life. He campaigned energetically for the Republican national ticket led by Benjamin Harrison; following its victory he sought a position in the new administration. TR expressed interest in becoming assistant secretary of state. He was rebuffed—given that the new secretary was James G. Blaine that cannot have come entirely as a surprise.

Harrison tossed him an unenviable consolation prize, appointing him one of three members of the U.S. Civil Service

Commission. Though civil service reform garnered some public attention, especially among "good government" types, the commission was universally regarded as a political backwater. One of Roosevelt's admirers explained:

> They already thought of him as a young man dangerous to all Machines and so they felt the prudence of bottling him up. To make him a Civil Service Commissioner was not exactly so final as chloroforming a snarling dog would be, but it was a strong measure of safety. Theodore's friends, on the other hand, advised him against accepting the appointment, because, they said, it would shelve him, politically, use up his brains which ought to be spent on higher work, and allow the country which was just beginning to know him to forget his existence.

Government positions are not commensurate with private sector jobs—in private sector terms they tend to be either "half a job" or "a job and a half." At the Civil Service Commission Roosevelt immediately set out to transform his pitiful little half job into something formidable. Undaunted by his own status as a presidential appointee, he sought to limit the patronage powers of the executive—inevitably occasioning open combat with Harrison's most influential cabinet members as well as key congressional committees. The more progress he made in reclassifying government jobs from patronage to civil service, the more he would alienate key political figures, up to and including the president himself.

Perhaps Harrison's evident discomfiture was a factor in the decision of Grover Cleveland, the Democrat who defeated Harrison in 1892, to reappoint Roosevelt (the two had been acquainted since Roosevelt was an assemblyman and Cleveland was New York's governor). A Republican in a Democratic administration, TR continued to advance the cause of civil service reform, with even less apparent connection to his own prospects.

As Washburn observed, Roosevelt's work was entirely disconnected from developing a constituency for elective office. No one understood this more than Roosevelt himself. In 1901, in response to a young admirer, he wrote:

> In spite of my own example to the contrary, I would not advise any friend of mine to accept an appointment on the National Civil Service Commission, if he had any view to what is called a political future for himself. I say "my example to the contrary," but as a matter of fact when I took the Civil Service Commissionership, I made up my mind definitely to abandon all thoughts of future political preferment, and this preferment came to me as a genuine surprise. . . . [N]ormally it is not the kind of work that leads to a future.

In 1894 Roosevelt was offered the support of New York City reformers for another mayoral bid. Against his inclinations he declined, acceding to the wishes of his wife, Edith. Roosevelt was downcast, writing Henry Cabot Lodge that he "would literally have given my right arm to make the race, win or lose. It was the one golden chance, which never returns." Indeed, the reform Republican William Strong won easily.

It must have been with mixed feelings that Roosevelt entertained Strong's suggestion that he become commissioner of street cleaning. TR declined. He was subsequently offered, and accepted, a commissionership on the four-person Police Board. One of Roosevelt's contemporaries, Albert Shaw, later wrote:

> A man of smaller caliber, of more calculating ambition, or of personal vanity and self-appreciation, would have refused this post as of lower rank than his merits deserved. Mr. Roosevelt had made the mayoral fight ten years earlier and could have done as well [as Strong]. . . . No official place in the entire

> United States would have seemed more undesirable or perilous to the public man who sought to climb the political ladder than the police commissionership of New York City, unless it were the civil service commissionership at Washington. To accept Mayor Strong's urgent invitation was to flop from the frying pan into the fire, in the opinion of all those who believed that the path of success lay in the skillful avoidance of enmities and controversy.

Immediately upon taking his position in the spring of 1895 Roosevelt threw himself into the challenge of reforming a department that slouched toward corruption through selective enforcement of the laws, notoriously including a ban on the sale of liquor on Sundays. Using the same tools he employed to expand the power of his post at the Civil Service Commission—strict law enforcement, publicity, activist management—TR turned a demoralized workforce around. Though cartoonists and editorialists took note of him from as far away as London, the reaction was by no means uniformly positive. TR faced unstinting attack from various quarters: the German-American community long accustomed to Sunday beer drinking, local newspapers, and political adversaries inside and outside the Police Board. In December 1895 he wrote to Lodge: "It really seems there *must* be some fearful shortcoming on my side to account for the fact that I have not one New York City newspaper or one New York City politician on my side." In 1896 he told another close friend, Owen Wister (fellow Harvard alumnus and author of Western novels, including *The Virginian*), that he was "politically dead."

Though the board was strengthened by his leadership, internal and external resistance were unremitting. Within a year's time prospects for additional progress appeared limited. With the election of Republican William McKinley to the presidency in 1896 Roosevelt's thoughts inevitably wandered toward Washington. Senator Lodge and other friends put his name forward for a place at the Navy Department. TR's sponsors emphasized his long-standing interest in naval affairs, going back to his first book, *The Naval War of 1812*. The suggestion of Roosevelt did not elicit unalloyed enthusiasm from the New York senatorial delegation or the White House. TR's activist approach to his previous positions had not gone unnoticed by the commander in chief. Lodge reported after a meeting with McKinley that the president was concerned lest Roosevelt have a "preconceived notion which he would wish to drive through the moment he got in."

After some back and forth Roosevelt was appointed assistant secretary of the navy and confirmed by the Senate in April 1897.

THOUGH ROOSEVELT was nearing forty—in an era when men routinely died before reaching fifty—his career was a curiosity. Many people—some supportive, others not—viewed him as a potential national leader, even president. Yet TR had not established a "career" in any usual sense.

Freed by a large inheritance from the necessity of making a living, as the father of six young children he was nonetheless not in a secure financial position. His business ventures—in publishing and ranching—were, in financial terms, a self-indulgence and a flat-out failure.

TR's career in elective office was estimable but brief. His accomplishments as civil service commissioner and police commissioner were tangible but tinged with lingering controversy. His heterogeneous work history did not lay the groundwork for advancement to the higher positions that his ability indicated, such as the U.S. Senate (then appointed by the legislature, highly influenced by machine politics) or the governorship of New York. As McKinley's reaction to his prospective appointment to a subcabinet position illustrated, TR's record and force of personality rendered him less rather than more likely to be selected for a cabinet chair.

In various ways, at various times, Roosevelt expressed the sentiment that he related in a letter to his sister: "[I]t is worse than useless for a man of my means and my methods in political life to think of politics as a career." Faithful to his approach, he had imposed his own terms on his life and leadership. As yet it was hard to see what it amounted to. No one could have foreseen the path that would take Roosevelt, in just over four years, into the presidency.

McKINLEY'S QUALMS about the temperament of his new assistant secretary of the navy were amply justified. Roosevelt swung into action almost immediately upon his appointment. He sought to impose his highly opinionated will on the Navy Department. Within weeks he delivered a major address to the Naval War College that read more like a presidential statement advancing the debate than a routine subcabinet reiteration of policy. TR pushed the secretary toward naval expansion and did not hesitate to jump the chain of command, importuning the president directly. He also felt no compunction about working directly with members of Congress across the range of administration policy, far outside his department's jurisdiction.

On the afternoon of Friday, February 25, 1898, while Secretary Long was taking a day off—but still in Washington—Roosevelt served as acting secretary. The "acting" designation was a formality, to ensure that bureaucratic and legal technicalities would not impede the flow of work in the principal's absence. TR used the occasion to unilaterally issue a series of orders edging the United States measurably closer to war with Spain. The most significant was a cable to Commodore Dewey directing that he prepare his ships for operations against the Spanish fleet in the Philippines in the event of a declaration of war.

Roosevelt had not taken precipitate action. He had coordinated his efforts with key naval personnel and supportive members of Congress. The secretary was understandably angry to find that his subordinate had taken such action without his prior approval, but the orders stood. Roosevelt was fortunate not to be countermanded, disciplined, or fired. He took a calculated risk in order to do what he believed right: "I may not be supported, but I have done what I know to be right; some day they will understand."

In addition to being committed to advancing his goals for national policy, Roosevelt had long been desirous of the chance to do his part in war for the United States. When war with Spain finally came, in April, he immediately sought a role. Having been among the most vociferous "jingoes" urging—and prompting—America into war, TR believed he was obligated to offer not only his best judgment, but also his body. Overruling objections and concerns expressed by family and friends, he resigned from the Navy Department and volunteered for army service in Cuba.

In seeking a commission Roosevelt declared: "I don't want to be in an office instead of at the front; but I dare say I shall have to be, and shall try to do good work wherever I am put. I have long been accustomed, not to taking the positions I should like, but to doing the best that I was able to do in a position I did not altogether like, and under conditions which I didn't like at all."

Roosevelt declined the highest military position on offer. He later explained:

> What I am interested in, remember, is not in the least holding the office, but doing a job that is actually worth doing; this is the position that to the best of my belief I have always taken,

> and always shall take . . . it was the position I took in the Spanish War, when I could have obtained a brigadier generalship, and refused a colonelcy in order to put the right man in as colonel [Leonard Wood] and serve under him as lieutenant colonel, because I was sure that would give me the best chance of getting into the game and doing the job as it ought to be done.

Roosevelt's heroism in the brief Spanish-American War that followed brought him national recognition and would catapult him into the governorship of New York several months later, in November 1898. Less well known but not unimportant—at least to Roosevelt—were the risks he took off the battlefield. Through open letters and information provided to the press he publicly challenged the top military brass, including the secretary of war (the precursor of today's secretary of defense). TR believed his actions were necessary to protect American soldiers unjustifiably posted in regions infected by disease, or supplied with unsatisfactory food or weaponry. Though not at risk for bureaucratic retribution in the manner of a career officer, he was nonetheless vulnerable. Roosevelt was brazenly desirous that the secretary of war approve recommendations in his behalf for a Medal of Honor for his service in the Cuban campaign. TR was not unaware of the likely consequences of a public challenge to the secretary, characterizing it as "calculated impudence." He added, "I have several times written him on similar subjects knowing I was taking risks but knowing also that they had to be taken and that I was the only man who would take them." Many concluded that TR's public advocacy for his troops sealed the decision of the secretary to deny him the recognition he sought with boyish zeal.

In the summer of 1898 Roosevelt returned to New York. He was a national hero. His military exploits had been reported in the press with faithful and favorable detail by some of the most renowned reporters of the day. His Republican

Party, facing steep odds in the forthcoming general election, could not avoid casting a glance in TR's direction in its anxious search for a credible gubernatorial nominee.

Suddenly Roosevelt was in a position to obtain high-level leadership on his own terms. The two major political parties in New York were run by "machines"—coteries of elected officials, businessmen, and others of influence. The identities and personalities of candidates for high office were generally of limited consequence. The prime movers in such a system would not ordinarily turn to the likes of Roosevelt; confronting imminent defeat, otherwise queasy Republicans suddenly found him palatable. The Republican boss, Senator Thomas Collier Platt, had never been comfortable with TR; the prospect of sharing close quarters with the Rough Rider was not a welcome one. When Roosevelt's name was raised, the "Easy Boss" responded: "But if he becomes Governor of New York, sooner or later, with his personality, he will have to be President of the United States. . . . aside from the question of whether he will be fair to me and to our organization, I am afraid to start that thing going."

As the summer drew to a close, Platt's lieutenant Lemuel Quigg journeyed to Long Island to visit TR, who was with his troops waiting to be mustered out. According to Roosevelt's *Autobiography:*

> [Quigg] said he wanted from me a plain statement as to whether or not I wanted the nomination, and as to what would be my attitude toward the organization in the event of my nomination and election, whether or not I would "make war" on Mr. Platt and his friends, or whether I would confer with them and with the organization leaders generally, and give fair consideration to their point of view as to party policy and public interest. . . . He simply wanted a frank definition of my attitude towards existing party conditions.

> To this I replied that I should like to be nominated, and if nominated would promise to throw myself into the campaign with all possible energy. I said that I should not make war on Mr. Platt or anybody else if war could be avoided; that what I wanted was to be Governor and not a faction leader; that I certainly would confer with the organization. . . . but that while I would try to get on well with the organization, the organization must with equal sincerity strive to do what I regarded as essential for the public good; and that in every case . . . I should have to act finally as my own judgment and conscience dictated and administer the State as I thought it ought to be administered.

Roosevelt was elected in November 1898, by a narrow margin of fewer than 18,000 votes of the 1.3 million cast. His two-year term began in January 1899. Platt acknowledged that the new governor kept his end of the bargain, consulting prior to significant personnel and policy decisions. In the end, however, TR would go his own way. Though he would accede on many lower-level personnel decisions, Roosevelt parted company with Platt (and often with the machines of both parties) on high-level appointments and major policies (including corporate regulation and taxation and conservation).

Roosevelt—and those who wished him well or ill—was aware that as the governor of the nation's most populous and economically powerful state, he was automatically a potent candidate for the presidency or a presidential cabinet post. He privately expressed interest in either possibility but maintained his attention to the job at hand, discouraging himself and others from a distracting focus on the future. He was uncertain whether the Republican bosses would consent to his renomination for governor or whether he would prevail in the general election that would occur simultaneously with the national election in 1900. TR understood that as chief executive of a large and complex organization, many factors beyond his control—ranging from poorly performing subordinates to unpredictable external forces—might decide his fate. In Albany, while stretching an already big job to the limit, Roosevelt completed three books and wrote numerous articles. His future uncharted, he kept open many doors, such as the possibility of editing a magazine upon leaving office.

The uncertainty of TR's future was intensified by the controversies he was touching off in the tumultuous present. Journalist Steffens, reviewing TR's unconventional course, wrote of "Governor Roosevelt as an Experiment." By 1900, Platt—who claimed he "[had] learned to love that man"—had been delighted long enough; he wanted to hustle TR out of Albany, ideally quietly smothering him into oblivion.

When Vice President Garret Hobart died unexpectedly in late 1899, Platt recognized a perfect opportunity to "kick Roosevelt upstairs." At the time there was no constitutional provision for replacing a deceased vice president, and the position would remain unfilled until the 1900 election.

TR resisted. He wrote Platt in February 1900, "The more I have thought over it, the more I have felt that I would a great deal rather be anything, say professor of history, than Vice President." The vice presidency was viewed as a political dead end. In those years its duties were limited to presiding over the Senate (which might convene for only a few days per year). The position had no institutional base; it did not have a physical office near the president; it did not include a mansion as did the presidency and the governorship of New York. His wife, Edith, voiced concerns that the vice presidency would mean a lower salary than the governorship as well as significant additional expenses. With the notable exception of one valued friend and adviser, Lodge, most close supporters urged him to decline the position were it offered.

The vice presidency was not Platt's alone to give. President McKinley's master strategist, Ohio senator Mark Hanna, was aghast at the thought of Roosevelt as vice president. Perhaps impelled by intuition, Hanna strenuously argued against his selection at the Philadelphia Convention in 1900: "Don't any of you realize there's just one life between this madman and the presidency?" An unlikely coalition including Eastern bosses hostile to Hanna and Western delegates enthusiastic for the Rough Rider moved the convention to select Roosevelt. The sole vote against the nomination was TR's own.

Platt witnessed the inauguration of McKinley and Roosevelt in March 1901, famously saying he was there "to see Teddy take the veil." In the vice presidency Roosevelt finally encountered a position he could not transform into significance by dint of personal force. His optimism fortified by defiance, TR declared, "If I have been put on the shelf, my enemies will find that I can make it a cheerful place of abode."

Roosevelt's path was lonely—as lonely as the carriage in which he unobtrusively trailed the triumphant president's inaugural parade on March 4, 1901. The new vice president's official duties presiding over the Senate lasted four days, after which adjournment was declared until December. McKinley did not tend to solicit his advice or respond directly to his letters of recommendation for office seekers. TR traveled, gave speeches, and, as ever, kept up his writing and correspondence. Along with some supporters he did some discrete politicking with a view toward the 1904 election. Such self-promotion was limited not only by Roosevelt's position vis-à-vis McKinley but also by the widespread assumption that he would be opposed by the party leadership of his home state. Recognizing that his public life would likely conclude with McKinley's term in March 1905, he kept his mind open to varied career possibilities. The new vice president wrote several judges (including Alton Parker, who would be his presidential opponent in 1904) seeking guidance on how he might complete his legal training (he had dropped out of Columbia Law School years earlier) while in office.

IN SEPTEMBER 1901, Roosevelt was suddenly thrust into the conductor's chair of the racing train that was American life at the dawn of the twentieth century. His unusual life experiences—that previously appeared fragmentary, not unified into a working whole—were brought together, rendering him extraordinarily well prepared for national leadership.

Roosevelt appears to have assumed, beginning as a young man, that he could serve successfully at high levels of leadership, including the presidency. Perhaps his singular self-confidence and a sense of destiny moved him beyond those whose leadership is hobbled by a desire to prove themselves by linking their names to a title or position, rather than a commitment to service.

His pledge to do his best in whatever position he found himself in, with the expectation that each job would be his last in public life, made his path unconventional.

Coexisting with his unrelenting determination and self-mastery was an understanding that "planning" one's life or career is ultimately a fool's errand. He recognized "that any man who has had what is regarded in the world as a great success must realize that the element of chance has played a great part in it. Of course a man has to take advantage of his opportunities; but the opportunities have to come." As for the highest level of leadership, he wrote to his son Theodore, Jr.: "as regards the extraordinary prizes the element of luck is *the* determining factor." TR appeared to follow generally the view he expressed to Lodge about one of his writing projects: "I will do my best and trust to luck for the result." The "luck" is not in the development of one's own abilities, but in having the occasion arise for their application.

Roosevelt understood that an individual can be a leader in *any* position. If one's aim is to serve, one must be prepared to take on tasks that might differ from what one would have chosen. Roosevelt did not await the "right" position to engage his extraordinary leadership skills. He would enthusiastically undertake tasks and positions that others might see as "beneath" his abilities or advantages—vitalizing and expanding them with the full force of his personality. On becoming president Roosevelt reiterated to Lodge the credo he had long applied: "Here is the task, and I have got to do it to the best of my ability; and that is all there is about it."

In a letter in 1899 Roosevelt declared, "Whatever good I can accomplish is largely accomplished because I am not nervously calculating the chances as to my future." Doing one's best where one is, minimizing distractions such as calculating one's prospects, may enable one better to achieve the tasks at hand. It may enhance performance by limiting one's anxiety about outcomes. Whether an enterprise is successful in meeting its goals—and whether it is recognized as such—of course cannot be ensured. The most anyone can do is to serve to the best of their ability, seeking to be worthy of success. In a letter to Wister dated November 19, 1904, at the zenith of his power and public approval, Roosevelt wrote of his presidency: "I was forced to try a dozen pieces of doubtful and difficult work in which it was possible *to deserve success*, but in which it would not have been possible . . . to be sure of commanding success."

TR's commitment to service endowed him with invaluable experience, showcasing qualities that would be called upon in the future. If his gifts and energy appeared disproportionate to his early leadership roles, others were given glimpses of his potential. Should a crisis or other opportunity arise requiring leadership, where it might be granted on his terms, Roosevelt would be ready. As he told his friend Jacob Riis, "I put myself in the way of things happening, and they happened."

Just as one should not await a leadership position based on one's personal desires rather than what service and fate dictate, one also should not avoid action on the basis that only perfection is worth achieving. The people who do the most good, TR found, "are those who have had ideals but . . . who have tried to do each his duty as the day came, and to fight each evil as they found it arise without bothering their heads as to the 'ultimate' evil."

Roosevelt sought to achieve "disinterestedness." When as a military commander he publicly challenged the top brass, or as a politician defied power brokers whose enmity could end his career, TR was showing, in the words of leadership expert John Maxwell, that he loved his people more than his position. To Roosevelt that was the basis for moral leadership. It was also eminently practical. As the often critical *New York Sun* wrote in 1900, "People got to saying, 'This man Roosevelt seems to do about what he thinks is right and doesn't care a rap for the consequences. He must be all right.'" Albert Shaw wrote: "He always seemed more interested in the things for which he contended than in his own fortunes or personal ambitions." The fact that Roosevelt was manifestly a highly skilled politician lured cynical people to search overly for calculation underlying his actions. Others recognized that his willingness to disregard political considerations he comprehended more than virtually anyone else was a tribute to his courage and commitment to service.

The resulting bond of trust that TR forged with the public allowed them to grant him the benefit of the doubt at critical junctures. Referring to blunders that came close to derailing TR's gubernatorial candidacy in 1898 (including having established legal residency outside of New York to lower his tax bill), historian Wallace Chessman writes:

> The fact that Roosevelt survived such episodes . . . affords a valuable insight into the nature of his career. The figure here revealed was a good deal less than a careful schemer with long-range ambitions; indeed in both instances he was singularly shortsighted and confused. Mistakes like these might well have been fatal for other politicians, but in his case they were taken as signs of his ingenuousness. If men thought he had done wrong they assigned the blame to others, to his family advisers and to the Platt machine. Roosevelt was the simple and good man loose in an evil world, and the world was the better for it.

TR ON LEADERSHIP

- Leaders should focus all energy on the job at hand, without regard to their own future prospects. In so doing, they will be of greater service in the present and more worthy of leadership responsibility in the future.
- To the greatest possible extent, leaders should seek leadership on their own terms. Where the terms are imposed by others, a position of authority may be drained of much of its potential for disinterested service.
- Leaders should visibly love their people more than their positions—and prove their love through their actions.
- Anyone can choose to become a leader at any time, irrespective of position. The key is a commitment to service.
- A leader should aim to build a life based on service, not a career based on advancing up a series of positions.
- Against the vagaries of fate, even the most brilliant cannot reliably discern their own interest, but almost anyone can understand and seek to do his duty.
- Rather than seeking success (which is generally outside of one's control), a leader should seek to *deserve* success.

CHAPTER TWO

CEASING TO BE AFRAID

First say to yourself what you would be;
and then do what you have to do.
—EPICTETUS, *DISCOURSES*

There were all kinds of things of which I was afraid at first, ranging from grizzly bears to "mean" horses and gun-fighters; but by acting as if I was not afraid I gradually ceased to be afraid.
—THEODORE ROOSEVELT

EXPRESSING HIMSELF in military terms, Roosevelt saw life as a continuing campaign. None of his many battles was more demanding than his 1912 run for the presidency as an independent "Bull Moose" candidate. Almost single-handedly, he simultaneously challenged the machinery of the two great American political parties, as well as their able candidates: his handpicked Republican successor, President William Howard Taft, and the Democratic nominee, New Jersey's Governor Woodrow Wilson.

Never before or since has a potentially victorious campaign for the American presidency been based so entirely on the personality, philosophy, and effort of one individual. By mid-October, in the furious final weeks prior to the November election, even the indomitable TR was showing the strain. After months of open-air speeches unaided by microphones, his apparently tireless voice was reduced to a raspy whisper. Yet he carried on . . .

On Monday October 14 Roosevelt made his way by train to Milwaukee, unwilling to cancel appearances and unable to arrange for appropriate substitutes from his shallow bench of high-level political allies. As aides and supporters bickered about his health and schedule, TR finally resolved the matter, agreeing to continue as planned in Milwaukee: "I want to be a good Indian."

Roosevelt made his way from the train station to the Gilpatrick Hotel in an open car, tipping his hat to enthusiastic crowds. Conserving his waning strength, he neither stood nor spoke. At the hotel, with a few minutes to spare before dinner, he surprised his staff by snatching some sleep. According to his able chronicler, former *New York Times* reporter O. K. Davis: "It was the only time, in all the campaign trips I made with him, that I ever saw him sleep before bedtime."

After dinner TR rested for a few additional minutes and then walked downstairs and outside, taking his seat in the open car that would carry him to the auditorium for his speech.

Responding to nearby cheers, Roosevelt stood and turned toward the rear of the vehicle, characteristically lifting his hat with his right hand.

From the friendly throng—did Roosevelt see it like a slow-motion dream? —a deranged man with a pistol thrust himself forward . . . the hand with the gun took aim at TR at point-blank range . . . the fire of a shot . . . the concussive blast into his chest, as if kicked by a horse . . . a flash of pain . . . collapse onto the car seat . . . blood and pain and cold and wet. . . .

Pandemonium . . .

The violent death he had so long courted—even taunted—had suddenly, cunningly grabbed him by the lapels, pulling so close its cold breath brushed his neck. Who would have thought the bullet would find him now? Why not where it was so much more likely, in the Wild West of his youth? Why not when he was conspicuously mounted on horseback, beckoning troops on the ground into a random rain of carnage in the Spanish-American War? Why not when he was president, recognizing that even the placid McKinley had been murdered by a half-witted anarchist?

Roosevelt appeared in absolute command of this most unpredictable moment. Had he prepared for it in forethought long before? Did his mind reel back to his writings of the deaths of heroes he offered as examples to others? Did he think of Stonewall Jackson or Robert Gould Shaw or Lord Nelson or Davy Crockett or William Barrett Travis or John Quincy Adams or Abraham Lincoln, each of whom exhibited dauntless courage as he faced, in his own ways and circumstances, "the rifle pits"?

A guard leapt onto the assailant, who tried to fire his gun again as he went down. The guard got a stranglehold on his prey, maneuvered his knee into the small of his back, set to snap the animal's neck on the spot . . .

Roosevelt, implored to reveal his condition, replied matter-of-factly: "He pinked me."

Hauling himself onto his feet, he coughed and touched his hands to his lips; finding no blood he concluded, he later wrote, "the chances were twenty to one that it was not fatal."

Witnessing the mauling of his assailant, TR ordered: "Don't hurt him! Bring him here! I want to look at him!" (He later wrote, "I would not have objected to the man's being killed at that very instant, but I did not deem it wise or proper that he should be killed before my eyes if I was going to recover."). Finding the trembling would-be killer unfamiliar—"the poor creature"—he directed the driver to proceed to the convention hall. Rebuffing the anguished pleas of staff and a family member, Roosevelt's weakened voice conveyed unalterable resolve: "You get me to that speech. It may be the last one I shall ever deliver, but I am going to deliver this one." During the ride to the convention center, the former president held his ground against a doctor's advice: "No, this is my big chance, and I am going to make that speech if I die doing it."

TR recognized he had been granted an incomparable stage on which to exhibit the disinterestedness that he said motivated his 1912 campaign, the most controversial—and legitimately questioned—assertion of leadership of his eventful career.

Following an introduction inadvertently too low-keyed to convey the seriousness of the situation, TR took the stage. As he removed the manuscript from his coat pocket, he likely realized for the first time that the fifty-page address, folded in two, may have provided the slim margin of life. He began to speak, unaided by a microphone:

> Friends, I shall ask you to be as quiet as possible. I don't know whether you fully understand that I have just been shot; but it takes more than that to kill a Bull Moose! . . . The bullet is in me now, so that I cannot make a very long speech, but I will try my best. . . .
>
> And now, friends, I want to take advantage of this incident and say a word of solemn warning to my fellow countrymen. First of all, I want to say this about myself: I have altogether too important things to think of to feel any concern over my own death; and now I cannot speak to you insincerely within five minutes of being shot. . . . I can tell you with absolute truthfulness that I am very much uninterested in whether I am shot or not. It was just as when I was colonel of my regiment. I always felt that a private was to be excused for feeling at times some pangs of anxiety about his personal safety, but I cannot understand a man fit to be a colonel who can pay any heed to his personal safety when he is occupied as he ought to be occupied with the absorbing desire to do his duty.

He opened his jacket and vest, exposing his blood-soaked shirt. The wounded leader beseeched the crowd to "be as quiet as possible for I am not able to give the challenge of the Bull Moose quite as loudly." Physically shaken but spiritually robust, TR brushed aside repeated requests from audience members and staff that he cut short his remarks. Drained of color, straining for breath, uneven in delivery, at times he weaved dangerously near the edge of the stage. Anxious lieutenants examined his every move, preparing to catch him should he fall. Soldiering on through his prepared text, TR let the completed pages fall to the floor, bequeathing bullet-torn mementos to those at his side in the greatest moment of his 1912 crusade.

TR spoke for fully one hour and a half. His eloquence arose more from his hard-won courage than his carefully crafted words.

Reaching the end, as the audience cheered, TR turned to the accompanying doctor: "Now I am ready to go with you and do what you want."

Medical personnel dressed the wound. Heeding the advice of a highly respected doctor from Johns Hopkins who happened to be visiting Milwaukee, Roosevelt proceeded by train to Chicago. He arrived after three the following morning. In a gesture foreshadowing Ronald Reagan's actions following an attempt on his life in March 1981, the Bull Moose declined the offer to be transported from the train into a waiting ambulance: "I'll not go to a hospital lying in that thing. I'll walk to it and I'll walk from it to the hospital. I'm no weakling to be crippled by a flesh wound."

Attending physicians located the bullet that had entered the right side of his chest and rested in his ribs. En route, the bullet encountered TR's speech text, a spectacle case, and, most important, the extraordinary chest built from the feeble foundation of a frail, asthmatic boy, beginning many years before. According to an attending surgeon, "Colonel Roosevelt has a phenomenal development of the chest. It is largely due to the fact that he is a physical marvel that he was not dangerously wounded. He is one of the most powerful men I have ever seen laid on an operating table. The bullet lodged in the massive muscles of the chest instead of penetrating the lung." TR's body would carry the bullet for the remainder of his life.

Even the most virulent opponents of Roosevelt's Bull Moose candidacy—whose attacks and "mendacity" had been, in TR's mind, nothing less than an incitement to assassination—showed respect. The *New York Times* editorialized: "Mr. Roosevelt showed the indomitable courage that is ingrained in his being. It was rash . . . an act of hardihood . . . even an act of folly, but it was characteristic, and the judgment of the country will be that it was magnificent." The *New York Herald* exclaimed in a headline: "We are against his politics, but we like his grit."

ROOSEVELT OFTEN SAID, "There are worse deaths than for a man to be killed in the service of his country." Corresponding with the British author and statesman James Bryce during the First World War, he wrote of the death of a gallant naval captain: "inasmuch as we must die, and it is a mere matter of a very few years whether we die early or late, the vital thing is that our deaths should be such as to help others to live."

TR viewed himself as a soldier in combat in Milwaukee. Though the precise circumstances were a complete surprise, his course of conduct was not entirely improvised. He later wrote to Sir Edward Grey, the British foreign secretary:

> There was then a perfectly obvious duty, which was to go on and make my speech. In the very unlikely event of the wound being mortal I wished to die with my boots on, so to speak. It has always seemed to me that the best way to die would be in doing something that ought to be done, whether leading a regi-

> ment or doing anything else. Moreover, I felt that under such circumstances it would be very difficult for people to disbelieve in my sincerity, and that therefore they would be apt to accept at face value the speech I wished to make, and which represented my deepest and most earnest convictions. If, on the other hand, as I deemed overwhelmingly probable, the wound should turn out to be slight, it was still likely that I would have little further chance to speak during the campaign, and therefore it behooved me to go on while I had the chance, and make a speech to which under the circumstances it was at least possible that the country would pay some heed. This is all there was to the incident.

Roosevelt considered assassination a "trade risk" to be accepted without qualm by any leader whose own decisions affect the lives of others. He said it is "not a question of courage: it is a question of perspective." If a leader is focused on the safety of those for whom he is responsible, he simply does not have room in his mind for anxiety about his own safety. He added: "I have never felt that public men who were shot whether they were killed or not, were entitled to any special sympathy; and I do most emphatically feel that when in danger it is their business to act in the manner we accept as commonplace when the actor is an enlisted man of the Army or Navy, or a policeman, or a fireman, or a railroad man, or a miner, or a deep sea fisherman."

In his *Autobiography* Roosevelt said that cowboys from the Badlands and the Rough Riders from his Cuban regiment were "puzzled" by the strong public reaction to his actions in Milwaukee. He characteristically turned the story around to praise them: "They would not have expected a man to leave a battle, for instance, because of being wounded in such a fashion; and they saw no reason why he should abandon a less important and less risky duty."

THE COURAGEOUS MAN who expressed—and gave life to—these sentiments had once been a "very small person" afraid of many things. He recalled himself variously as "a sickly, delicate boy," "a wretched mite." Wracked by asthma, he was sometimes too weak to blow out a bedside candle. Young Teedie and his family were hostages of a sort, understanding that their lives might be disrupted at any moment to accommodate the demands occasioned by his illness. In an unconsciously amusing letter written during his presidency, distinguishing the boy from the man he became, TR wrote, "my belief is that I was rather below than above my average playmate in point of leadership."

In his *Autobiography* Roosevelt described a fateful encounter:

> Having been a sickly boy, with no natural bodily prowess, and having lived much at home, I was at first quite unable to hold my own when thrown into contact with other boys of rougher antecedents. I was nervous and timid. Yet from reading of the people I admired . . . , I felt a great admiration for men who were fearless and who could hold their own in the world, and I had a great desire to be like them. Until I was nearly fourteen I let this desire take no more definite shape than daydreams. Then an incident happened that did me real good. Having an attack of asthma, I was sent off to Moosehead Lake. On the stage-coach ride thither I encountered a couple of other boys who were about my own age, but very much more competent and also much more mischievous. I have no doubt they were good-hearted boys, but they were boys! They found that I was a fore-ordained and predestined victim, and industriously proceeded to make life miserable for me. The worst feature was that when I finally tried to fight them I discovered that either one singly could not only handle me with easy contempt, but handle me so as not to hurt me much and yet to prevent my doing any damage in return.

From this incident he learned "what probably no amount of good advice could have taught me." TR determined to remake his body, soon finding that the project was necessarily even more far-reaching: "Having been a rather sickly and awkward boy, I was as a young man both nervous and distrustful of my own prowess. I had to train myself painfully and laboriously not merely as regards my body but as regards my soul and spirit."

At an early age Roosevelt grasped the wisdom of Winston Churchill's dictum that courage is the first virtue, since it is the foundation that underlies all the others. He resolved to overcome the fears that stood as obstacles to his personal development:

> There were all kinds of things of which I was afraid at first, ranging from grizzly bears to "mean" horses and gun-fighters; but by acting as if I was not afraid I gradually ceased to be afraid. Most men can have the same experience if they choose. They will first learn to bear themselves well in trials which they anticipate and which they school themselves in advance to meet. After a while the habit will grow on them, and they will behave well in sudden and unexpected emergencies which come upon them unawares.

Harnessing his spirit, body, and mind, TR transformed the remainder of his life into a catalog of moral and physical courage. At Harvard College he became a lightweight boxer. Although this might not appear a tremendous accomplishment at first glance, it likely was a momentous step for Roosevelt. The fact that later in life he occasionally may have given the erroneous impression that he was lightweight champion may be viewed as indicative of its significance in his mind.

Historian John Morton Blum, sympathetic yet unsentimental about TR, suggests that his decision to enter politics required courage, given that the choice was, at least among his social class, generally considered "disreputable." Even assuming that he was animated by a desire for power, Blum continues, Roosevelt needed "not only courage but stamina to discipline that craving, to manage himself so that he could earn the chance to manage other men."

However one interprets his initial motivations, Roosevelt unquestionably exhibited moral courage in the political arena, beginning almost immediately upon his election to the New York Assembly and continuing through the remainder of his life.

In the Badlands he displayed physical courage. TR earned the respect of cowboys and completed his transformation into the figure we would recognize. In *Hunting Trips of a Ranchman* he wrote from personal experience: "Clumsiness and, still more, the slightest approach to timidity expose a man to the roughest and most merciless raillery; and the unfit are weeded out by a very rapid process of natural selection." The cowboys were accustomed to young aristocrats from the East passing through on self-indulgent sojourns. TR was something different. He had, in the words of one who knew him there, "a brass monkey's nerve," verging on recklessness. His lack of fear was constantly in evidence, whether he was arresting and transporting criminals or punching a drunken cowboy who attempted to humiliate him in a bar, calling him "four-eyes," or not backing down from an apparent challenge from a renowned duelist.

As a hunter he appeared fearless, confronting deadly animals at short range in situations where men were routinely disabled or killed. Memorably, Roosevelt once was held upside down over a cliff as he took aim at a mountain lion. Eager to show himself able to hold his own in the outdoors, he ignored discomfort, ranging from inclement weather to disjointed fingers and broken limbs.

TR's decision to enlist for the Spanish-American War required courage. One of his closest friends and most trusted career counselors, Lodge, declared that his resignation from the Navy Department would end his political career. His heroic action in the battle of San Juan became the stuff of legend. The noted war correspondent Richard Harding Davis witnessed Roosevelt, on horseback, leading—from the front—his troops on the ground in a charge. "No man," Davis wrote, "who saw Roosevelt take that ride expected he would finish it alive." TR proudly wrote Lodge that he "was singled out by the Generals in command on the ground . . . on that particular day in the big fight of the war" as the most deserving of the Medal of Honor. Roosevelt went to his grave believing that "San Juan was the great day of my life."

TR WAS NOT, in his terms, "naturally fearless." One wonders whether any sane person—at least anyone of reasonable intelligence—could be naturally fearless. TR's bold project of re-creating his mind, body, and spirit required courage. Striving to exile fear from the totality of his personality, he henceforth exhibited courage throughout his life. In the doing he summoned other essential leadership qualities—including will, forethought, learning, and judgment.

Fearlessness, as important as it is, is a means to an end. A psychopath may be fearless. A wicked despot such as Hitler or Stalin or Mao may be fearless. Fearlessness is valued where it is harnessed for moral purposes, though, as Samuel Johnson observed, it is "so necessary for maintaining virtue, that it is always respected, even when it is associated with vice." Generally we use the term "courage" to describe fearless actions for moral purposes.

Though courage may be regarded as the most important virtue, it should not be viewed in isolation. Roosevelt believed that the qualities of a good hunter were much like those of a good soldier—and he saw the best citizens as having soldier-like qualities. To give courage effect, one must also train oneself from undue nervousness. TR referred to it as "buck fever":

> [A] state of intense nervous excitement which may be entirely divorced from timidity. It may affect a man the first time he has to speak to a large audience just as it affects him the first time he sees a buck or goes into battle. What such a man needs is not courage but nerve-control, cool-headedness. This he can get only by actual practice. He must, by custom and repeated exercise of self-mastery, get his nerves thoroughly under control. This is largely a matter of habit, in the sense of repeated effort and repeated exercise of will power. If a man has the right stuff in him his will grows stronger and stronger with each exercise of it.

In 1896, under strain from confrontations with fellow commissioners on the New York City Police Board, TR wrote to a friend:

> I have always been nervous before a contest, although I have not a particle of nervousness once the fight is actually on, and indeed rather enjoy it. In the old days I was always nervous before a boxing match. . . . I felt very nervous before I actually got to grips with my foe [on the police board]. I did not try to control the appearance of nervousness as much as I should have done, partly because I knew it would disappear the minute I came down to actual fighting, and that then I should be perfectly cool and collected; but I see now that it was a mistake not to try to command myself as much in advance as in the contest; I shall do it hereafter.

Roosevelt viewed mastery of the reality and appearance of nervousness as necessary to make him a better fighter—both to fortify his own performance and to dispirit a foe.

TR regarded courage and honesty as "twin virtues." Honesty without courage—as exhibited by the "timid good"—is not effective. Fearlessness allied with honesty is the basis for moral courage. Roosevelt exhibited moral courage throughout his political career, as acknowledged by many among his most severe detractors.

Roosevelt's combination of courage and honesty impelled him to confront persons and situations directly. When the speaker of the New York Assembly publicly tore up Governor Roosevelt's message for corporate regulation, TR walked into the capitol and directed that the message be read—otherwise he would force his way into the chamber and deliver it himself. Years later, speaking in Reno, Nevada, he warned of the consequences of the city becoming a "divorce colony." When America was divided—and some ethnic groups inflamed—on the question of entry into the First World War, former president Roosevelt went on the rhetorical offensive, declaring he would not "pussyfoot." As Jacob Riis wrote, "It has been Theodore Roosevelt's lot often to be charged with rashness, what his critics in the rear are pleased to call his 'lack of tact.' It is the tribute paid by timidity to unquestioning courage." Paradoxically, his directness, his evident boldness heedless of risk—even when headed toward apparent, certain defeat—left many adversaries with a sneaking affection, if not admiration, for this leader who so evidently gave of himself without reserve in the heat of battle.

TO ROOSEVELT, "life is a great adventure, and you cannot win the great prizes unless you are willing to run certain risks, unless you are willing to pay certain penalties." TR was no stranger to risk. A fair question is whether he courted death unnecessarily. In the immediate aftermath of the Cuban battles that made his name, on a hot beach with his regiment, he swam in shark-infested waters. As president he mingled with crowds and faced frightening moments—such as when a woman tossed a bouquet his way, leaving the Secret Service to look on with bated breath, hoping against hope it did not conceal something lethal (it did not). While president he could not pass up an opportunity to dive into the ocean in a prototype submarine. After the presidency he ventured skyward in an early airplane near St. Louis with a noted aviator, Arch Hoxey (Hoxey was killed in an aviation accident shortly thereafter). Biographer Henry Pringle listed six times—the first in 1886, the last for World War I in 1917—that Roosevelt volunteered for wartime service (only twice did war actually occur).

In part he assumed risks because it was fun, quenching what he called his "thirst for the sensational." He wrote Lodge after breaking his arm in an accident: "I am always willing to pay the piper when I have had a good dance; and every now and then I like to drink the wine of life with brandy in it." Perhaps he saw such situations as opportunities for further cultivation of his fearlessness, maintaining the attitudes and habits that would be called on in more urgent situations. He likely viewed all examples of his courage as service to others, gifts of his example.

With respect to his loved ones, TR did not urge risk taking for its own sake. He wrote to his son Ted in 1903 that risk should be "balanced by reward." During the First World War he urged his son Archie not to decline offers of staff assignments where he might be "more useful" to the cause, once he had proven his mettle in combat. With respect to himself, TR's decisions to assume risks tended to follow much more forethought than one might infer from the lightning speed with which they were made. In his *Autobiography* he wrote that a person "can do his part honorably and well provided only he sets fearlessness before him as an ideal, schools himself to think of danger merely as something to be faced and overcome, and regards life itself as he should regard it, not as something to be thrown away, but as a pawn to be promptly hazarded whenever the hazard is warranted by the larger interests of the great game in which we are all engaged."

Ultimately, attitudes about risk reflect beliefs about life and death. In Roosevelt's view, "the worst of all fears is the fear of living." In the early twentieth century death was a visible, constant companion. Roosevelt's life was touched by his own early vulnerability as well as the loss of loved ones far too young to die. Perhaps these experiences led him to see clearly that the additional risks he assumed were not always as significant as they might appear to others.

Roosevelt's sense of life was heightened by his awareness of and readiness for death. As president he often carried a gun (memorably tossing one onto a table in the home of the shocked president of Harvard—it being illegal to carry a firearm in Massachusetts). On safari in Africa or exploring South America, he transported morphine in case suicide became an attractive option; during horrendous travails in Brazil in 1914, injured, delirious, and near death, TR asked his son Kermit to allow him to die rather than burden the group. Perhaps from having cheated the death that had so many opportunities to catch him as a young man; perhaps from guilt for surviving when so many others were taken too soon; perhaps from his admiration of the romantic lives and deaths of heroes he heard and read about from childhood; Roosevelt defied death by throwing himself fearlessly into life.

THE FEARLESSNESS THAT makes courageous action possible is an essential quality of leaders. Courage, while not the sole virtue of leadership, is without question the foundation on which the others ultimately rest.

Roosevelt's example demonstrates the extent to which courage can be cultivated as an act of will. It also illustrates that what he called (paraphrasing Napoleon) "three o'clock in the morning courage" (required for an immediate, instinctual response to unforeseen circumstances) can be developed through forethought and learned habits of fearlessness.

The significance of courage to Roosevelt's leadership cannot be overstated. His national political career was based on the courage he exhibited in combat in Cuba, supplemented by his well-known assumption of physical risk in going out West and political risk in fighting entrenched interests.

Irrespective of one's views of the Spanish-American War, Roosevelt's conduct showcased important leadership qualities. Most important was the unambiguous heedlessness of self—he was manifestly willing to give his life for his nation and his regiment. TR was thereby empowered to ask others, then and later, to give their all as well. Where a leader or organization exhibits, in his words, "courage united with skill," the results can be extraordinary.

TR's fearlessness was a launching pad for audacity. This can ignite a chain reaction across an organization, multiplying the abilities of the entire team. For good or for ill, people tend to follow a leader whose manifest fearlessness has resulted in tangible achievements in the past. Questions, doubts, disagreements relating to a leader's actions may well be discounted in the face of his undaunted courage, especially when expressed with conviction and confidence.

Finally, courageous leadership can be empowered by the perception that the leader—and by extension the enterprise—is marked by destiny, favored by fortune. Whatever TR thought of his fate in not being killed while hundreds under his command fell on the muddy, blood-soaked ground of Cuba, others recognized the good fortune embedded in the tableau. This in no way minimizes the courage or the accomplishment; it is not "luck" in the sense of winning the lottery. The leader serves others by hurling himself directly and first into the unknown vicissitudes of fate that all will ultimately share. Such a leader is often characterized as charismatic. Those seeking direction, order, and security from his leadership may be more likely to trust his judgment on matters of great consequence—decisions inevitably made on the basis of insufficient information, reliant on intuition, instinct, and other unquantifiable factors, sometimes altogether outside the realm of reason.

TR ON LEADERSHIP

- Courage is the "first virtue" because it underlies all the others.
- Courage (physical and moral) can be developed as an act of will.
- Courage can convey a heedlessness of self that confirms a leader's complete commitment to service of others.
- Fearlessness is not recklessness. Acceptable risk should be calculated, based on the value of the endeavor at stake.
- Proven courage under fire can impart to a leader an aura of destiny, of being favored by fortune. This may cause others to repose confidence in him under circumstances marked by great uncertainty and risk.

Chapter Three

ALWAYS LEARNING

[A]s soon as any man has ceased to be able to learn, his usefulness as a teacher is at an end. When he himself can't learn, he has reached the stage where other people can't learn from him.
—Theodore Roosevelt

Looking back on his decision to transform his personality by overcoming his fears, Roosevelt wrote that he was inspired in part "from reading of the people I admired—ranging from the soldiers of Valley Forge, and Morgan's riflemen, to the heroes of my favorite stories." Over the remainder of his life he found, "Books are the greatest of companions." He told a friend, "Reading is a disease with me."

The images of Roosevelt we most readily evoke are those of the man of action—rancher, cowboy, soldier, explorer, hunter. Anyone close to him was keenly aware of his relentless drive to learn. He had the advantage of a college degree and some graduate study in an era when perhaps one out of five thousand young American men (and far fewer women) graduated from college. Yet he did not view education as beginning or ending in a classroom—he was skeptical of learning not linked to action in the world. TR warned with characteristic vigor of those he called the "educated ineffectives": "if, in any individual, university training produces a taste for refined idleness, a distaste for sustained effort, a barren intellectual arrogance, or a sense of supercilious aloofness from the world of real men who do the world's real work, then it has harmed that individual."

Many people veer too far in the other direction, viewing reading books as separating them from practical things, even self-indulgent. They consider it a diversion from value-added work.

For one aspiring to leadership such a view is shortsighted and self-defeating. Leadership scholar Warren Bennis found that dedication to ongoing learning is a constant among top leaders. It is reported that Bill Gates, co-founder of the Microsoft Corporation, sets aside a half hour of each working day, and an additional two weeks per year, for reading intended to advance his education.

Even as president TR routinely read one, two, or even three books a day. With pardonable hyperbole, his son Quentin, as a small child, informed intimates that his father read every new book arriving at the Library of Congress—"right off." Roosevelt plucked any available bit of time for a quick read, commonly carrying a book in his pocket or leaving one strategically stashed behind a pillar in the White House. On November 4, 1903, toward the end of his second full year in the presidency, responding to a query from the president of Columbia University, Roosevelt provided a list of books he had read, in whole or in part, over the previous two years. They ranged from the classical histories of Herodotus, Thucydides, and Plutarch to Carlyle and Gibbon in modern times; from Aeschylus and Aristophanes to Shakespeare and Milton; from Aristotle's *Politics* to Lincoln's *Speeches and Writings* (Lincoln's place as one of his most admired heroes prompted Roosevelt not only to read his books from beginning to end, but to read certain parts "again and again"). He read literature from Sir Walter Scott to Tolstoy, Twain, and Dickens. He might also turn for "an occasional half hour's reading in Keats, Browning, Poe, Tennyson, Longfellow, Kipling," as well as numerous other authors less familiar today.

In late 1908, as he prepared to leave the White House, TR conceived a "pigskin library" for an extended African safari. Though he had "no sympathy whatever with writing lists of *the* One Hundred Best Books or *the* Five-Foot Library," his own selection is revealing. It included the Bible, *The Federalist*, works by Shakespeare, Spenser, Marlowe, Macaulay, Homer, Carlyle, Shelley, Emerson, Longfellow, Tennyson, Poe, Keats, Milton, Bret Harte, Browning, Twain, Bunyan, Euripides, James Fenimore Cooper, Thackeray, and Dickens—and much more. He explained, "the books themselves are of unequal value and . . . they were chosen for various reasons, and for this particular trip."

They shared one attribute: "They were for use, not for ornament." Roosevelt captured the unity of reading and action that characterized his life:

> I almost always had some volume with me, either in my saddle-pocket or in the cartridge-bag which one of my gun-bearers carried to hold odds and ends. Often my reading would be done while resting under a tree at noon, perhaps beside the carcass of a beast I had killed, or else while waiting for camp to be pitched; and in either case it might be impossible to get water for washing. In consequence the books were stained with blood, sweat, gun-oil, dust, and ashes; ordinary bindings either vanished or became loathsome, whereas pigskin merely grew to look as a well-used saddle looks.

TR believed reading should reinforce one's best moral instincts. In his essay "Books for Holidays in the Open," he wrote that while tastes would vary, "this does not mean permitting oneself to like what is vicious or even simply worthless. . . . It is clear that the reading of vicious books for pleasure should be eliminated. It is no less clear that trivial and vulgar books do more damage than can possibly be offset by any entertainment they yield." He offered the cautionary example of Tolstoy as a talented writer but "an exceedingly unsafe moral adviser." Referring to the earthy work of François Rabelais, TR wrote to one of his sons, "I have no doubt that he has a certain merit of his own, but after vain effort I find that I no more care to read him than I would to examine a gold chain encrusted in the filth of a pigpen."

Though today we might draw the lines rather differently, the point merits reflection. Roosevelt would likely have agreed with business consultant James Rohn, who urges would-be leaders to consume "vitamins for the mind" just as they ingest supplements for their physical health.

In his *Autobiography* Roosevelt wrote that leaders "need more than anything else to know human nature, to know the needs of the human soul; and they will find this nature and these needs set forth as nowhere else by the great imaginative writers, whether of prose or poetry." Where such books include beneficial moral content they "will enable [the reader] to furnish himself with much ammunition which he will find of use in the battle of life."

PROPELLED BY HIS restless curiosity, TR trained himself to assimilate knowledge that might be of use from any conceivable source. His manner of reading periodicals—tearing out the pages as he consumed their offerings and then dropping them to the floor—was apt.

Observers marveled at his ability to read rapidly and retain vast amounts of information. Owen Wister recalled a visit to the White House:

> In the train going to Washington one afternoon, I finished a book just published which I felt sure would interest him. When he came into my bedroom for a talk about half-past five, which was his habit to do, I put the book in his hand, *The New South*. He turned the leaves over, decided to read it, and took it away. Next morning at breakfast, he reviewed the whole volume and discussed its main points. . . . Now, he had left my room after six, we had a large dinner party, and additional guests after it until bedtime about eleven. . . . Somewhere between six one evening and eight-thirty next morning, beside his dressing and his dinner and his guests and his sleep, he had read a volume of three-hundred-and-odd pages, and missed nothing of significance that it contained.

Roosevelt was blessed with a photographic memory, enabling him to summon up entire pages and quote from memory long after the initial encounter (he could do the same with people, often recalling names and brief conversations from years earlier). He was, by all accounts, a speed-reader (this may have resulted in part from his pursuit of knowledge for use in action, prompting him to hunt valued information rather than passively follow authors' arguments).

Winston Churchill wrote of a British statesman, "The Past stood ever at his elbow and was the counsellor upon which he most relied. He seemed to be attended by Learning and History, and to carry into current events an air of ancient majesty." Roosevelt would ponder current events with the assistance of knowledge gained from the past. His daughter Alice recalled, "I can hear my father and Cabot Lodge talking about Jefferson as if he were an obnoxious neighbor of theirs."

TR's reading was omnivorous, cutting across numerous disciplines—from history and literature, to science and philosophy, in several languages. This allowed for a continual cross-fertilization of information that would later find expression in thought and action.

Roosevelt was a notably prolific writer. To be sure, the quality of his writing varied jarringly. His *Naval War of 1812* remains a standard reference. His *Winning of the West,* though not fulfilling his ambitious goal of carrying him into the front rank of historians, includes passages of brilliance, suggesting what might have been. Some of his biographies and essays on topics of the day from birth control to the arts to modern politics are of more interest in casting light on TR and his time than on his ostensible subjects. His *Oliver Cromwell*—one of three books published while he was governor of New York—was playfully described as "a fine, imaginative study of Cromwell's qualifications for the governorship of New York."

Nonetheless, Roosevelt's writing, like his reading, was critical to his leadership. It required that he systematize and discipline his thinking across a range of subjects. The requisite study provided the opportunity, perhaps even more than his reading, of pulling forth the "forethought" that would become the basis for subsequent actions and decisions. Roosevelt as author has been fairly criticized as limited by an inability to get beyond himself. Granting that, writing necessarily entails a degree of separation from subject conducive to attaining greater objectivity and perspective. Through reading and writing, Roosevelt absorbed the experiences and judgments of others—enabling him to draw even more value from his own life experiences.

AS MUCH AS he valued books, TR stated that he reached his mature conclusions on major issues "not so much as the result of study in the library or the reading of books . . . as by actually living and working with men under many different conditions and seeing their needs from many different points of view." Roosevelt unified the life of action and the life of thought into a dynamo of continuous learning.

Beginning as a boy, travel made him respectfully aware of other cultures and languages, spurring creativity. Though he did not particularly enjoy his first visit to Europe at the age of ten, when he was fourteen he returned with a more mature appreciation, also sightseeing in the area now known as the Middle East. His focus on bird life in Egypt stimulated a lifelong interest. Such experiences were almost certainly behind his insistence in later life that Americans overcome prejudice against learning from the work of foreign nations, particularly in an age of instantaneous communication through the telegraph and telephone.

Throughout his life TR would turn to travel for learning and perspective. He came to regard his time in the Badlands "as the most educational asset of all my life." His African safari in 1909–1910 not only provided the lessons of team cooperation and hunting, but also enabled him to bring back hundreds of specimens for scientific study and preservation in America. His Amazon expedition in 1914 resulted in the exploration of a major river; in his honor the name was changed from the "River of Doubt" to Rio Teodoro. His travel was enriched by his continual reading in transit and on tour, combined with his usual practice of writing articles, books, and letters about his experiences.

AN EARLY LOVE of nature and a rather late correction for nearsightedness helped TR to develop heightened powers of observation. He could identify animals, especially birds, as well as leading naturalists of the day (in his *Autobiography* he recounted, with boyish pride, that he identified forty-one birds during an afternoon walk in the English countryside). Doubtless this ability spilled over into the whole of his daily experience.

He could be an attentive listener. To be sure, Roosevelt was a legendarily vigorous talker—some claimed, only partially in jest, that perhaps a handful of minutes during a several-hour dinner might be seized by someone else. Nonetheless, he was able to listen with care and then rapidly interpret and distill information. TR has been compared with his distant cousin Franklin in his capacity to listen productively even while speaking. This could be applied not only in gauging group reaction to a presentation but also in one-on-one meetings. Both Roosevelts were known for holding occasional interviews in which they spoke without pause, simultaneously gleaning information from their observations of their visitors' countenances.

It might be glib to say simply that Roosevelt had an "open mind"—rarely has someone been so opinionated—but he certainly was open to information from virtually any source. This included competitors. William Jennings Bryan—the Democratic presidential nominee defeated three times in campaigns in which Roosevelt characterized his ideas as "dangerous" and far worse—had a fair point in observing that TR eventually adopted most major planks of Bryan's platform. Roosevelt would study his opponents' ideas, challenge those he found wanting, and not hesitate to adopt those he found convincing, constructive, or consistent with his own approach.

As Roosevelt sought multiple sources of information at any given time, he was also able to bring to bear learning from earlier in his life. Lewis Einstein noted that conclusions Roosevelt developed as a young assemblyman attacking a "wealthy criminal class" did not reemerge publicly until years later, when he directed his gaze toward "malefactors of great wealth." TR was able to focus his attention entirely on one matter, then focus just as intently on subsequent matters as they arose—and return later with renewed, undivided attention to the first. Einstein explained, "He could take up a cause and invest it at once with the fierce ardor of an intense conviction. He would make it his own and attach to it the loyal devotion and enthusiasm of others who recognized the power of his leadership even when they mistook the exclusiveness of his interest."

TR applied lessons learned in one phase of his life to new circumstances. His experience as an assemblyman informed his consideration of issues such as industrial justice, the power of special interests corrupting business and political life, and the need to make the legal system more accountable to the public. His service as police commissioner was strengthened by his previous experience as an assemblyman examining New York City governance issues. His presidential policies on military affairs were illumined by his four months of active duty, his service as assistant naval secretary, and his lifelong study and writing on naval affairs. TR's views on the American character were based not only on historical study but also on firsthand experience, especially in the West. He found empathy with people far outside the small circle of privilege into which he was born. His frustration in subordinate roles early in his career enhanced his ability to perform as chief executive, resulting in nuanced sensitivity to management issues such as delegation of authority.

A related attribute is seen in Roosevelt's culling information or a phrase from earlier reading and suddenly applying it to a new situation. In characterizing President Woodrow Wilson's notorious circumlocution as "weasel words" he apparently called forth reading from a periodical more than a decade earlier. When he cautioned reformers to avoid repeating the mistake of Mrs. Jellyby, he drew on the Dickens character who committed herself to saving the distant oppressed, overlooking the chaos of her own household. When he affixed the term "muckraker" to overly zealous journalists who belabored the negative and the notorious, he turned to Bunyan's then-familiar *Pilgrim's Progress*. When he warned against "meddlesome Matties," Americans recognized the term from *McGuffey's Readers,* the ubiquitous children's books of moral instruction.

IN HIS ROLE as executive, TR understood that his ongoing learning was of critical importance. Despite his own knowledge—one might say, *because* of his own knowledge—he was, in the words of one associate, "the most advisable man I ever met." This was not always understood, in part because Roosevelt might react instantaneously to someone who he felt was wasting his time. As Senator Albert Beveridge recalled, "Stupidity disgusted him; even when one who was his friend would do or say anything stupid he could be very harsh. And dullness irritated him. It was hard for him not to show his impatience with the pallid and the commonplace."

Among those whose opinions he valued TR was a careful, respectful listener, more than willing to accept suggestions. Roosevelt understood that most people had something of value to add on one topic or another; a few people, such as his close friend and adviser Elihu Root, had something to add on almost every topic; and a group of well-chosen team members might add additional value within the discipline of a well-run meeting.

He recognized that a chief executive's information about his organization and its performance could not come entirely from his own staff—even with the best of intentions inevitably it would be filtered through a sieve of self-interest. Nathan Miller reports that as president, TR "insisted that every news article, no matter how unfavorable to him or his administration, be shown to him, and a staff member was assigned to look through 350 newspapers each day and to clip items that reflected the mood of the nation." He regularly received members of Congress and citizens, hearing their concerns personally. No less significant was his extraordinarily active correspondence, encompassing not only average citizens but also accomplished individuals across the world, representing the full range of his rampant curiosity.

Roosevelt did not hesitate to turn to experts for advice. His bonds with journalist Jacob Riis were built on his admiration of Riis's book *How the Other Half Lives,* which exposed the dreadful underside of New York life. Riis recalled that TR "came to my office one day when I was out and left his card with a simple message written in pencil: 'I have read your book, and I have come to help.'" From George Bird Grinnell he learned of the destruction of big game, increasing his receptiveness to novel notions of wildlife preservation. As a member of the Civil Service Commission he read Captain Alfred Mahan's *The Influence of Sea Power upon History, 1660–1783,* which greatly influenced his subsequent policy actions at the Navy Department and the White House. In 1906, in the same period he was decrying "muckrakers," he read Upton Sinclair's exposé of the meatpacking industry, *The Jungle.* Based on the book's information and its public impact, Roosevelt successfully pushed for sweeping regulatory authority. Many more examples could be offered in this vein.

As an executive TR frequently developed special relationships with such experts, going beyond the transmission of information and knowledge. Riis worked at his side at the Police Board and would remain a valued friend and journalistic ally. Grinnell and other conservationists became a network of activists. As assistant secretary of the navy Roosevelt turned to Mahan not only for historical perspective but also for input on ongoing policy and political decisions. Such relationships lengthened his executive reach; they also resulted in durable partnerships that might reemerge as significant in the future.

TO ADD VALUE, the learning of a chief executive must be reflected in the performance of the organization he leads. A central goal for any living enterprise is to continuously learn.

A chief executive can accomplish this in part by attracting and motivating outstanding individuals to run operating divisions. Roosevelt distinguished his presidential administration by assembling and leading a conspicuously talented team.

TR initiated the modern presidential commission to serve as a prototype management consultancy. Through this vehicle he injected the best thinking, up-to-date information, and unconventional but promising ideas into stolid executive bureaucracies. He thereby might obtain information from his own organizations that may have been blocked from reaching the top of the chain of command. The commissions were also an informal vehicle for the identification and training of promising personnel who might not otherwise have come to TR's attention.

Roosevelt established six study commissions during his presidency. Each included prominent figures from relevant fields and was staffed by executive branch employees, at no additional cost to taxpayers. One, the Keep Committee, rooted out bureaucratic waste. Another examined the multifarious approaches taken by government agencies to scientific issues, seeking to make their policies consistent and up-to-date. The commission vehicle was utilized most extensively in the conservation arena. This reflected Roosevelt's personal interest and the presence of enterprising staff such as Gifford Pinchot. It also reflected the reality that conservation, as defined by TR, was a new organizing principle cutting across longstanding boundaries of thought and organization.

The most controversial was the Commission on Country Life. Roosevelt's concern was that while agricultural policy was a top priority of government, the broader questions of rural life, in a time of transition from an agricultural to an industrial-based economy, were insufficiently considered. Congress refused to pay for the publication of its report—and expressly prohibited the establishment of any future presidential commissions absent prior congressional approval. Roosevelt, nearing the close of his time in office, was disinclined to place value on congressional relationships as opposed to tangible accomplishments. With jaunty disregard for legal niceties, TR publicly dismissed the prohibition as unconstitutional. He added, lest there be any doubt, that were he remaining in office he would expressly disobey it.

Underlying the controversy was recognition of the power of outside reviews to disrupt existing arrangements. Information might be updated, or gathered together in a new manner, challenging longstanding assumptions. Additional groups might enter the process or bring public focus on issues heretofore resolved behind closed doors, if at all. The reaction of the general public or affected parties might allow—or require—the chief executive to reconfigure priorities. Congressional critics (and those who stimulated their concerns) and Roosevelt were justified in finding this worthy of a fight. In many circumstances, in the words of Thomas Jefferson, "information is power."

ROOSEVELT'S THIRST FOR learning was never quenched. Wister suggested that his White House was an American *salon*—a place of sophisticated conversation in the European tradition. If so, it was a decidedly American variant, as likely to include gunslingers as tea sippers. TR was on an "incessant lookout for merit in any worthy talk, and his instant impulse [was] to give merit his emphatic recognition and encouragement." Wister continued:

> Bat Masterson would be coming to lunch. If you were to be there, Roosevelt would manage to tell you of Bat's formidable pistol and his use of it in discouraging murderers in the alkali. If Seth Bullock were invited, you would hear in advance about his friendship and admiration for Seth Bullock in the lawless Bad Lands. . . . Or it would be a geologist, an ornithologist, a Danish authority on tropical diseases, a German who had written a

remarkable work about crustaceans, or somebody who had got farther south, or farther north, or farther up Mount Everest, than anybody else. Or it would be some Balkan historian who had brought letters, and there were indications that he would turn out a distressing bore; but you were not to worry, he would put the Balkan next to himself and do his best.

He might see Buffalo Bill Cody one day; boxing champ John L. Sullivan the next; the president of Harvard on the third; a Rough Rider on the fourth. TR's curiosity about ideas and his bent for activity were reflected in his taste in companions. In the words of one writer during TR's lifetime, "He likes prize fighters, painters, cowboys, poets, diplomatists, hunters, sculptors, soldiers, naturalists, football players, novelists, men who can tell him about Irish or Norwegian sagas, about ancient Greek coins, or about almost anything else." More than one observer saw his curiosity and delight in learning about life as indicative of a "boy's mind." One expects TR would not have disagreed.

LEARNING WAS, LITERALLY, a *vital* part of Roosevelt's leadership—a living force. His preparation for leadership through self-mastery began with books at his side. His years of leadership were constantly informed and enlarged by reading and writing, conversation, correspondence, and an extraordinarily broad—yet methodically bounded—quest for experience. One of a leader's key roles is to educate—a word derived from the Latin "to lead forth." Roosevelt understood that a leader must continuously learn if he is to remain an effective teacher. TR's approach to learning unified his forays into the realms of thought and action; it also bound together his life and his leadership.

Roosevelt avoided the error of those afflicted with what John Maxwell calls "destination disease." Such individuals labor under the delusion that if they achieve a particular goal, position, award, or degree, they will no longer need to learn. That would mean, of course, that they would no longer grow. A leader dedicated to service, recognizing that his enterprise can always improve—and that additional possibilities of service always arise—will make certain that his learning is perpetual. A leader's added value tends to arise *not* from what he has learned, but from the capacity to *continue* to learn.

TR ON LEADERSHIP

- To maintain usefulness as a teacher, a leader must always continue to learn.
- Become a voracious reader. Seek information, knowledge, and experience from every available medium.
- Examine the content of your learning experience—reading, writing, entertainment, time with companions—just as you monitor your nutrition. Leaders should strive for balanced mental and spiritual nourishment, including "vitamins for the mind."
- Develop your powers of observation and listening so that more and more of your daily experience yields knowledge, perspective, inspiration, and insight.
- Utilize lessons derived from earlier times in your life as ready reserves that can be cross-fertilized and deployed in future situations.
- Effective executives make themselves—and their enterprises—perpetual-motion learning machines.

Chapter Four

WORKING BRAVELY IN THE DARKNESS

Black care rarely sits behind a rider whose pace is fast enough.

—Theodore Roosevelt

On the morning of Wednesday, February 13, 1884, Assemblyman Theodore Roosevelt was surrounded by well-wishers in the capitol at Albany. Whatever misgivings colleagues harbored toward the hyperactive representative from Manhattan's Silk Stocking district were for the moment overcome amidst joyous news: a telegram reported that TR had become a father. A baby girl, named for his wife Alice, had been born on the evening of February 12. Roosevelt had anticipated the birth might occur on the fourteenth, Valentine's Day—the fourth anniversary of the announcement of their engagement. Nonetheless, his sense of the significance of dates likely gave him satisfaction that his firstborn arrived on the anniversary of Lincoln's birthday.

Later the same morning, the happiness was suddenly eclipsed by foreboding. Roosevelt's ebullience buckled as he read a second telegram. He immediately arranged to return home on the next available train.

Finally departing at dusk, he would endure an excruciatingly long train ride—at least five hours. The customary bleakness of an East Coast winter had become something rather different in February 1884. The sun had relinquished its dominion, yielding to a fog the likes of which rarely had been encountered. New York life was rendered torpid. The *New York Times* for the thirteenth editorialized: "It is suicide weather. Life does not seem worth living to a sensitive person easily influenced by atmospheric conditions. There is something comfortless and unhappy in the raw and chilly air, something suggesting of death and decay in the dampness that fills the world." One expects Roosevelt—doubtless habituated to regular reading of the most important daily newspaper in New York—saw these words.

They would have added a suitably dark background to the anxieties crowding his mind. Just over six years previously, in February 1878, TR, then a college student, sped by train from Boston to the deathbed of the father he idolized. Theodore Roosevelt, Sr., whom his son revered as "the greatest man I ever knew," died before his eldest son's arrival. He was forty-six.

As the train crawled through a fog so thick that ships at sea and pedestrians on the streets struggled to find their way, Roosevelt must have pondered the changeability, the apparent randomness of human affairs. Though the second telegram has not survived, it seems to have reported that his wife was gravely ill from complications from childbirth (perhaps with forced optimism, TR corresponded with a friend on the thirteenth, describing his wife as "only fairly well"). The second telegram may also have disclosed the appalling coincidence that his vibrant and beautiful mother, Martha Bulloch Roosevelt ("Mittie"), was herself in serious condition, likely from ingesting tainted food or water.

In young TR's eyes Alice Lee had always had an otherworldly quality. She was undeniably attractive. Her facial features were sculpted, marked by striking blue eyes, framed by blond tresses, warmed by a smile radiating her sunny temperament. Almost invariably described as "willowy," she was unusually tall for a woman of the time, standing just an inch shorter than Roosevelt. Her manner was cultivated and considerate, in part reflecting her privileged background. More than a century later, faded photographs readily convey her appeal. It is hardly surprising that Roosevelt would decide that he had fallen in love with her at first sight in the autumn of 1878. She was seventeen; he was turning twenty.

Young TR—bespectacled, dandified, intense suitor, awkward dancer, redolent of laboratory chemicals (he would later, apparently in part because of Alice's objections, turn away from a scientific career), explosive in speech, unable to contain nervous tension, as yet not having attained the charm for which he would later be noted—may not have immediately ascended to the top rung in Alice's eyes. As historian Betty Boyd Caroli gently put it in *The Roosevelt Women,* "he courted her with a passion that exceeded hers." He would not be deterred. Utterly ignoring the counsel reflected in Yeats's poem—"Never give all the Heart"—Roosevelt laid siege. He wrote in his diary in February 1880: "for a year and a quarter now I have *never* (even when hunting) gone to sleep or waked up without thinking of her; and I doubt if an hour has passed that I have not thought of her." Her self-esteem was sufficiently strong to withstand the full weight of his extravagant admiration and its concomitant expectations.

There were anxious moments, doubtless magnified by TR's restless imagination. At one point he purchased dueling pistols lest a rival interpose himself. Finally, on October 27, 1880, his birthday, they were married, bringing to a successful conclusion one of Roosevelt's earliest and most important campaigns.

The marriage was successful. By all accounts he continued to feel as he wrote near the end of their engagement, "I am so happy that I dare not trust my own happiness." Elsewhere he declared: "you have made my happiness almost too great." Gazing from the train into the fog, did he fear that his happiness had been so great that by some incomprehensible decree it must now be shattered? Did he reflect then, as at other times, on Emerson's law of compensation, whereby so many of the joys and pains of life might be viewed as inexorably tied, one to another?

Roosevelt had not yet made his way to the family home on West Fifty-seventh Street when his sister Corinne arrived at approximately 10:30 P.M. Their handsome, doomed, alcoholic brother Elliott threw open the door: "There is a curse on this house! Mother is dying, and Alice is dying too."

TR arrived shortly before midnight. He rushed to his wife's bedside, finding her in a semi-comatose, delirious state. He took her in his arms; it is not clear whether she recognized him. At about 3 A.M. he was told that his mother was dying, and he joined the other three children at her bedside. Mittie died shortly thereafter. She was forty-eight.

He returned to Alice, holding her until she died at 2 P.M. She was twenty-two.

Roosevelt had foreseen that Valentine's Day, Thursday, February 14, 1884, would be an important day in his life. It turned out very differently from what his charmed, cocooned, privileged existence had accustomed him to anticipate. He was twenty-five.

His diary for February 14 was marked by a large "X" and a single sentence: "The light has gone out of my life." The entry for the following day, Friday, the fifteenth, was left blank. On Saturday, after the joint service and burial of his mother and wife, TR summoned strength to compose a brief summary of Alice and their life together. In self-consciously deliberate, youthful handwriting, he concluded: "For joy or for sorrow my life has now been lived out."

In a privately circulated memorial Roosevelt wrote of Alice:

> We spent three years of happiness such as rarely comes to man or woman. . . . As a flower she grew, and as a fair young flower she died. Her life had been always in the sunshine. . . . None ever knew her who did not love and revere her for her bright, sunny temper and her saintly unselfishness. Fair, pure, and joyous as a maiden; loving, tender and happy as a young wife; when she had first become a mother, when her life seemed to be but just begun . . . by a strange and terrible fate, death came to her. And when my heart's dearest died, the light went from my life forever.

Henceforth, following the advice of a fellow legislator, Roosevelt would learn "to work bravely in the darkness."

IT WOULD BE difficult to overstate the force of the blow Roosevelt sustained. The intensity of his emotions for Alice, beginning with their courtship, led to outpourings that many today would consider almost incredible. Even by the standards of the Victorian era, TR was the ultimate romantic. It may be significant that his emotional life was not complicated by the hypocrisy that we often associate with the Victorians. At the time of her death, Alice was the first and only woman he had loved in every way a man can love a woman.

In 1908, nearing the end of his presidency, Roosevelt wrote one of his sisters with advice for her young daughter, whose fiancé had died unexpectedly:

> The one and only thing for her to do now is to treat the past as past, the event as finished and out of her life; to dwell on it, and above all to keep talking of it, with you or anyone else, would be weak and morbid. Let her try not to think of it; this she can not wholly avoid; but she can wholly avoid speaking of it. Let her

> show a brave and cheerful front to the world, whatever she feels; and let her never speak one word of the matter, henceforth, to you or to anyone else. In the long future, when the memory is too dead to throb, she may if she wishes again speak of it.

He never again spoke of Alice. Their daughter, the embodiment of their love, would never hear her father discuss her mother. Alice Lee Roosevelt remains forever young, a figure of possibility, her brief life noted on a simple gravestone in Greenwood Cemetery in Brooklyn.

DURING THE First World War, TR spoke with his friend Owen Wister about resolving difficulties:

> There are two kinds of troubles a man can be in: trouble that he can do something to cure, and trouble that nothing he can do will cure. If he is in the first kind of trouble, the longer he thinks about it, the worse he'll be: let him start at once, let him get into action and try to remove the trouble. That will help him to feel better very soon. But if it's a trouble he can't cure, let him dismiss it from his mind and think of something else.

For all cases Roosevelt prescribed action. In the immediate aftermath of the loss of Alice and his mother, Roosevelt gave himself entirely to his work. After the close of a hectic legislative session, he entered the national political fray, working against the inevitable nomination of James G. Blaine at the bitterly divided Republican convention of 1884. As part of their process of moving on, the surviving Roosevelts sold the home on West Fifty-seventh Street. TR decided not to seek reelection to the Assembly. He had followed this same approach—hard, almost manic work—after the death of his father. He would continue this practice for the remainder of his life. For example, in 1918, he insisted on keeping all appointments, including a speech to the Republican state convention at Saratoga, in the week he learned of the loss and then death of his son Quentin, a U.S. aviator in World War I. This approach combined whatever therapeutic value Roosevelt derived for himself with his serving as an example of putting the good of the cause before oneself.

As a next step after Alice's death, Roosevelt arranged for a complete change of scene. He returned to the distant, desolate Badlands he had first encountered in happier times. He was repeating, on a larger scale and in a new area, a similar outdoor sojourn he had undertaken following the loss of his father. He would meet new people, learn new skills, and constantly challenge himself. TR was developing a custom of using sustained, active travel to effect a boundary separating his present and future from his past and loss. He would live much of the next two years on the mythic American frontier, fortifying himself—mentally, physically, spiritually—for the next phase of his life.

The act of writing, reinforced by his ongoing, voracious reading, may have played a significant role, giving him greater perspective and a degree of closure. In addition to a tribute to Alice, he wrote extensively in two areas to which he would return for the remainder of his life: history and first-person accounts of his experiences in the outdoors. The act of writing redoubled his attention to his new tasks and surroundings and enhanced the acuity of his observations. It was likely in the summer of 1887 that Roosevelt penned the words that his friend Owen Wister believed to be central to understanding him: "Black care rarely sits behind a rider whose pace is fast enough." Writing brought together Roosevelt's worlds of thought and action. Perhaps, in a moment of lonely vulnerability to the changing winds of fortune, it may also have provided him, in the words of Shakespeare, a sense of being "author of himself."

A distinct individual emerged from this process of renewal and development in the frontier West. His friend and biographer William Roscoe Thayer wrote, "I recall my astonishment the first time I saw him, after a lapse of several years, to find him with the neck of a Titan and with broad shoulders and stalwart chest, instead of the city-bred, slight young friend I had known earlier." Others reacted similarly in 1910, observing significant changes following his return from the yearlong African safari he undertook after leaving the White House in 1909. Roosevelt used such recreation (which included a great amount of work ranging from physical labor to writing) in the original sense, *re-creating* himself.

TR observed, "Life brings sorrows and joys alike. It is what a man does with them—not what they do to him—that is the true test of his mettle." TR often expressed the view that he would never have become president without his western interlude. Biographer Carleton Putnam quoted Roosevelt's emotional reaction on returning to the Badlands in 1900: "[H]ere the romance of my life began." Since his extended time in the West was in reaction to Alice's death, one wonders if he pondered the implications of such statements.

Roosevelt's aggressive assertion of will—reflected in his self-discipline, his penchant for action, and his writing—coexisted with an acute awareness of the inability of humans to control their fate. In one sense this awareness rendered his project all the more courageous and poignant. It afforded him a sense of perspective beyond his years. In the first spring after Alice's death he wrote, "Although I am not a very old man, I have yet lived a great deal in my life, and I have known sorrow too bitter and joy too keen to allow me to become either cast down or elated for more than a very brief period over success or defeat."

Consciously or not, TR was following a saying passed from his mother's Southern family into the Roosevelts: "Live for the living, not the dead." In 1886 he ended his dual East-West interlude, restoring New York City as his full-time home, running unsuccessfully for mayor in November. He became engaged—after considerable anguish as to whether remarriage might be disloyal to Alice's memory—to his childhood companion and sweetheart, Edith Kermit Carow. Together they built a durable partnership, producing five children.

MISFORTUNE SUCH AS the loss of a loved one falls in TR's category of problems one cannot do much about. Mistakes, defeats, and failures more often fall in the category of problems one may be able to affect. For the latter he recommended study and reflection on the errors, followed by action to rectify them.

At least in private, and after the fact, Roosevelt could discuss and be forgiving of his own mistakes. For example, he wrote to one of his sons that he "rose like a rocket" in the state assembly but "came an awful cropper and had to pick myself up after learning by bitter experience the lesson that I was not all-important and that I had to take account of many different elements in life. It took me fully a year before I got back the position I had lost, but I hung steadily at it and achieved my purpose." Roosevelt's self-image as a leader was not redefined by his missteps; he altered his attitude to bring his performance back into line with his self-image.

In some situations TR publicly declared his mistakes. In a speech before the Assembly, he acknowledged that his vote in favor of a bill intended to cut the railway profits of speculator Jay Gould was in error. This was made all the more difficult by the fact that he shared the sentiment underlying the effort, memorably characterizing Gould and his associates "as . . . part of that most dangerous of all dangerous classes, the wealthy criminal class." Several Rough Riders commented favorably on his practice of immediately acknowledging his own error when he incorrectly applied drill manuals in training. Late in his career, picking up the mantle of woman's suffrage, he acknowledged that his earlier vacillation on the issue was mistaken.

Lincoln Steffens wrote that Roosevelt understood that confessing error not only was the right thing to do morally, but could also have positive consequences. According to Steffens, TR recognized that in so doing a leader could draw others near: "It'll make the people see that I'm just like them; one of them."

The beneficial side of apologies has its limits. Roosevelt warned Wister: "Never indulge yourself on the sinner's stool. If you did any harm, that won't undo it, you'll merely rake it up. The sinner's stool is often the only available publicity spot for the otherwise wholly obscure egotist."

The roll of Roosevelt's conspicuous mistakes is long. His financial investments in the Badlands yielded a flood of red ink. He failed in a bid to become speaker of the New York Assembly. He opposed the inevitable presidential nomination of Blaine in 1884, eventually incurring the wrath of all sides. He placed third in the three-way race for mayor of New York in 1886. Several years later, bowing to family pressure, he declined the mayoral nomination when victory may well have been assured. He left the New York City Police Board in frustration, stymied by the recalcitrance and passive-aggressive tendencies of at least one of his fellow commissioners. He repeatedly sought to avoid the vice presidential nomination in 1900, seeing it as the likely end of his public career. In 1906 President Roosevelt discharged three companies of African-American soldiers in response to a "conspiracy of silence" he suspected was shielding a small number from accountability for violence, including a murder, against civilians in Brownsville, Texas. As president, he blundered in prematurely declining to run for a third term and then in the selection of his successor, William Howard Taft. His post-presidential campaigning in 1910 was linked to a string of Republican defeats. His 1912 third-party candidacy split the Republicans, allowing the loathed Wilson to take office as a minority president, leaving TR isolated and in some cases shunned by long-time allies and friends.

TR said he would have no trouble identifying ten mistakes he had made for every one noted by others. The key is how he chose to handle them.

Roosevelt understood and accepted the dynamic whereby the home-run king may also be the strikeout king: "[T]he man who has never made any mistakes has never made anything." The more activities one undertakes, the more likely the errors; the more significant the activities, the more significant the errors. In a letter in 1900, Roosevelt sought perspective by reference to "one of the two greatest of all Americans, Abraham Lincoln. Lincoln committed mistake after mistake." TR expected mistakes from himself and others, sought to learn from them, and would then move on—not lingering and becoming, as he was wont to say, "morbid" about it. In the same vein, he had little patience with the "timid good," who avoided error by forsaking action.

Some mistakes, not going to core questions of leadership and character, can rapidly be rectified or contained. One of Roosevelt's, which seems almost comic today, involved the early twentieth-century movement for simplified spelling. Curiously for one so highly educated and said to be gifted with a photographic memory, TR was an atrocious speller. As president he expressed sympathy with the efforts of the Spelling Reform Association to simplify and systematize spelling. In 1906 he directed that government agencies adopt more than 300 spelling changes proposed by academic experts.

Though the reforms might be defensible on the basis of logic, public reaction ranged from derision to anger. The chief justice of the Supreme Court defiantly refused to adopt the new spelling. When Roosevelt sent his annual message to Congress, employing the new spellings, opponents grasped the opportunity to focus their long-simmering rage against what they considered a pattern of executive overreaching. A typical reaction was that of the *Louisville Courier-Journal:*

> Nuthing escapes Mr. Rucevelt. No subject is tu hi fr him to takl, nor tu lo for him to notis. He makes tretis without the consent of the Senit. He inforces such laws as meet his approval, and fales to se those that du not soot him. He now assales the English langgwidg, constitutes himself a sort of French Academy, and will reform the spelling in a way tu suit himself.

The *Baltimore Sun* queried: "How will he spell his own name? Will he make it 'Rusevelt' or will he get down to the fact and spell it 'Butt-in-sky'?" A humorist summed up the general reaction: "This is 2 mutch."

The House of Representatives, after days of debate, unanimously rebuked the president, directing that government documents should reflect "the standard of orthography prescribed in generally accepted dictionaries of the English language." TR saw the risk that the symbolic resonance of such a non-essential issue could damage his ability to lead on more significant matters. He rescinded his executive order and abandoned the cause—other than saying he would continue to use simplified spelling in his own correspondence.

One of Roosevelt's fateful mistakes occurred on election night 1904. Having won by the largest margin in history to that time, TR issued a surprise announcement to the press: "The wise custom which limits the President to two terms regards the substance and not the form. Under no circumstances will I be a candidate for or accept another nomination." His wife, Edith, visibly blanched when she—along with everyone else—heard this vow for the first time on election night.

In one sense the renunciation of power at the moment of his maximum strength is attractive and even admirable. Perhaps Roosevelt was stung by criticism that his obvious enjoyment of power indicated a tendency toward the authoritarian. In following Washington's two-term custom voluntarily (there was as yet no constitutional term limit on presidents), and beyond its letter (he had just been elected president for the first time, his first three years having been as successor upon McKinley's death), he might have seen himself making a gesture of historical magnitude. Was he thinking this act might add weight to comparisons of his presidency with those of his heroes, Washington and Lincoln, demonstrating beyond peradventure that his service was "disinterested"? Was he thinking of Oliver Cromwell, the English leader of whom he had recently written, who also renounced power voluntarily?

Whatever the rationale, he soon regretted the statement. TR repeatedly said he would have given his right hand to be able to take it back. In making himself a "lame duck" so early in his term, he tangibly weakened his presidency. Had he made the same announcement later, it would have had the same direct consequences without unnecessarily weakening his ability to lead. One might view his error, disinterested on its face, as arising from undue focus on himself rather than on those he served.

This was a mistake that could not be rectified or mitigated. Roosevelt knew that to reverse himself would make a bad situation much worse. He recognized that the "plain people" of the nation from whom he derived support—ordinary Americans such as today would be called the "middle class"—would have their faith shaken by such a reversal. He was immobilized: As with the renunciation, he said he would give his right hand rather than forfeit their trust. There was no way to go back on his word without appearing to be self-interested, irrevocably denuding his moral authority.

ROOSEVELT COMPREHENDED that an individual's reaction to and interpretation of adverse events and mistakes may be at least as important as the events and mistakes themselves. Whereas such events cannot be predicted, much less affected by any individual, anyone can determine his reaction by an act of will. Roosevelt manifestly did not allow his view of himself to be diminished by according undue significance to setbacks, either of his own doing or imposed. Neither would he allow his self-perception to be affected by others' negative characterization of his mistakes. If he could not correct an error or otherwise recover a loss, he would nonetheless transform it into an occasion for personal growth and a dividing point separating the past from the present and future.

Nonetheless, his reaction to the loss of his first love and first wife, Alice, can fairly be criticized as brutal. It would be difficult to defend his lifelong refusal to discuss her even with their daughter, particularly in light of the younger Alice's poignant attempts to win her father's attention if not approval. At the same time, his approach of moving on, not lingering in the past, living entirely in the moment to the best of one's ability, is worthy of emulation.

With respect to mistakes, Roosevelt applied a similar approach. He understood that missteps, properly understood and utilized, can be a path to greater achievement. They are to some extent inevitable, especially when a person takes an unconventional path, bereft of the reassurance that accompanies one who follows a familiar, rutted road.

When he made a mistake that could be rectified, he would act rapidly. He would try to cut his losses, as with the simplified spelling example, where he sensed additional danger from persisting on a doomed course. Where a mistake could not be corrected, as with his renunciation of a third term, Roosevelt would do his best not to linger over it. As he wrote in reviewing a book by Brooks Adams, "men who break new ground [tend] here and there to draw a devious furrow."

TR tended to speak of organizations and individuals in the same terms (thus able to offer his own life, and the lives of other leaders, as examples for collective action). He urged: "A strong and wise people will study its own failures no less than its triumphs, for there is wisdom to be learned from the study of both, of the mistake as well as of the success." He described "the whole period of the marvelous growth of the United States . . . [as] a constant and uninterrupted stream of failure going side by side with the larger stream of success." Roosevelt continually sought to learn from the experiences of others, whether from history or personal observation or otherwise.

Roosevelt applied a degree of calculation in deciding whether to publicly discuss his own mistakes. He likely understood that many people do not take a forgiving view of the mistakes of others, particularly those of controversial leaders. Should the fact of one misstep be utilized effectively by adversaries against achievement of an ongoing priority, acknowledging it might constitute an additional, perhaps more damaging error, at least without careful consideration of options of timing.

In some situations Roosevelt reacted to his own mistakes just as he reacted to misfortune; having done all he could, he moved on without looking back. He often said, as to students at Cambridge University in 1910, "I never took much interest in defeats." If an action could not be redefined credibly by him into a victory, he might banish it from his discussion. For example, his *Autobiography* included no mention of Alice Lee; his first, unsuccessful run for the New York City mayoralty; the Brownsville incident; even the excellent past performance of erstwhile allies (most notably Elihu Root) from whom he had become estranged. This might be understood as related to his occasional exaggerations of his accomplishments, as well as his craving for recognition, ranging from the

Medal of Honor to a boyish appreciation of uniforms. Determined to live to the fullest, in the moment, Roosevelt seemed to view his ups and downs as related parts in the construction of a life with many sides and experiences. Mistakes and misfortune could be made to be as useful as successes. They need not be understood as "failures." This approach is, of course, very different from that of an individual who seeks a career up a ladder where each rung unambiguously represents an advance; where "success" and "failure" appear more clearly defined—but defined almost entirely by others.

Without the comfort—and limitations—of such externally imposed definitions, one must be able to draw on resources within oneself. For Roosevelt, a critical factor, enabling him to do the best he could, wherever he was, was his indomitable optimism. Wister and others detected a wistful undertow in TR's ebullience. Many witnessed his dispiriting pessimism at key turning points in his career, such as before the 1904 election he ultimately won by a landslide. He would not allow himself to remain down for long.

Roosevelt tended to define his actions in moral terms. Focusing on the consequences of his actions for others may have helped him move on from mistakes more readily than individuals who think primarily in terms of their own perceived interests. To be sure, many people, then and now, have taken Roosevelt's moral pronouncements with a grain of salt, seeing him primarily as a professional politician with an uncanny ability to attract and use power. Without engaging that issue—but noting that such criticism awaits any leader avowing moral purposes—the fact remains that a focus on the needs of others may lead to an enlarged capacity to forgive oneself and be forgiven by others. There can be little question it empowered Roosevelt to move forward at various times in very difficult circumstances, as in the aftermath of his ill-starred 1912 Bull Moose presidential campaign.

Far from restraining his efforts or undermining his self-confidence, TR strove to convert his mistakes and misfortune into occasions for transformative personal growth. Tolerant of his own mistakes, as an executive he applied a sophisticated sense of which mistakes should be forgiven—or even encouraged—by members of his team. His ability to bounce back from disappointment showcased qualities of character that inspired others and fortified his leadership.

TR ON LEADERSHIP

- How an individual chooses to interpret a misfortune or mistake can be at least as significant as the objective facts at hand.
- One should not dwell on a misfortune or unavoidable mistake, where nothing can be done to rectify the situation. Renewed action can establish a boundary separating the past from the present and future.
- Leaders should strive to view mistakes as learning opportunities.
- Where appropriate, a leader should acknowledge error and apologize—but not take the "sinner's stool."
- Where a leader makes a mistake in a manifest effort to serve others, forgiveness—by oneself as well as from others—is more readily achievable than where one appears to be acting in one's own interest.
- An individual's ability to carry on in the face of calamitous adversity showcases critical leadership traits, including perseverance, self-containment amidst difficult circumstances, courage, perspective, and an ability to focus on the needs of others rather than oneself. Individuals who have mastered such challenges in their own lives are more apt to be viewed as leaders able to serve others.

CHAPTER FIVE

WIELDING THE BIG STICK

[Y]ou are probably acquainted with the old proverb: "Speak softly and carry a big stick—you will go far." If a man continually blusters, if he lacks civility, a big stick will not save him from trouble; and neither will speaking softly avail, if back of the softness there does not lie strength, power.

—THEODORE ROOSEVELT

ONE IMAGE OF Roosevelt stands out among all others: fighter. The boy who could not hold his own against his school-age tormentors came to view life as a succession of battles. It was not surprising that TR replaced the billiards table in the governor's mansion at Albany with a wrestling mat. A spirited if not physically imposing boxer since his youth, as president he lost the sight in his left eye in a sparring match.

TR saw fight and struggle in every aspect of life. Entering politics he separated himself from the "timid good": "You can't govern yourselves by sitting in your studies and thinking how good you are. You've got to fight all you know how, and you'll find a lot of able men willing to fight you." For the individual, the group, the nation, the rule was the same: "There is only one effective defense, and that is the offensive. There is only one way to win a fight, and that is by hitting and not parrying." As assistant secretary of the navy he urged:

> In public as in private life a bold front tends to insure peace and not strife. . . . Diplomacy is utterly useless where there is no force behind it; the diplomat is the servant, not the master, of the soldier. . . . Peace is a goddess only when she comes with sword girt on thigh.

Far from incompatible with virtue, aggressive fighting is necessary to achieve it: "[Y]ou have got to make up your mind in life that you can only be as good and affectionate as you are willing to fight for. It is easy enough to be the opposite, but you have to fight to be good." As for opponents, they must be made to understand "that if they go to war they must expect to be shot at." This requires "a man who is willing to fight, who knows the time to fight, and who knows how to fight."

Compared in life to Wordsworth's "happy warrior," Roosevelt declared: "Aggressive fighting for the right is the noblest sport the world affords." His temperament matched his analysis that "the forces of good [are] in [a] ceaseless contest with the forces of evil." At home, he brandished the Big Stick with relish against individuals or groups he saw acting at variance with his nationalist vision of America. Most famously, "malefactors of great wealth" felt the sting of the stick, but so did some on the other side of the political fence, such as anarchists and socialists. Some critics claimed to see a lust for war in his fighting spirit. To those who labeled him a warmonger, TR responded: "'Blessed are the peacemakers,' not merely the peace-lovers; for action is what makes thought operative and valuable." He did not hesitate to wield the Big Stick against any nation. To meet the requirements of his policies, Roosevelt made the stick larger and larger, culminating in a world-class

American navy. As in other areas, he generalized from his own experience: "the very fact a nation can fight often obviates the necessity of fighting. It is just so with a boy."

And just so with a president. Roosevelt could shift rapidly from the clenched fist to the open hand; the combination made him a remarkably successful negotiator. His mediation of the Russo-Japanese War in 1905 resulted in his winning the Nobel Peace Prize. He extended the Monroe Doctrine, to ensure that foreign nations could not use debt collection from Latin American nations as a pretext for military intervention in the Western Hemisphere. Backing his policy with growing American military might, Roosevelt's administration launched no U.S. invasions of Latin American nations. He was the first world leader to submit an international dispute to the Court of Arbitration at The Hague. He led the effort to include representatives of Latin American nations at the Second Hague Conference and succeeded in winning its adoption of the Drago Doctrine, outlawing the use of force in collecting foreign debts. Roosevelt was pleased with the characterization of an admiring admiral: "[Y]ou knew how to use force without committing violence."

TR employed the Big Stick in negotiating landmark agreements in the domestic arena. He successfully mediated the Anthracite Coal Strike of 1902 that threatened to shut down the nation's economy and unleash violent unrest. His negotiations with Congress yielded numerous achievements, including the Hepburn Act, regulating the nation's railroads, and legislative acquiescence to the construction of the Panama Canal. In 1910, shortly after TR departed from the White House, cereal magnate C. W. Post unsuccessfully recruited him as prospective president of the Trades and Workers Association of America, an organization advocating mediation of labor disputes.

In some circumstances, perhaps including his 1912 Bull Moose candidacy, the temptation to join a good fight may have overcome Roosevelt's better judgment. In general, though, he skillfully used his renown as a fighter as a tool to resolve conflict through negotiation.

Among the elements of Roosevelt's negotiating approach are the following:

Preparation is critical. On the "substantive" side, Roosevelt sought a strong negotiating stance—making sure he had his Big Stick ready for action. This might mean military preparedness, the initiation of a lawsuit, or the adroit use of publicity. As he once said as governor, "When I go to war, I try to arrange it so that all the shooting is not on one side."

From a process standpoint, negotiation often necessitates that parties make decisions in rapid fire, in a sequence that is not necessarily foreseeable. As with all decisions, forethought can be of vital importance. Roosevelt spent three to four months, for example, in pre-negotiations with the Japanese and Russians prior to mediating their dispute. It is important to identify one's *interests* with exactitude prior to negotiations, so they can be understood and communicated clearly, even as parties' bargaining *positions* change. TR also studiously examined the backgrounds and negotiating techniques of the individuals with whom he would deal.

Make timing your ally. Roosevelt was fond of the saying "Ninth-tenths of wisdom consists in being right in time." To the extent one can control the timing, one can not only ensure one's own preparedness but also disadvantage the adversary. Taking the initiative enabled TR to "do [his] fighting in the adversary's corner."

Roosevelt deliberately timed actions to obtain maximum leverage in negotiations. An example occurred in his 1906 parley with House Agriculture Committee chairman James Wadsworth over federal regulation of the meatpacking industry. TR had ordered a Department of Agriculture investigation into sensational allegations leveled in Upton Sinclair's best-selling book, *The Jungle.* The resulting report was damning. To break through Wadsworth's intransigent opposition to new regulation, Roosevelt indicated that he would not make the report public if the chairman would let his bill pass the committee. When Wadsworth acquiesced—but inserted disabling amendments—TR released portions of the report, further inflaming public concerns over food safety. He privately threatened to disclose additional investigative findings as necessary to overcome the opposition of Wadsworth and his allies. This pattern persisted throughout the negotiation. In the end, Roosevelt got his bill, and Wadsworth lost the congressional seat he had held for a generation.

Timing can provide necessary context within which a negotiation will occur. TR took decisive actions early in his presidency, exhibiting his willingness to bring to bear all power at his disposal. In 1902 he quietly threatened force against Germany should it intervene in Venezuela, sending an unmistakable signal throughout the diplomatic community. In the same year he took a strong public position in the Anthracite Coal Strike, laying the groundwork for credibly threatening a government takeover of the mines should labor-management negotiations fail. In 1903 he declined to arbitrate long-standing Alaska boundary disputes with Great Britain—until he was assured of settlement terms favorable to the United States. Thus defined in public and expert opinion, Roosevelt would have greater room for potential compromise in future negotiations without creating an appearance of weakness.

Define your negotiating role based on the interests you represent. Roosevelt assumed various roles in negotiations. In some situations, including a number of legislative and foreign policy settings, he acted as an advocate for a set of interests. At other times he served as a mediator among contending parties (it should be noted, however, that his service as a mediator was itself an assertion of presidential power in domestic affairs, and an assertion of U.S. power in international affairs). With his sights set on advancing the interest for which he was responsible, TR consciously tailored his role in negotiations, in turns tending toward facilitation, direction, advocacy.

Seek to delegate your negotiating authority. While maintaining decision-making authority, Roosevelt did not hesitate to utilize staff to handle negotiations. For example, Elihu Root, while serving as his secretary of state, was afforded wide latitude. This extended TR's reach while simultaneously providing him distance should a contingency disrupt the process or make a renegotiation necessary. Having others negotiate also allowed him, as in the Russo-Japanese War mediation, to gain perspective while continuing to gather information from sources outside the negotiation. His separation, combined with his studied neutrality, provided the contending parties with the safety valve of seeking his involvement at critical junctures.

Ensure that the other side has complete authority to negotiate. Roosevelt made certain that the representatives with whom he would negotiate had complete authority to bind the entities represented.

Seek direct communication with principals. Where the negotiation was with a representative of the ultimate decision-maker, TR would seek direct access to the decision-maker. In dealing with foreign nations, he might intervene personally in negotiations among diplomats, while not forgoing his option to communicate directly with his counterpart heads of state and governments. When Roosevelt negotiated with the New

York political boss Senator Platt, delineating their prospective relationship should TR become governor, he obtained express assurance that he would have direct access to the political and business leaders in whose name Platt spoke. In the case of elected officials generally, Roosevelt considered his recognized skill in communicating directly with their constituents—their principals—to be one of his negotiating advantages.

Focus resolutely on interests. Negotiations, like other group endeavors, can take on lives of their own—with distinctive rhythms, personalities, and tendencies. In the heat of a contentious negotiation participants may lose sight of their underlying interests, instead becoming embroiled in conflicts arising from bargaining positions. In *Getting to Yes,* Roger Fisher, William Ury, and Bruce Patton explain that reconciling interests rather than positions succeeds for two reasons: There may be more resolutions possible for an underlying interest than a bargaining position; even though bargaining positions are opposed, there may be shared or compatible interests underlying them.

Roosevelt understood this distinction and acted on it. In dealing with Senator Platt, for example, one of his fundamental interests was to protect his independent authority, as governor, from incursions by Platt's machine. When Platt requested that they meet in New York City (rather than the capital, Albany), Roosevelt readily obliged, insisting only that the fact of such meetings be publicly disclosed. From Platt's perspective, having TR meet with him in New York City was significant in signaling the continuing clout of the "Easy Boss." Roosevelt viewed it as a compromise over a matter of small significance. As he wrote to a reformer in 1900, "Mr. Platt is very sensitive about his dignity and position. I am not in the slightest degree sensitive in these matters. I want results. I am only too glad to call on Mr. Platt, or to have him to dinner, or take breakfast with him, and to discuss with him first and at length all projects, provided, in the end, I have my way about these same projects."

To critics of his practice of meeting with individuals with whom he disagreed on one or more major issues, TR responded: "If my virtue ever becomes so frail that it will not stand meeting men of whom I thoroughly disapprove, but who are in active official life and whom I must encounter, why I shall go out of politics and become an anchorite. Whether I see these men or do not see them, if I do for them anything improper then I am legitimately subject to criticism; but only a fool will criticize me because I see them."

When Platt attempted to foist an appointment on the new governor, Roosevelt immediately balked, even though the prospective officeholder may have been objectively "qualified." Politely but firmly rejecting the attempt to dictate the selection, TR underscored that as governor he welcomed recommendations but reserved final decision-making authority. Platt was not pleased with this approach, but he found that Roosevelt would indeed accept input on personnel matters. In some cases Roosevelt would passively await proposed appointments from Platt or other political leaders. If the suggestions proved unacceptable, TR would turn them back, and the process would resume until a suitable individual was proposed. Roosevelt would give all possible credit to those who backed successful applicants and seek their assistance for his own priorities (which tended to be legislative proposals.) For more significant posts, TR might present Platt or other relevant leaders with a list of candidates he found acceptable, seeking their reactions. For the most important jobs, Roosevelt would ascertain and communicate an objective standard of qualification. Thereafter Platt or others would propose individuals who could meet the standard, achieving the aims of all sides. If in the end Roosevelt decided on a course of action he had reason to believe would disappoint or provoke Platt, he would grant the proud older gentleman the respectful courtesy of advance notice—but he would not seek his consent.

A disciplined focus on interests, advanced through skilled listening and flexibility in positions, can set the stage for novel solutions, "thinking outside the box." When TR was police commissioner he found himself enmeshed in a controversy concerning the visit of a notorious German anti-Semite named Ahlwardt. Some urged that Ahlwardt be banned from speaking. Others declared that the right to free speech must not be abridged, even though the city would have to deploy its police to protect this most undesirable of guests. Roosevelt, after broad consultation, determined that the interests of all sides could be met by providing security protection—with a detail of forty Jewish policemen. TR recalled, "Herr Ahlwardt delivered his violent harangues against the men of Hebrew faith, owing his safety to the fact that he was scrupulously protected by the men of the very race he was denouncing."

In the Anthracite Coal Strike of 1902, the nation faced imminent, widespread privation and civil disorder. President Roosevelt strove to mediate a bitter dispute between the mining companies and the miners' unions. Negotiations reached an impasse over the appointment of a presidential Commission of Arbitration. Though the appointments would be at the president's discretion, each member was to represent a specified interest or qualification. The operators adamantly refused to legitimize a representative of organized labor.

With winter looming and negotiations near the breaking point, Roosevelt divined the operators' underlying interest within their bargaining position. He reframed a point of contention:

> After about two hours' argument, it dawned on me that they were not objecting to the thing, but to the name. I found that

> they did not mind my appointment of any man, whether he was a labor man or not, so long as he was not appointed *as* a labor man, or *as* a representative of labor; they did not object to my exercising any latitude I chose in the appointments so long as they were made under the headings they had given. . . . I announced at once that I accepted the terms laid down. With this understanding, I appointed the labor man I had all along had in view, . . . calling him an "eminent sociologist."

Another notable instance of President Roosevelt's concentration on interests occurred in 1906. He was engaged in pitched battle with Senate grandees who opposed his legislation establishing national regulation of railroads. Senator Nelson Aldrich of Rhode Island—respected, intelligent, shrewd, calculating—was the leader of the Republican majority resisting the will of the forceful president of their own party. Reckoning that Roosevelt was motivated as much by power lust or pride as concern for the legislation, Aldrich came upon an ingenious and unexpected stratagem: he tapped a Democrat to sponsor TR's bill, Senator Benjamin R. Tillman of South Carolina.

Tillman was anathema to Roosevelt, personally and politically. According to historian William H. Harbaugh, Tillman was "a beak-nosed, one-eyed master of personal invective whom Roosevelt had once compared to Robespierre and Marat and had not spoken to for four years." Shortly before Aldrich's artful maneuver, TR had banned "Pitchfork Ben" from the White House.

Roosevelt was likely annoyed by this turn of events, but he was not cowed. He later wrote, "I did not care a rap about Mr. Tillman's getting credit for the bill, or having charge of it. I was delighted to go with him or with any one else just so long as he was traveling my way—and no longer." Later in the process, with success in sight, other legislators stepped forward to assume the lead, and TR abandoned Tillman. Roosevelt's focus on interest (or, as he termed it, "the essentials") rather than personality was determinative.

Protect ongoing relationships. One of the most important interests in many negotiations is the relationship between the parties. For example, a business leader dealing with a financial institution, a government agency, or a competing company may need to consider, even in the most heated dispute, the consequences to an ongoing relationship.

Roosevelt's vigorous use of the Big Stick coexisted with an unusual, hard-earned capacity to maintain relationships. This may have resulted in part from his steadfast focus on interests rather than personalities. In the heat of the fight over railroad regulation, historian George E. Mowry reported, TR and Aldrich maintained "cordial personal relations . . . even dined together in the White House." As governor, he lost no opportunity to publicly and privately praise Senator Platt, for example, in areas where they agreed (even though this meant that during his governorship, Roosevelt most often praised his stance on national rather than state issues).

He made a practice of sending draft copies of speeches and other important documents to various individuals with whom he would negotiate, simultaneously seeking their input and giving notice of his thoughts.

As with Platt, Roosevelt paid great heed to issues of protocol in dealing with heads of state. He maintained cordial relations with the famously prickly Kaiser Wilhelm II of Germany, even after compelling him to retreat from several threatened actions against U.S. interests. President Roosevelt revealed his approach to an American diplomat:

> I have always been most polite with him, have done my best to avoid our taking any attitude which could possibly give him legitimate offense, and have endeavored to show him that I was

> sincerely friendly to him and Germany. Moreover, where I have forced him to give way I have been sedulously anxious to build a bridge of gold for him, and to give him the satisfaction of feeling that his dignity and reputation in the face of the world were safe. In other words, where I have had to take part of the kernel from him, I have been anxious that he should have all the shell possible, and have that shell painted any way he wished.

After TR proposed a second international conference at The Hague to advance the cause of international law, he discreetly backed off, acceding to the wish of Czar Nicholas II of Russia to be the official convenor. Mediating the Russo-Japanese War at Portsmouth, New Hampshire, in 1905, TR gave his personal attention to such details as serving lunch buffet-style, obviating the need for protocol determinations on order of service that might have taken on undue significance in an international dispute involving disparate cultures.

TR regarded his capacity to rein in his temper to be a significant accomplishment. Throughout his career he expressed frustration that too many people were quick to quarrel but slow to fight; he tended to be prepared for a fight but slow to quarrel. As governor he reported that his success in one of his most controversial negotiations was the result "of combining inflexible determination with extreme good nature, and resolutely refusing the advice of [those] who wanted me to quarrel [with opponents]." Even archrival President Wilson acknowledged—following a personal meeting as he prepared to deny TR the opportunity to lead troops on the battlefield in the First World War—that Roosevelt had an engaging "sweetness." We would now call it extraordinary charm. One political observer granted that TR was "as sweet a man as ever scuttled a ship or cut a throat."

In addition to recurrent declarations of "disinterestedness" and commitment to broader issues, Roosevelt's apparent eagerness for a fight may have led some people to avoid personalizing their disagreements with him. TR likely was attempting to meet the standard set by Lincoln, whom he quoted admiringly: "So long as I have been [president], I have not willingly planted a thorn in any man's breast."

Become a skillful, active listener. Roosevelt was, famously, a talker. He was also a highly skilled listener, an indispensable attribute for negotiating success. His power of observation, combined with finely tuned intuition, increased his effectiveness. For a person as intelligent and assertive as TR, the necessity of listening could tax his low reservoirs of patience. He recalled his frustration with a querulous corporate executive during the Anthracite Coal Strike: "If it wasn't for the high office I held I would have taken him by the seat of the breeches and nape of the neck and chucked him out of that window." As the Russo-Japanese mediation wore on, Roosevelt confided, "To be polite and sympathetic in explaining for the hundredth time something perfectly obvious, when what I really want to do is to give utterance to whoops of rage and knock their heads together—well, all I can hope is that the self-repression will be ultimately helpful for my character."

TR suppressed these potent urges and applied his ability to listen actively—not merely yielding the floor to others, but also drawing out valuable information and subtly guiding their thought processes. An observer at the Russo-Japanese mediation wrote:

> His conduct during the whole time that the peace negotiations lasted has been a marvel of tact. Without appearing to inject himself into the course of the conversations and discussions which took place between the delegates, he contrived to keep himself exactly informed as to all that was going on, and more than once intervened in the most discreet manner by conveying a hint or a message to the plenipotentiaries which cleared the

> skies and brought things back to their true level. . . . That he contrived to do so without showing openly his hand, and while abstaining from everything that could have been interpreted as an attempt to interfere in matters which were not supposed to concern him, was a work which perhaps no one in the whole world outside of himself would have been able to perform.

Be manifestly willing to walk away from the table. One of Roosevelt's great strengths as a negotiator was his manifest willingness to walk away from the table, to abandon negotiation altogether, if his "bottom line" was not met. Through his public and private actions and words, TR left no doubt that there were lines he would not cross.

Another example comes from his work with Senator Platt. Governor Roosevelt decided against reappointment of an ally of Platt's who held a high position in the state government. Platt arched his back, determined that the incumbent be retained. He reminded Roosevelt that the state senate—over which Platt had great influence—would not only have to approve a new nominee but also have to act affirmatively to remove the incumbent. TR later wrote that he "persistently refused to lose [his] temper, no matter what [Platt] said," and "explained good-humoredly" that he would take whatever actions he could, including testing the limits of the appointment powers of the governor, to work his will.

The back-and-forth continued for weeks, Platt remaining obdurate and threatening "war to the knife" that would cut short TR's career. A lieutenant of the machine boss followed up on the evening prior to Roosevelt's planned announcement of the new nominee. According to Roosevelt's *Autobiography:*

> My visitor went over the old ground, explained that the Senator would under no circumstances yield, that he was certain to win the fight, that my reputation would be destroyed, and that he wished

> to save me from such a lamentable smash-up as an ending to my career. I could only repeat what I had already said, and after half an hour of futile argument I rose and said that nothing was to be gained by further talk and that I might as well go. My visitor repeated that I had this last chance, and that ruin was ahead of me. . . . I shook my head and answered, "There is nothing to add to what I have already said." He responded, "You have made up your mind?" and I said, "I have." He then said, "You know it means your ruin?" and I answered, "Well, we will see about that," and walked toward the door. He said, "You understand, the fight will begin tomorrow and will be carried on to the bitter end." I said, "Yes," and added, as I reached the door, "Good night." Then as the door opened, my opponent, or visitor, whichever one chooses to call him, whose face was . . . impassive and . . . inscrutable, . . . said: "Hold on! We accept. Send in [the new appointee]. The Senator is very sorry, but he will make no further opposition!"

Roosevelt concluded, "I never saw a bluff carried more resolutely through to the final limit." His credible willingness to risk his career—something unusual in any time, and likely altogether unfamiliar to Senator Platt—not only enabled him to prevail in this negotiation, but also affected his overall relationship with the "Easy Boss."

Do not bluff. In the preceding example, Platt violated one of TR's tenets: "I never make a bluff, either in public or private life." He recognized that having a bluff called in any circumstances could undercut his credibility in future negotiations (another reminder that all negotiations are interrelated).

Roosevelt also understood that bluffing might endanger third parties. In 1903 he publicly criticized Russia's czarist government for pogroms in which hundreds of Jews were murdered. Though he set a precedent in using the presidency to direct international attention to humanitarian problems within the jurisdiction of other nations, he took care not to promise direct American assistance to the oppressed Russians. TR acknowledged that the Russian Jews received little direct benefit as a result, explaining: "out in the [W]est we always used to consider it a cardinal crime to draw a revolver and brandish it about unless the man meant to shoot. And it is apt to turn out to be sheer cruelty to encourage men by words and then not to back them up by deeds."

Maintain open negotiations. Whenever appropriate, Roosevelt opened his negotiations to the public. This had several consequences.

Individuals seeking favored treatment that would not bear public scrutiny were discouraged from coming forward. For example, Roosevelt held daily office hours in the White House for members of Congress. It soon became known that the new president might repeat and deny their more dubious requests loudly, in front of a group that often included reporters and other interested observers.

TR's written communications in negotiations were crafted with the assumption that they might become public documents at any time. This ensured that his negotiating positions and approaches would be publicly defensible. Roosevelt was keenly aware that people would pay scant attention to a dispute pitting one politician against another (such as himself versus Platt); they wanted to understand how their own interests would be affected. TR disciplined his negotiations and related communications through an unrelenting focus on those broader interests.

Should negotiations deteriorate, TR would have the option of publicly releasing, directly or through others, his written positions. If his opponents were not as dexterous—many congressmen and foreign leaders were not—he might threaten to share their documents with outside parties.

By focusing on communications, he helped keep his adversaries' attention on their own interest in achieving a resolution that would bring them all credit. Roosevelt anticipated the now common exercise in dispute resolution of having the parties draft, in advance of agreement, press announcements outlining the results and significance of their successful negotiations. Since TR was gifted in his ability to communicate with opinion leaders as well as the public at large, he had the additional leverage of being able to influence and rouse relevant external voices during the course of negotiations.

Create a historical record. In important negotiations, Roosevelt methodically established a historical record, creating files of relevant documents, sometimes supplemented with related correspondence. It is not happenstance that the sole surviving contemporaneous records of historic meetings—including some with Senator Platt, others with financier J. P. Morgan—are often Roosevelt's. During the Panic of 1907, as Wall Street tottered toward general insolvency, Roosevelt agreed not to intervene with antitrust action against a controversial plan by which the behemoth U.S. Steel Company engorged the Tennessee Coal and Iron Company. Some years later, accusations were leveled in Congress about the transaction, and President Taft's administration initiated an antitrust suit against U.S. Steel likely intended to embarrass Roosevelt. TR's contemporaneous correspondence, memorializing the critical decision meeting and its context, was invaluable in defending his earlier decision in Congress, in court, and before opinion leaders.

Communication of the ultimate agreement is a critical phase of negotiation. Parties engaged in the intense give-and-take of negotiation understandably might think their work largely complete once terms are agreed upon. Roosevelt understood that much remained to be done. The communications presenting the final agreement are of vital importance. This is especially true in high-stakes negotiations, where the necessity of movement from initial bargaining positions might obscure the extent to which the interests of those represented have been furthered.

TR took pains to present his compromises in terms of the interests advanced and their consistency with his broader vision. He recognized that this was of importance not only for the negotiation at hand, but also for future negotiations, and, perhaps, for the enforcement of existing agreements. In some cases this suggested a need not only to plan one's own communications, but also to coordinate with the other parties.

Roosevelt also exercised care in *not* communicating information that might prove embarrassing to other parties, especially if they were apparently "bested" in a negotiation. In international affairs this was critical in dealings with Germany and Japan, whose leaders were irrationally sensitive to perceived slights.

Scrupulously honor and enforce agreements. Agreements have value only to the extent to which they are honored by the parties. Roosevelt's history and evident temperament as a fighter, an individual who backed up his words with action, imparted the great advantage of trust in implementation and enforcement of agreements. Since all agreements must rely, to a greater or lesser extent, on trust, one's credibility must remain high. Negotiations past, ongoing, and prospective are affected by evolving perceptions of a party's veracity and power.

Where future performance is problematic because of variables such as long duration or prospective changes in parties' representation, Roosevelt's practice of meticulous (at times self-serving) written documentation could be of great value. Even Senator Platt acknowledged that TR had fulfilled his commitments. Since Roosevelt maintained and published the correspondence outlining the terms of their working partnership, as well as other key documents, we all can see that Platt was right.

TR ON LEADERSHIP

- A willingness to fight aggressively for one's principles and interests empowers a leader, setting the stage for productive negotiation.
- Preparation is critical. The contours of many agreements come into view prior to commencement of formal negotiations.
- Make timing your ally.
- Define your negotiating role—facilitator, mediator, arbitrator, or advocate—based on the interests you represent.
- Seek to delegate your negotiating authority.
- Ensure that the other side has complete authority to negotiate.
- Seek direct communication with principals.
- Focus resolutely on interests. Do not confuse interests with bargaining positions.
- Protect ongoing relationships.
- Become a skillful, active listener.
- Be manifestly willing to walk away from the table.
- Do not bluff: "Never draw unless you mean to shoot."
- As far as practicable, maintain open negotiations.
- Create a historical record.
- Communication of the ultimate agreement is a critical phase of negotiation.

- Scrupulously honor and enforce agreements. Trust is of paramount importance. All negotiations and agreements—ongoing and future—are interrelated and affected by evolving perceptions of a party's veracity and power.

CHAPTER SIX

ACTION, ACTION, AND STILL MORE ACTION

Whatever I think is right for me to do,
I do. I do the things that I believe ought to be done.
And when I make up my mind to do a thing, I act.
—THEODORE ROOSEVELT

ON TUESDAY EVENING, February 18, 1902, the legendary American financier J. P. Morgan hosted business associates to dinner at his home on Madison Avenue in New York City.

An invitation from Morgan would not have been taken lightly.

At the turn of the twentieth century the political affairs of the nation were run in Washington, but financial power was directed from New York. Morgan was the preeminent figure in public and private finance. In the Gilded Age, before the creation of the Federal Reserve in 1913, private citizen Morgan served as America's de facto central banker. As the United States became a global economic power, Morgan emerged, in the words of biographer Jean Strouse, as "the most powerful banker in the world." Morgan's financial genius lay behind the restructuring of much of the American economy, accelerating the transition from an agricultural to an industrial base. In early 1901 he spearheaded the creation of the world's first billion-dollar corporation, U.S. Steel. As the nation assessed the significance of that gargantuan entity in its midst, Morgan suddenly served up another in November 1901: the $400 million capitalization of the Northern Securities Company.

Northern Securities was intended to consolidate and rationalize the railroads of the growing Pacific Northwest. It would provide critical infrastructure necessary for future trade with Japan and China. Morgan hoped it would bring to a close ruinous competition among some of Wall Street's most powerful tycoons (which incited a brief but unsettling "Northern Securities Panic" in the spring of 1901). The new venture brought together a number of the most renowned—and reviled—financial leaders of the era. In addition to Morgan, included were William Rockefeller, E. H. Harriman, James J. Hill, Jacob Schiff, and James Stillman.

Morgan excused himself from his dinner guests to receive an urgent telephone call. A member of the press tracking the wires had happened on a bombshell: The new president, Theodore Roosevelt, had directed the attorney general to file suit against the Northern Securities Company, alleging antitrust violations. Without warning through the customary official and unofficial channels, the preeminent position of Morgan—as well as the other financiers joined together in Northern Securities—was publicly challenged by the president of the United States.

In his history of the period, Mark Sullivan wrote that Morgan made his way back to the dinner table, "his countenance showing appalled dismay, but little anger." Why was Roosevelt taking such an immense and irrevocable step away from the cooperative attitude of the McKinley administration? Why hadn't he given Morgan the courtesy of notice? Why had he not afforded an opportunity for Morgan's Wall Street lawyers—who had provided every assurance that the scheme was legal under the law as it was then interpreted and enforced—to make whatever additional changes might be required? Why hadn't TR at least spoken with Morgan satrap Robert Bacon, Roosevelt's revered Harvard classmate? The new president was a New Yorker, in at least some senses a "gentleman," and though not close to Morgan, their paths had crossed many times over the years. Perhaps Morgan recalled that shortly after the 1900 election, Vice President–elect Roosevelt held a dinner in his honor, including other financial barons and opinion leaders who had exhibited trepidation at the elevation of their boy governor.

All at once, all that was far away. Morgan's intuition doubtless informed him that an earthquake had occurred; perhaps shock rather than anger would be an appropriate immediate reaction.

Anger would follow soon enough. In the ensuing days the market wavered as investors anxiously sought to comprehend the new financial-political landscape. Newspapers that had, perhaps wishfully, praised the new president for his restraint in continuing the McKinley policies were violently shaken to their senses.

How would Morgan, aptly labeled "Jupiter" by a New York journalist, respond? Though the term "imperious" is irrevocably tied to the financier, it is insufficiently descriptive. In the words of Edward Page Mitchell of the *New York Sun:*

> Mr. Morgan was dynamic both in intelligence and in will. There seemed to radiate something that forces the complex of inferiority . . . upon all around him, in spite of themselves. The boldest man was likely to become timid under his piercing gaze.

> The most impudent or recalcitrant were ground to humility as he chewed truculently at his huge black cigar.

Over six feet in height, more than 200 pounds in weight, his thinning white hair often covered by a formal top hat, Morgan strode purposefully, leaning heavily on a mahogany cane. His nose was oversized, deformed, and discolored into a startling red, the results of a disease, rhinophyma, that afflicted him in his fifties. Perhaps in part a purposeful rebuke to those who found themselves, despite themselves, gawking at the nose so often called "rubicund," Morgan's gaze was searing, unforgettable. The photographer Edward Steichen recalled that meeting the financier's eyes was akin to looking into the lights of an oncoming locomotive.

Morgan decided he must have a word with the president, face to face, man to man.

On Saturday, February 22, the financier and his entourage arrived for a meeting at the White House. According to TR's description of the encounter (his is the only contemporaneous record that remains), Morgan expressed dismay and disappointment that he had not been afforded advance notice. Roosevelt responded: "That is just what we did not want to do."

Morgan persisted, "If we have done anything wrong, send your man [the attorney general of the United States] to my man [meaning Morgan's lawyer] and they can fix it up."

Roosevelt replied simply, "That can't be done."

"Are you going to attack my other interests, the Steel Trust and the others?"

"Certainly not, unless we find out that in any case they have done something we regard as wrong."

After the meeting concluded, TR told the attorney general, "That is a most illuminating illustration of the Wall Street point of view. Mr. Morgan could not help regarding me as a big rival operator, who either intended to ruin all his interests or else could be induced to come to an agreement to ruin none." Roosevelt's authorized biographer, Joseph Bucklin Bishop, wrote that Morgan, on returning to his hotel, drafted "a very indignant and violent letter" to the president. One of Morgan's lawyers intercepted it prior to delivery, after succeeding with difficulty in convincing the aggrieved financier of its "unwisdom."

THE NATION WAS caught unawares by the bold action of its new president. Roosevelt had methodically prepared his assault against Northern Securities, from a legal and communications standpoint, so as to ensure the element of surprise. He worked directly with his attorney general and deliberately did not consult other cabinet members, most especially Secretary of War Elihu Root. Root was one of TR's closest personal and political advisers, with whom he shared a history going back to his first assembly race; he was also one of the nation's most respected lawyers and had unmatched ties to Wall Street.

Root would almost certainly have shared the judgment of other informed observers that the administration's legal position was dubious. The Supreme Court had some years before eviscerated the Sherman Antitrust Act, and there was no particular reason to assume that his administration's position on the Northern Securities case (which inevitably would wend its way to the high court) would pass legal muster.

What is more, Roosevelt's political position was precarious. In the White House because of an assassin's handiwork, he could claim no public mandate other than that of McKinley's last election (in those days before public polling, he could not credibly point to other indicators of public sentiment). He did not enjoy the unified support of his party nationally. He could not rely on the backing of the party organization of his home state, New York. The machinery of government was manned by McKinley's appointees. The Northern Securities suit would strain an already uncomfortable relationship with the financial community—making him blameworthy, in the eyes of the credulous, for future market downturns—while not silencing the attacks of partisan critics.

Nevertheless, Roosevelt was determined to act. He later recalled: "When I became President, the question as to the *method* by which the United States Government was to control the corporations was not yet important. The absolutely vital question was whether the Government had power to control them at all." Roosevelt would justifiably claim success when the Supreme Court upheld his antitrust action against Northern Securities in 1904.

At the same time, TR's action against Northern Securities was far more than a legal matter. Selecting his target with care, awaiting the right moment, Roosevelt struck a blow against the preeminent symbol of the arrogant, abusive, unaccountable overlords of Wall Street. Without public accountability, the financial elite ran roughshod over legislatures and courts, trampling long-standing economic and social arrangements. They had become, in the memorable term uttered by Edmund Burke a century earlier in characterizing the British East India Company, "a government in merchant's clothing."

If Wall Street considered itself a sovereign on par with Washington, D.C., many among the wealthy few saw themselves as a caste apart from their fellow citizens. The term "conspicuous consumption" hardly does justice to their luxurious lifestyles, unabashedly emulating the European nobility whose excesses had motivated millions to immigrate to America in the first place. Though the elite were adding great wealth to the nation, TR believed their heedless economic power demoralized ordinary Americans. For many families, the connections between traditional virtues (hard work, honor, thrift, concern for neighbors, patriotism) and economic well-being were loosening. Roosevelt intended that ordinary citizens' faith would be reaffirmed when they learned that the names of Morgan and Rockefeller and Hill and Schiff were on the receiving end of a hostile legal pleading brought by the United States of America. Those who feared Wall Street the most (perhaps exaggerating its importance) may have had particular admiration for Roosevelt's direct assault. As TR once wrote in another context, "when I get angry my impulse always is to move up as close to my antagonist as possible"; here he moved in very close as an entranced public looked on.

As biographer H. W. Brands points out, the decision to challenge Wall Street power in a case relating to railroads was well placed. "Roosevelt knew firsthand the tribulations of small cattlemen in their unequal contest with the railroads; in attacking . . . Northern Securities, Roosevelt possessed a peculiar credibility." The new president from the East reinforced his identification with the West; the new president from the aristocracy threw his lot with ordinary people everywhere who felt impotent in the face of the changes unleashed by distant financiers who appeared oblivious to the worth and values of their fellow Americans. TR was not declaring war against all trusts; he simply sought to make them answerable to the nation of which they were a part.

At the time that he authorized filing of the Northern Securities suit, Roosevelt cannot have known its ultimate legal disposition. What TR did know was that by not providing advance notice to Morgan—a fact that agents of Wall Street publicized widely as evidence of the purported instability and recklessness of the new president—he unambiguously signaled that the long-standing covenant between government and business had been revoked. The national government had asserted its primary role in defining and executing the public interest. Henceforth, Mr. Morgan would come to Washington, rather than Washington going to Mr. Morgan. Mr. Morgan would not stand as an equal to the president of the United States. The president would serve as the ultimate arbiter of the public interest, taking into account the needs and beliefs of ordinary Americans as well as those of Wall Street.

The Northern Securities suit was the first in a series of actions by which Roosevelt established that the presidency would be, for the first time since Lincoln, the preeminent branch of the national government. As he wrote several years later, "my ambition is that, in however small a way, the work I do shall be along the Washington and Lincoln lines. While President I have *been* President, emphatically; I have used every ounce of power there was in the office and I have not cared a rap for the criticisms of those who spoke of my 'usurpation of power.'"

Five months after McKinley's assassination, Roosevelt's suit against Northern Securities set the tone for the remainder of his presidency. Though tactically the announcement of the lawsuit was a surprise, in a larger sense it should not have been. Morgan's dumbstruck reaction brings to mind the old phrase: Everything is sudden to the blind. TR's view of Wall Street and its responsibilities was a matter of public record, most recently in his first annual message to Congress as president, in late 1901. Through decisive action—and his willingness to act in the face of multiple, manifest uncertainties—Roosevelt's words would henceforth be taken seriously.

As people in business tend to do, Morgan begrudgingly but rapidly adapted to the new circumstances. Later in 1902, when Roosevelt intervened in the Anthracite Coal Strike, Morgan lent his influence to dislodge the mining companies from suicidal obduracy. In the course of one year the new president established his office as the accepted forum for resolving disputes between labor and capital. Though this was termed "mediation," TR was no ordinary mediator. His efforts to effect an agreement were backed up by his apparent willingness to push the Constitution to its limits, taking over operation of the mines. It was far from clear that seizure would have been held constitutional. Yet with stakes so high—and a president so audacious—a judicial joyride would have been perilous for all sides.

Though Roosevelt would not cease to be "His Accidency" until winning election on his own in November 1904, the presidency was, after the initiation of the Northern Securities suit, indisputably *his* office.

TR WAS CONSTANTLY criticized for being impetuous—rather like a boy with too much steam in his boiler (to borrow a phrase of his own). He often made decisions, especially the most consequential decisions, with amazing speed. Though he had a quick mind, well furnished by learning, reasonable people might ask the question shouted at Owen Wister by an intemperate railroad magnate during the Anthracite Coal Strike negotiation: "Does your friend ever think?"

Roosevelt declared that he "would never act except upon the most careful deliberation." In some cases that deliberation might occur in large part at the time a decision was required. At other times, it might have occurred earlier. Roosevelt's sharp eye and sensitive intuition often discerned emerging issues in embryonic form.

Writing about military commanders, TR consistently identified "forethought in preparation" as a leadership quality of the greatest importance. Courage, intelligence, daring were essential, but not sufficient. In any situation where life is accelerated and concentrated—as at the height of battle, where fateful decisions must be made instantaneously—a leader must rely on forethought. Forethought might be defined as a store of the raw material for future decisions.

One's moral values represent a critical source of forethought. Roosevelt appraised many circumstances almost instantaneously by the lights of his own moral code. In today's terms, he would be labeled "judgmental." TR was most surefooted in situations where he could comprehend and communicate questions in moral terms—casting himself as a fighter against omnipresent manifestations of evil.

Forethought can be harvested from one's personal experience. Though significant, one's own experience cannot be the sole or predominant reference for leaders who would assume responsibility for decisions affecting others.

TR added the experience of others, from direct observation as well as from his reading, study, and writing of history. Confronting a decision, President Roosevelt might look not only to his able staff or outside experts, but also to the experiences of Washington or Jefferson or Lincoln or Admiral Nelson or Marlborough or numerous others. The forethought occasioned by experience, reading, or discussion enabled him to view contemporary problems in unconventional ways. He might discern patterns among disparate issues—past, present and future—unnoticed by others. The resolution might then appear inevitable, simple, or obvious.

TR applied forethought to his overall leadership approach and style. Though he had harsh words for Carlyle, the British historian associated with the "great man" theory of history, Roosevelt believed that the influence and actions of individual leaders could be paramount in achieving success for an enterprise. His understanding of history and other fields, replenished and deepened by ongoing learning, more often than not concentrated on leadership. From a young age TR unselfconsciously passed judgment on military and political leaders of the past and present, enumerating their strengths and shortcomings. Continuing such ruminations while serving in positions of responsibility, Roosevelt seamlessly internalized lessons from Lincoln and other exemplary figures.

TR's ability to combine, without inhibition, the life of action and the life of the mind made his imagination a dynamo, cross-fertilizing ideas and experiences. An admiral who was a supporter of Roosevelt, William S. Sims, wrote: "Just as Napoleon's brilliant decisions were not an inspiration of genius, but were arrived at . . . by continuous reflection, so it was with Roosevelt."

In addition to what might be called general forethought (that has been accrued over time and might be applied in any number of situations), TR prepared assiduously for specific decisions where circumstances allowed. Lewis Einstein observed:

> Roosevelt was far more cautious than is commonly believed. His methods of inquiry before taking a decision were conducted with the utmost prudence. He was artist enough to hide this aspect of his skill, and to serve his dishes without any indication of their ingredients or of the care he had generally taken in their preparation. His method was that of the military commander who conceals his reserves until ready to hurl them at the foe. Roosevelt's system of attack when it came into the open was so frontal that men forgot the wariness of his approach and the craft with which he prepared his assault.

One should not assume, with some critics, that instantaneous decision making and action necessarily suggested that TR thought about an issue half as much as they. It was more likely he considered it many times, from more vantage points, over a far longer period of time.

Armed with forethought Roosevelt would have the confidence necessary for decisive action. Unhindered by hesitation or half-heartedness, a leader can follow his dictum: "If you must take a nettle in your hand, grasp it firmly."

ONE OF PRESIDENT ROOSEVELT'S top international priorities was the construction of the Panama Canal. For centuries visionaries had sought a "path between the seas," linking the Atlantic and Pacific Oceans. For the United States, the canal was of paramount strategic importance. Since it would be built, if at all, in the Americas, there was concern lest it be controlled by European powers. The United States, with coasts on both oceans, had an interest in lowering the cost of shipping from Los Angeles to New York by dramatically cutting the length of the voyage. America's naval power and overall international position also would be greatly enhanced by the proposed canal.

TR acted with what his critics termed great "suddenness" in 1903, concluding a treaty with the new nation of Panama as it broke away from Colombia. The transaction would long be questioned by those who raised what Roosevelt considered "legalistic" or overly "meticulous" objections. Often bypassing his cabinet, regarding Congress as merely an obstacle on a course that could not be observed clearly from Capitol Hill, Roosevelt acted on convictions he had established and publicly presented over many years. Speaking in California in 1911, unfettered by the constraints of office, he declared: "I am interested in the Panama Canal because I started it. If I had followed conventional, conservative methods, I should have submitted a dignified state paper to the Congress and the debate would have been going on yet, but I took the canal zone and let Congress debate, and while the debate goes on the Canal does too."

The other action that Roosevelt regarded as most significant in his foreign policy was the sailing of the Great White

Fleet in 1907–1909. Again he bypassed much of his cabinet and turned a deaf ear toward overheated congressional demands for time-consuming discussion and debate. Advised that a united fleet could be made battle-worthy (and credible for power projection) only after a significant period of actual use—and wishing to demonstrate America's resolve and newfound strength to Japan and other nations—TR overlooked or overcame many objections to accomplish his goal. Correctly concluding that the legislative branch would do the right thing when confronted with a fait accompli, Roosevelt audaciously launched the Great White Fleet on his own schedule, not waiting for congressional approval of appropriations to purchase sufficient fuel for its return stateside.

His penchant for action was also revealed in dealings with individuals. From early adulthood, when he shot dead—after fair warning—a neighbor's harassing dog, TR exhibited directness verging on ruthlessness in personal confrontations. An example was his elimination, in 1903, of McKinley's friend and sponsor, Ohio senator Mark Hanna, as a potential competitor for the presidential nomination for the following year.

TR's opportunity came unbidden, but he was not unprepared. In his quest for dominance of the state Republican Party, the other Ohio senator, Joseph Foraker, set a trap for Hanna. Foraker publicly proposed that the Ohio Republicans endorse the nomination of incumbent President Roosevelt a year early. Whatever his intention with respect to the nomination, Hanna's prestige benefited from his prospective candidacy. Now he was forced either to support TR (and renounce his own ambitions) or, by not granting support, to appear to oppose the president and titular head of his own party.

Like a child tossed into the ocean without benefit of swimming instruction, Hanna flailed about, pitiful and forlorn. He publicly stated that Foraker's proposition had been "forced upon me in a way which makes it necessary for me to oppose such a resolution." He dispatched a personal telegram to Roosevelt expressing his unwillingness to give early nomination support, suggesting the president would understand his rationale when passed along, presumably in subsequent private conversation.

TR seized the moment. He publicly ignored the telegram, responding only to Hanna's prior statement: "I have not asked any man for his support . . . of course those who favor my administration and nomination will endorse them, and those who do not will oppose them."

Hanna, isolated and embarrassed, reversed course, announcing he would no longer resist an early presidential endorsement. Roosevelt displayed magnanimity after victory. The Ohio senator, who had opposed adding the "madman" from New York to McKinley's ticket, died early in 1904. TR expressed thanks for Hanna's grace in the uncomfortable period after McKinley's death, concluding, "No man had larger traits."

ROOSEVELT'S TRANSPARENT directness fortified his negotiating stance in many situations, imparting the aura of the Big Stick. At other times, where an indirect approach might have been more efficacious, he may have missed opportunities.

When circumstances imposed an indirect approach—direct action was foreclosed—Roosevelt would respond accordingly. A memorable example occurred in 1907.

TR's premature withdrawal from consideration for the 1908 presidential nomination, combined with the loss of congressional supporters in the 1906 midyear election, emboldened his adversaries. Among them was a group of Western congressmen, embittered by the president's unprecedented conservation policies, which removed or restricted millions of acres from private development. They passed an amendment to curtail the president's ability to set aside additional national reserves.

Roosevelt found himself in a quandary. He felt compelled to sign the agriculture appropriation to which the dreaded amendment was attached (there was no option of a partial veto). He remained committed to major expansion of protected lands. The president had ten days in which to decide how to handle this troublesome legislation.

At the suggestion of Gifford Pinchot, his close ally and head of the Forest Service, Roosevelt decided he would sign the legislation—after annexing an additional sixteen million acres of forest reserves.

Roosevelt later recalled, "The opponents of the Forest Service turned handsprings in their wrath; and dire were their threats against the Executive; but the threats could not be carried out, and were really only a tribute to the efficiency of our action."

FROM THE COMFORTABLE distance of a century, hearing that congressmen "turned handsprings in their wrath" elicits a smile. Picturing J. P. Morgan in full anger is entertaining. Such things are far from us now. We know how things turned out, who was proved right, at least by our lights. But then it was different.

A leader who takes the initiative not only has the advantages of the first mover; he must also accept the likelihood of greater controversy and criticism. Roosevelt recognized this reality. He wrote in his *Autobiography:*

> If I were on a sail boat, I should not ordinarily meddle with any of the gear; but if a sudden squall struck us, and the main sheet jammed, so that the boat threatened to capsize, I would unhesitatingly cut the main sheet, even though I were sure that the owner, no matter how grateful to me at the moment for having saved his life, would a few weeks later, when he had forgotten the danger and his fear, decide to sue me for the value of the cut

rope. But I would feel hearty contempt for the owner who had so acted.

The leader must have confidence that he has served his enterprise well, even if, foreseeably, some will not in the short run—if ever—understand or praise actions done in their behalf.

ROOSEVELT'S PHILOSOPHY—"Action, action and still more action"—encompassed initiative, improvisation, and attack. Seizing the initiative enhances a leader's capacity to take action on his own terms—based on more information over a longer period and from more sources—than is likely when responding defensively. Since taking the initiative necessarily entails going into uncharted territory, one must be prepared to improvise. Roosevelt believed that being on the attack made it possible to assemble a larger coalition of otherwise incompatible forces. In his *Autobiography* he stated that his foreign policy "was based on the exercise of intelligent forethought and of decisive action." He might well have said the same about any aspect of his life.

Roosevelt's restless, activist temperament imposed a bias for action. When action was the best means to serve, that was a great advantage. In situations where the best course for the enterprise might be nonaction, to act directly would be to meet one's own needs rather than to serve. Elihu Root, a dispassionate observer as well as loyal friend, recognized this tension. In early 1912 Root worried aloud that TR would not be able to restrain himself from a premature decision on whether to enter the presidential election later that year (which would split the Republicans between Roosevelt and Taft). Root reminded him that "your temperament . . . [imposes] the urgent need of your nature for prompt decision and action." Roosevelt's temperament may have made it hard for him to understand that in some cases the best "action" is, for the time being, no action.

With that caveat, TR's approach of intelligent forethought followed by decisive action, relentlessly taking the initiative, remains a model of effective leadership. When leaders and their enterprises cease to take bold actions as a matter of course, they may have become dangerously comfortable or more attuned to their own concerns than the needs of those they would serve.

Late in his life, in conversation with Owen Wister, Roosevelt summarized his estimate of his own gifts—and something larger about leadership. At home at Sagamore Hill, "spacing his words in that way of his for emphasis," TR told his longtime friend: "I have—only—a second rate brain—but—I think—I—have—a—capacity—for action."

TR ON LEADERSHIP

- Decisive action, backed by intelligent forethought and timed to seize the initiative, is a hallmark of effective leadership.
- Audacious action, especially when taken early in a leader's tenure—and manifestly exposing the leader to risk—can establish a position of enduring strength.
- Forethought is the raw material of decision making. Where a leader's learning and life experiences are intermingled, continuously growing, the ongoing process of reflection can endow a leader with creative, rapid decision making.
- "If you must take a nettle in your hand, grasp it firmly."
- Leaders who cease to seize the initiative through decisive action may no longer be advancing, as far as possible, the interests of those they serve.

Part Two

LEADERSHIP IN ACTION

[Roosevelt] became for me the image of a great leader and the prototype of Presidents.
—Walter Lippmann

[Roosevelt] was . . . the greatest executive of his generation.
—Gifford Pinchot

CHAPTER SEVEN

GETTING THE BEST ON YOUR TEAM

Personally I have never been able to understand why the head of a big business, whether it be the Nation, the State or the Army, or Navy should not desire to have very strong and positive people under him.

—THEODORE ROOSEVELT

ROOSEVELT WAS in a delicate position as he began the work of his presidency in late September 1901. President McKinley was understood to have had a rather different vision and a very different approach to governing than TR. The new president appropriately promised to carry out the McKinley agenda. Roosevelt's only policy option, for the moment, was no action.

Personnel matters would not wait. As soon as he was sworn in at the Wilcox home in Buffalo on September 14, TR asked the members of the McKinley cabinet to remain in place. Some, like Elihu Root, then serving as secretary of war, were familiar and close to the new president. Others were little known to him (as vice president he did not sit with the cabinet, did not have an office or staff in the White House, and had no formal voice in McKinley administration councils). The entire cabinet—even the redoubtable secretary of state, John Hay, inclined to retirement at the end of a career reaching back to Lincoln's administration—acceded to Roosevelt's request.

During the week of September 23, his first on the job as president, he turned his attention to lower-level personnel issues. Roosevelt went further, faster than people were accustomed to expect. He consulted widely, seeking input on appointments, signaling a high degree of personal, direct presidential supervision.

TR most likely devoted more attention to personnel matters than any president before or since. Beginning as a New York assemblyman he fought for reform of the civil service. As a member of the U.S. Civil Service Commission, he worked extensively on issues of testing and promotion, hiring and firing of government employees. Within days of becoming president of the New York City Police Board he initiated efforts to design and institute a system of nonpolitical appointment and promotion. During his brief tenure as assistant secretary of the navy, Roosevelt led reform of personnel practices. He raised a regiment for the Spanish-American War—welding an effective fighting force from amateurs from across the nation. His preparation was capped by two years as governor of New York, where he held a chief executive position analogous to the presidency.

Among the elements of Roosevelt's approach to personnel:

Hire people more talented than oneself. Roosevelt sought conspicuously talented individuals for his team. He understood that a chief executive has no more important task than attracting and retaining the ablest possible group.

In *The Effective Executive*, Peter Drucker explains: "[N]o executive has ever suffered because his subordinates were strong and effective. There is no prouder boast, but also no better prescription, for executive effectiveness than the words

Andrew Carnegie, the father of the U.S. steel industry, chose for his own tombstone: 'Here lies a man who knew how to bring into his service men better than he was himself.'" Though each member of the team may have been, in Drucker's words, "a 'better man' in one specific area and for one specific job . . . Carnegie . . . was the effective executive among them."

For the biggest jobs—in terms of priority to the enterprise and demands on the occupants—Roosevelt would brook no compromise on quality. The construction of the Panama Canal called for "the biggest man we can get." For the U.S. Supreme Court—of particular importance to Roosevelt, given the high court's propensity to strike down assertions of legislative and executive power at the turn of the twentieth century—his insistence on excellence yielded Oliver Wendell Holmes, Jr.

First as secretary of war and later as secretary of state, Elihu Root, the legendary Wall Street lawyer, served Roosevelt and the nation with distinction. He advised the president on matters large and small. TR acknowledged that Root was well qualified for the chief executive role. Had the politics of the time been different, he likely would have sought to install Root as his successor. Though their paths diverged when Roosevelt bolted the Republican Party in 1912, Root's career was one of historic accomplishment, including a Nobel Peace Prize.

William Howard Taft—with whom Roosevelt later split in a spectacular fashion—served estimably in the Philippines and in the cabinet; he eventually became the only person to have served as president and chief justice of the United States. Gifford Pinchot—one of the founders of the modern conservation movement and a future governor of Pennsylvania—was a protégé of TR and a dynamic public administrator.

Talented people attract talented people. Roosevelt was proud of the considered judgment of one of the most respected observers of the era: "At the end of my administration Mr. [James] Bryce, the British Ambassador [author of *The American Commonwealth*], told me that in a long life, during which he had studied intimately the government of many different countries, he had never in any country seen a more eager, high-minded, and efficient set of public servants, men more useful and creditable to their country, than the men then doing the work of the American Government in Washington and in the field."

Members of his team continued to serve the nation in succeeding decades, some through the presidencies of Franklin Roosevelt and his successor, Harry Truman. Having been credentialed by TR, such individuals would be recognized as experts in their various fields and veterans of an extraordinary group. They were a living legacy, extending Theodore Roosevelt's influence into the future.

Look for the best in each person. In 1900, during a campaign swing through the West, Roosevelt recalled, "I had studied a lot about men and things before I saw you fellows, but it was only when I came here that I began to know anything or measure men rightly." In the preface to *The Winning of the West,* he wrote of the people he encountered in the Badlands, "I am not blind to their manifold shortcomings, nor yet am I ignorant of their many strong and good qualities." His friend Bill Sewall, a woodsman who helped introduce the young Manhattan tenderfoot to outdoor life (and who was appointed by his friend, the president, as a collector of customs in Maine), said, "[H]e was quick to find the real man in very simple men. He didn't look for a brilliant man when he found me; he valued me for what I was worth."

In Drucker's terms, Roosevelt focused on the prospective contribution that an individual might make to the success of the enterprise. Rather than asking if someone is a "good man," one should ask, "Good for what?"

TR focused on individuals' strengths. He overlooked differences—in style, temperament, or point of view—which were outweighed by the candidate's prospective contribution.

A striking example was William Moody, whom Roosevelt appointed secretary of the navy, attorney general, and associate justice of the Supreme Court. As a member of the House of Representatives, Moody was a harsh critic of TR at the Navy Department. Even after McKinley's death he persisted in spewing insults about the new president. Roosevelt, like his hero Lincoln, was willing to bring on disagreeable persons if they would achieve results. He understood, to borrow terms his wife Edith used about their children, that one could not assume eagles to have the virtues of sparrows. This perspective allowed TR to extol the heroism of Admiral Nelson, despite personal behavior—"unfaithful to his wife and faithful to his mistress"—that he would never condone in himself.

As chief executive of enterprises including diverse talents and personalities, Roosevelt often had to defend the selection or retention of one team member to others. In the Progressive Party—like other insurgency movements, tending to attract "prima donnas"—he frequently shielded Wall Street financier George W. Perkins from the slings and arrows of colleagues whose contributions might fairly be described as less practical and more philosophical. Roosevelt made his case entirely in terms of the results being achieved for the enterprise. TR's celebrated comment—"When I spoke of the Progressive party as having a lunatic fringe, I specifically had you in mind"—was aimed at an associate who luxuriated in posing as an implacable Perkins critic.

Where one must bargain over personnel, set standards for selection. Personnel decisions inevitably become intermingled with other priorities—especially when a chief executive has communicated widely that personnel issues are a top priority.

Roosevelt attempted to circumscribe such negotiations by publicly establishing standards for selection. He often said that Washington and Lincoln set lasting standards for public service; as a practical matter TR insisted on the highest standards largely for the appointments he considered most significant. Nonetheless, he might intervene in lower-level appointments when doing so sent important messages inside and outside the organization. On one occasion, resisting political pressure to appoint a felon, TR wryly proposed a baseline: First he would review the non-felons; then, if a proper candidate were not found, he would turn to the list including felons.

Publicly establishing selection and performance criteria enabled others, outside and inside the organization, to find and publicize deviations—especially given TR's penchant for openness. A result was that TR's will could be imposed further into his organizations than would otherwise have been practicable. Tendencies toward favoritism were nipped in the bud. He set the tone early in his presidential administration, moving decisively to investigate and remove executive branch employees enmeshed in a postal scandal.

Spend the time necessary to evaluate and acculturate prospective team members. Roosevelt devoted substantial amounts of his own time, as chief executive, to personnel matters. He understood that choosing the right person, and making his own expectations clear from the start, could save immense time and effort over the long term. Not only top-level appointments, such as to the Supreme Court, but also sensitive lower-level appointments received his hands-on attention. Characteristic was a letter to a controversial appointee, the newly installed U.S. Attorney for Delaware, whom TR warned to "walk even more guardedly than the ordinary public official walks."

TR's proclivity to appoint individuals of preexisting stature to prominent positions meant that he would rely on their shared commitment to his vision at least as much as their personal loyalty. Spending significant amounts of time in the selection process could reinforce both aspects.

Do not prolong consideration of people who will not receive a position. In his first weeks in office as president, Roosevelt summarily rejected a nominee for the federal bench whom he considered unqualified: "[M]y experience has taught me that in such a case a quick decision really prevents bitterness." He distinguished between applicants who were manifestly unqualified and those passed over because of the vagaries of circumstances at a particular time. Many in the latter category might well be the most desirable applicants for one or another position in the future, and TR encouraged them by expressing his appreciation of their continuing "usefulness."

Ceaselessly search for new talent. In each executive position he held, TR tirelessly sought to identify talented individuals and reward outstanding performance. Perhaps from his own experience in subordinate positions, he was dubious of promotion based on seniority rather than results. At the Navy Department, he advocated changes along those lines. Acknowledging that subjective factors in judging performance created a risk of rewarding "courtier" qualities, he concluded that the exigencies of war would incline toward a down-to-earth emphasis on tangible, measurable achievements.

In the presidency, Roosevelt's cultivation of talent prompted him to rummage around in distant organizational levels under the direct authority of his subordinates. When he personally intervened to attract a particularly able assistant secretary of state, he coordinated his efforts with the secretary's, made clear his goal was to fortify the secretary's office—and implicitly reminded all involved that they were part of the larger Roosevelt team.

Ruthlessly replace individuals who do not meet the standards of the enterprise. New talent—new people with skills required for new challenges, new skills developed in existing team members—is impeded whenever a position is occupied by someone less able to advance the enterprise. Just as a forest renews itself through the removal of old growth, an organization must continuously be shorn of less productive elements.

In a time of unprecedented change, Roosevelt did not hesitate to cashier those who could not keep pace. In 1908 he wrote to the expendable head of the Government Printing Office: "I do not believe you are able to manage this particular office—one of particular difficulty and needing a peculiar combination of traits in the man who is to do the work successfully. If the opportunity comes I shall be glad to place you in some office commensurate with your abilities."

TR held relevant questions of character to be non-negotiable. He frequently told of a capable ranch hand whom he found stealing others' cattle and marking them with the Roosevelt brand. TR fired him forthwith: "[I]f you will steal for me, you will steal from me."

When in command, Roosevelt viewed insubordination as grounds for summary action. To be sure, this was a shortcoming he was peculiarly qualified to judge. In a controversial series of incidents arising early in his presidency, TR rebuked a popular hero of the Civil War and Indian conflicts, General Nelson Miles. Roosevelt backed up Secretary of War Root in establishing a record of Miles's alleged deceit. TR stipulated that the old general "ought only be employed when we are certain that whatever talents he may possess will be used under conditions which make his own interests and the interests of the country identical."

Roosevelt's method of firing was situation-specific. The key was the good of the enterprise. When a top-level individual could be pushed aside quietly, transferred to another position better suited to his skills, TR might oblige. If a broader message was necessitated by circumstances, he would not hesitate to fire an employee personally and publicly.

Work with the tools at hand. TR's ability to find the best in each person was in line with Lincoln's dictum: "We must use the tools we have." He wrote Taft in 1901, "[W]hen we get down to the actual work-a-day world, the man who in the long run succeeds is the man who understands from the beginning that his tools will often be imperfect . . . and who goes on and does the best he can in spite of the mistakes and shortcomings of his associates, and in spite of the imperfections of what he has to work on."

Whether holding together the cabinet selected by McKinley or assembling his own team in various settings, Roosevelt did his best with the tools at hand. The greater the enterprise, the larger the executive responsibility, the higher the stakes, the more an executive's prospects of achieving success lies in the hands of others. A leader adds value by assembling a group of talented individuals and inspiring them to extraordinary achievement working as a team.

TR ON LEADERSHIP

- Hire people more talented than oneself.
- Look for the best in each person.
- Where one must bargain over personnel, set standards for selection.
- Spend the time necessary to evaluate and acculturate prospective team members.
- Do not prolong consideration of people who will not receive a position.

- Ceaselessly search for new talent.
- Ruthlessly replace individuals who do not meet the standards of the enterprise.
- Work with the tools at hand.

CHAPTER EIGHT

GETTING THE BEST FROM YOUR TEAM

If I want a man under me to do a job, I will give him the power to do it, and I will say: "I want you to do that piece of work." Now if he says: "How am I to do it?" I will say: "I will take another man. I will take someone else to do it." If I am trusted to do a job, I want the power given to me and then I will be held accountable for it. But give me the chance to make or mar that job myself.

—THEODORE ROOSEVELT

NO LEADER walks alone. A chief executive adds value by eliciting outstanding team performance. A superbly functioning group can accomplish far more than can be foreseen by adding the sum of its parts.

Roosevelt was an extraordinary team leader. He repeatedly lifted group morale and performance to new heights—as president of the New York City Police Board, assistant secretary of the navy, colonel of the Rough Riders, governor of New York, president of the United States, and head of an insurgent political movement, as well as on numerous hunting and exploring adventures.

TR frequently framed management issues in martial terms. His experience in the civilian and active-duty components of the military—looking from the bottom up as well as the top down—was a school for making large organizations operate effectively, including corporate and public bureaucracies today.

His four months of active duty as commander of a regiment included many of the same challenges rediscovered in start-up companies in the twenty-first century's New Economy: selecting and motivating team members, training them as a unit, imparting a unifying vision while encouraging individual initiative, recognizing and rewarding performance in the field as more significant than pre-existing rank or credentials, and ultimately disbanding the team and maintaining it as an ongoing network. The Rough Riders were guided by few rules and fewer certainties; time moved with remorseless rapidity. The stakes were far greater—and the consequences more final—than in the most unforgiving business environment. Roosevelt's team faced and fired real bullets.

Among the key elements of TR's approach to leading his team:

The welfare of your team is your overarching responsibility. The cornerstone of TR's success as a team leader was that he consistently placed the welfare of the group ahead of his own. Perhaps this is best encapsulated in a single statistic. As Roosevelt repeatedly emphasized in *The Rough Riders,* "In my regiment, as in the whole cavalry division, the proportion of loss in killed and wounded was considerably greater among the officers than among the troopers, and this was exactly as it should be."

Throughout the brief Spanish-American War, TR reliably took the perspective of the troops for whom he was responsible. He declined the offer of the top command of a regiment in favor of a more experienced officer. He butted heads with the bureaucracy to ensure that his troops would be outfitted with summer clothing. He twisted arms to make certain they were equipped with smokeless rather than outdated black-powder rifles. He demanded decent food for them and was prepared to purchase it himself if necessary. He paid out of his own pocket to move the regiment to its port of embarkation for Cuba. As enemy batteries showered death on the Rough Riders, TR at once protected and inspired his team, remaining on horseback while they were on foot. After the close of the hostilities—likely at the cost of the Medal of Honor he coveted—he signed a public letter to the military brass, demanding immediate action to protect the troops from rampant malarial fever (at one point he reported to his sister Corinne that of approximately 400 men in his camp, 123 were in doctors' care, with the rest of the 600 he started with either dead or in rear hospitals). When his regiment returned to Long Island, Roosevelt declined the offer that would have allowed him—but not those under his command—to leave camp and visit his nearby home and family.

TR asserted: "[T]he best work can be got out of the men only if the officers endure the same hardships and face the same risks." Throughout his life—beginning in the Badlands—Roosevelt lived by the code he expressed shortly before his death: "No man has a right to ask or accept any service unless under changed conditions he would feel that he could keep his entire self-respect while rendering it." With few limitations on what he would give of himself, TR faced few limitations on what he could ask from others.

A leader should develop leaders, not merely direct followers. John Maxwell calls it the "Law of Explosive Growth." When a chief executive methodically cultivates the leadership abilities of his subordinates, he exponentially enhances the potential of the organization. This requires a significant investment of time and resources by the chief executive. In subordinate roles TR had been frustrated by lack of authority to act, unclear accountability, absence of high-level support, and inability to communicate vital information up the chain of command. Becoming the executive he had wished for, he empowered—indeed required—his subordinates to lead.

Demonstrate faith in your team by delegation of authority. Roosevelt's selection of the "very strong and positive men under him" enabled him to delegate authority expansively. TR wrote in 1899, "[The leader] has the reins always and can shape the policy as he wishes it, and it is for his interest to have each department run by a man who will carry out his general policy, but will be given large liberty as to the methods of carrying it out."

Roosevelt's approach was vividly demonstrated in his historic, successful effort to construct the Panama Canal. The strategic value of a canal connecting the Atlantic and Pacific Oceans had long been recognized, but numerous attempts to realize it had foundered. TR faced extraordinary challenges. Once the necessary foreign policy hurdles had been cleared, the president confronted what one historian aptly concluded was "as difficult a task as an administrator can be asked to do":

> He had to create and staff an entirely new administrative organization which had to perform an unprecedented job. This organization had to be responsible for digging, dredging, and constructing locks and dams on a huge scale. It had to provide for the regular and systematic flow of supplies and materials from the United States over 2,000 miles of water to the Isthmus. It had to recruit a laboring force of skilled and unskilled labor, to transport the force to Panama, and then to house and feed these men. The care of their health required a large medical staff to fight yellow fever and other tropical diseases. Furthermore, this administrative unit had to govern the Canal Zone and handle relations between the Americans and the Panamanians. Finally, the organization had to operate under pressures from Congress, labor officials, the press, and the American public.

TR understood that every foreseeable threat looming over this vast public works project would be exacerbated with the passage of time. It would not be completed during his term of office under any scenario (it was actually finished in 1914, during the Wilson administration). Seizing the initiative, TR would leave his policy too far in gestation to be reversed responsibly by others.

Through the many twists and turns of this unprecedented undertaking, Roosevelt was constant in his method for getting the best from his team: He defined the mission; he hired the best available personnel; he delegated authority from his office and centralized it in the hands of an accountable subordinate; he backed and protected the accountable subordinate's team with every appropriate tool at his disposal.

Administrative problems initially placed the entire enterprise at risk. Prominent members of Congress, professing concern over Roosevelt's full-throated assertions of executive power, imposed a seven-person Isthmian Canal Commission. The commission, based in Washington, was hobbled by an unclear mandate and a structure incompatible with accountability. The result resembled what Roosevelt found at the New York City Police Board years earlier: "a complete divorce of power and responsibility, and it was exceedingly difficult either to do anything, or to place anywhere, the responsibility for not doing it."

TR asked Congress to restructure the commission and to authorize him to appoint an administrative staff to supervise the work in Panama. Slouching supinely into the passive-aggressive posture routinely assumed by legislative bodies, Congress indulged in vehement discussion—and took no action. Undeterred by the failure of his attempt to observe legal niceties, Roosevelt drove into the void with an executive order channeling administrative authority into three departments to be directed by presidential appointees. Ultimately Roosevelt moved further, placing power in the hands of a single individual, Colonel George W. Goethals. The commission survived as a shell, with Goethals as chairman and a protégé of TR serving as staff director in charge of day-to-day activities.

In Goethals, Roosevelt secured the accountability he believed essential for achieving results. As he had written in the context of municipal reform: "What we must have is some one man to hold to a definite responsibility." He took the same approach in other important areas of his administration. For example, he reorganized the Forest Service to affix "undivided responsibility" for paramount environmental priorities.

Roosevelt's approach to delegation—backed by his practice of expressing and enforcing high ethical standards—afforded him distance from activities that were necessary but perilous to the overall mission of the enterprise. George Cortelyou, whose highly productive fundraising efforts for the 1904 election campaign have never been fully documented, met TR's high expectations while apparently not burdening him with unnecessary details. John King, who played a similar role in later years, veered off the road of legality only after Roosevelt's death.

Back up and protect your team consistently. Having affixed accountability, Roosevelt would unfailingly back his team. This was particularly important with respect to the Panama Canal because of the many obstacles confronting the novel, gargantuan enterprise. He regularly asked Goethals and other top officials to let him know what they needed—a presidential statement here, legislation there, executive orders everywhere—and he would do whatever he could. If the Congress was restive and harassing—as when spitefully cutting the salaries of top officials for the project—he would swing into action. When a lawyer employed by the commission questioned the legality of a plan to build recreational facilities for workers, the president instructed the top staff: "You go back and tell that man to keep his mouth shut. He is not there to find objections. . . . I want to build the canal; I do not want to be told how not to do it, but how to do it. . . . I'll take the responsibility."

When a cabinet member was under fire following credible accusations of wrongdoing arising from his prior employment in the railroad industry, Roosevelt examined the facts and determined that his man was "straight as a string." Unfortunately the facts were difficult to explain concisely; the secretary's actions were foreseeably vulnerable to distortion and as such would not have been condoned had they occurred in the Roosevelt administration. Nonetheless, TR would not allow his associate to be run out of office on that basis.

Resolutely backing up staff reinforces accountability, focuses the chief executive on the areas where he can best add value, protects the chief executive's time and tactical flexibility by discouraging appeals from lower-level decisions, and promotes loyalty.

Delegation, though extensive, should be bounded by clear standards. Roosevelt tended to delegate most extensively in the most important projects, the Panama Canal being the most important of all. He distinguished between the setting of policy—which requires the decision of the chief executive—and implementation, which he largely left to the discretion of the accountable officials. Roosevelt negotiated agreements for the accomplishment of specific actions by specific dates, defining the "success" by which he would evaluate and enforce performance.

Roosevelt provided continuing feedback. His first secretary of the interior, inherited from McKinley, had difficulty adjusting to the torrent of expectations aroused by TR's pioneering commitment to environmental protection. In an effort to give him a stable toehold, Roosevelt dispatched detailed reactions, suggestions, and instructions. He gradually took the department into managerial receivership. When the secretary was ultimately replaced, the reasons were clear to all concerned. The accumulated letters and memoranda transmitting feedback would be available as an invaluable training and acculturation manual for his successor.

Fortify delegation with selective intervention. TR routinely intervened in the operations of well-run organizations within his responsibility. At first glance it might appear contradictory to his commitment to delegation, but generally it was not.

Roosevelt was renowned for communicating directly with subordinates far down the chain of command—sometimes implementing their recommendations against the expressed wishes of their supervisors. It was not a surprise when he accepted the counsel of seamen, overruling naval authorities on the types of vessels allowed to become part of the Great White Fleet. Obviously, were it taken too far, this approach could undermine the authority of TR's top appointees. In the case of the navy, President Roosevelt found it difficult to resist the temptation to be what he would characterize, in other contexts, a "meddlesome Mattie." This was surely a factor in the high turnover in the position of navy secretary during his administration.

In some cases TR's hand reached deep into the machinery of his organizations, directly and visibly safeguarding the welfare and raising the morale of his larger team. President Roosevelt intervened in military affairs, ranging from training curricula to the color of shirts worn by troops; from the dimensions of cavalry spurs to reversing a War Department decision affording more respectful notification to the families of officers killed in battle than to those of enlisted men. When such interventions were immediately recognizable as being within his vision and priorities, strains on the violated chain of command could be minimized. Roosevelt's proclivity in this regard encouraged lower-level employees—often facing realities entirely different from what was reported to decision makers—to share information with the chief executive without fear of penalty.

President Roosevelt publicly overturned actions by high-level subordinates that may have been necessary or justified from their perspective but appeared counterproductive from the singular vantage point of the chief executive. He reversed rulings of his administration restricting the use of popular food additives—including saccharine, on which the increasingly imposing chief executive personally relied. He cited fears of a backlash "upsetting the whole pure food law" that he had worked assiduously to achieve. Perhaps he was also concerned about other priorities being disordered by the timing or tone or substance of such errant decisions. In the aftermath of the saccharine intervention, TR prepared correspondence explaining his actions and reiterating his support for the chastened decision maker, whom he considered to be useful in some respects.

Even in the White House, TR interjected himself in matters that at first glance might appear picayune or tending toward "micromanagement." In fact, they generally related to issues of great symbolic importance, communicating values and priorities inside and outside his administration. Almost immediately on taking office as president, he ordered the Board of Commissioners of Washington, D.C., to halt air pollution from nearby public and private facilities—or, if they did not have requisite authority, to draft enabling legislation. On a later occasion he directed the secretary of war to ensure that African-American regiments have African-American bandmasters as soon as possible. In his capacity as "First Reader," he instructed the Public Printer to put a stop to "rough edges and gilt tops" and other unnecessarily expensive covers for government publications, in favor of "the plainest and simplest kind of bindings."

Roosevelt's approach to delegation was made effective by his wide-ranging interests, insatiable curiosity, technical competence, capacity to obtain information from outside the usual organizational channels, and methodical follow-up to prior directives. Every member of his administration, from cabinet members to assistant secretaries to clerks, labored with the sobering awareness that TR's energy and intellect might—at any time—furiously bore into an issue or an organization, questioning practices, personnel, arrangements, and accomplishments. Those to whom he delegated significant authority were energized—and disciplined—by this ever-present possibility.

Recognize strong performers. Writing to his son Quentin in 1914, TR recalled his own father's concern about passing along too many compliments, "because he did not think a sugar diet was good for me." It might be said, though, that Roosevelt had no compunction about providing a sugar diet for productive members of groups he led.

Elihu Root (before their falling out in 1912) "was *the* man of my cabinet, the man on whom I most relied, to whom I owed most, the greatest Secretary of State we have ever had, as great a cabinet officer as we have ever had, save Alexander Hamilton alone." Shortly after the 1912 election defeat, deploying flattery that would have alarmed many across America and around the world, TR addressed Gifford Pinchot, "O Mr. Secretary of State that-was-to-have-been!" Some of his fulsome praise—at times rather promiscuously bestowed on unexpected, dubious beneficiaries—caused observers to cringe. His custom, consistent with focusing on the best in each person, was in line with Goethe's dictum: "Treat people as if they were what they ought to be and you will help them become what they are capable of becoming."

Throughout his executive career, Roosevelt strove to lift morale and reinforce virtue through timely, public recognition of accomplishments. Doubtless with an eye toward Lincoln, who established the Medal of Honor during the Civil War, TR initiated the custom of White House presentations of the nation's highest military decoration. Critics chortled about the Panama Canal medallions prominently featuring TR's likeness and dramatically inscribed: "The Land Divided, The World United." Roosevelt sought to create among the Panama Canal workers an esprit de corps comparable to that of the dwindling band of aging Union Army veterans who gathered together annually to commemorate their service during the great days of 1861 to 1865, poignant and resplendent in their dress uniforms and glittering medals.

Roosevelt's sword cut a line in the sand between recognition that he conferred on members of his teams and that which they assumed for themselves. When Secretary of State John Hay died in 1905, TR expressed boundless admiration for "a man whose position was literally unique." He vociferously asserted, with respect to Hay and others, "I do not care a rap as to who gets the credit for the work, provided the work is done." Yet when Hay's posthumous papers appeared to claim credit for accomplishments the president viewed as his own, TR wrote a detailed account to Henry Cabot Lodge, declaring that Hay "accomplished little. . . . [H]is usefulness to me was almost exclusively the usefulness of a fine figurehead." Perhaps feeling the hand of history on his shoulder, he wrote somewhat similarly about Hay's successor Root in a letter to Andrew Carnegie near the close of his presidency. After enumerating the greatest foreign policy achievements of his administration as those he had "personally" handled, TR saluted Root for his primary role in the remainder.

Depending on one's viewpoint and temperament, this aspect of Roosevelt can be disappointing or amusing. His claims of personal credit were generally accurate and sufficiently infrequent so as not to drain the force of his customarily generous recognition of his subordinates' contributions.

Acknowledge and forgive acceptable mistakes—including your own. TR recognized that mistakes were inevitable whenever a leader or a group took action. The improvisation and creativity sparked by expansive delegation inevitably occasion missteps.

Roosevelt could be forthright in acknowledging his own mistakes to his team. Troops in his Spanish-American War regiment were touched by his candor in detailing his misinterpretations of the training manual. They surmised that a leader marked by such a high degree of self-confidence might display a correspondingly understanding attitude toward others.

Where a team member's mistake did not involve an essential matter, TR could be forgiving. In one memorable incident, Roosevelt unilaterally freed a Rough Rider court-martialed for violation of camp regulations. According to Jacob Riis, the soldier was in "agony" over not being able to join the fight in Cuba. TR, unrestrained by notions of due process incompatible with his personal judgment, relented, "All right, you deserve to be shot as much as anybody. You shall go."

In TR's subsequent campaign for governor of New York, opposition papers gleefully circulated one Rough Rider's inadvertently damning praise: "[H]e led us up San Juan Hill like sheep to the slaughter and so he will lead you!" Roosevelt had the good sense to share in the general merriment.

TR could be less forgiving of mistakes made by subordinates acting in his name, especially when he was directly implicated and had not approved the action in advance. Journalist O. K. Davis recounted an embarrassing incident in which an ungrammatical diplomatic message was dispatched by a State Department functionary over President Roosevelt's signature. Widespread criticism and ridicule ensued. TR summoned reporters, telling them "off the record" what had occurred, identifying the clerk who was responsible. In a single transaction Roosevelt protected his reputation, avoided disclosing to the other nation that the cable was not actually his handiwork, and accurately transferred responsibility to the offending civil servant without resorting to unbecoming public censure.

TR understood that an organizational culture that was unforgiving of mistakes could become dangerously inflexible in a time of accelerated change. As he wrote of the navy, "If there is one thing more than any other which our bureau chiefs and technical experts need to learn it is that they must never for a moment consider the question of acknowledgment of error in the past as a factor in doing what is best possible in the present. . . . To refuse to accept any change until its advantages have been demonstrated by actual experience means that we must always be behind the times."

Overlook minor differences. Roosevelt recognized that he could effect more change on more fronts if he did not allow himself to be distracted by what he called "minor differences." As he wrote to Gifford Pinchot about the Progressive Party after the 1912 election, "almost every man of any prominence in this movement has been both a burden and an asset."

It likely never crossed Pinchot's mind that Roosevelt might be describing him. There is no question he was an invaluable assistant to TR—he was loyal, bright, visionary, determined, and monomaniacally dedicated to his work. He was also abrasive, self-righteous, shortsighted, eccentric, and egocentric. Roosevelt once wrote, "Gifford Pinchot is a dear, but he is a fanatic, with an element of hardness and narrowness in his temperament, and an extremist." Following the fateful blow of the unexpected death of his young fiancée many years earlier, Pinchot remained a bachelor until late middle age—a status for which Roosevelt, a strident advocate of large families, had scant regard. He could be infuriatingly demanding of TR's time on trivial matters—as when he caused the president of the United States to decide whether Pinchot would be allowed to sign his (Pinchot's) entire name, or only his initials, on bureaucratic documents. Patiently placing such annoyances in perspective, Roosevelt obtained prodigious performance from his mercurial associate. TR even found value in Pinchot's disagreeable side, utilizing him as a "lightning rod" for controversial environmental policies.

Roosevelt extended his effectiveness by working in harness with individuals with whom he agreed on a given project, even though they shared little else in common. To the chagrin of purists, he worked well with numerous "machine" politicians on issues of mutual interest. The key was TR's unswerving focus on the essential in any given situation.

Create an "inner circle" of leadership. This chapter has used the term "team" broadly. For example, Roosevelt as president might be viewed as leading several teams, including his cabinet, his administration, the national government, and the nation as a whole.

Apart from those groups, Roosevelt relied extensively on what John Maxwell calls an "inner circle" of leadership. Most notable was an informal set during the White House years known as the "Tennis Cabinet." It included some of his cabinet members, some subcabinet officials, diplomats from foreign nations, and sundry friends and family. The Tennis Cabinet bridged TR's work and play, enabling him to cross-fertilize information and perspectives that otherwise would not have come together.

The president regularly visited the home of Secretary of State Hay after Sunday church services. Hay, and sometimes others such as Root or Taft, could use this setting to educate and inform TR in ways not possible in twice-weekly cabinet meetings. In addition to his responsibilities as secretary of state, Hay was a living link to Lincoln and the Civil War generation, to whom Roosevelt looked for inspiration and perspective. TR relied on the political and personal skills of his sister Bamie, whose home he frequented and used for many important meetings, first in New York and later in Washington. He unflaggingly maintained a lively correspondence with accomplished individuals close to home and in foreign lands.

TR's inner circle helped him maintain high standards. This is important for chief executives, whose ascendancy is often accompanied by a muting of longtime sources of feedback. Undercurrents of benign competition ran through the Tennis Cabinet, sometimes reaching Roosevelt. This likely kept TR at his best, just as an athlete may achieve peak performance while training with or competing against other accomplished athletes.

Manage by wandering around. Roosevelt perceived the value of what Tom Peters later popularized as "managing by wandering around." Emerging from behind the desk of authority and moving throughout his organization, he could learn far more than could be conveyed within the four corners of formal memoranda.

As a state legislator and again as governor, he visited tenements in New York City, uncovering a reality far more oppressive than depicted in faraway jurists' elegant dicta about the sanctity of freedom of contract. As a police commissioner he roamed the mean streets, often in disguise and late in the evening, rousting sleepy and corrupt officers and bolstering the resolve of those doing the right thing. At the Navy Department TR toured ships and shipyards rather than rely on the lifeless, sanitized words of routine reports.

In November 1906, as president, TR went to Panama to inspect personally progress on the construction of the Panama Canal (incidentally making him the first president to leave the continental United States while in office). As he wrote his son Kermit, "I went over everything that I could possibly go over in the time at my disposal."

As president, he ventured to Yosemite with preservationist John Muir, examining the giant Sequoias, whose "majestic trunks, beautiful in color and in symmetry, rose round us like the pillars of a mightier cathedral than ever was conceived even by the fervor of the Middle Ages." TR's personal observations enabled him to distinguish those trees he believed could be harvested from those that should be preserved for antiquity.

In 1907, President Roosevelt visited the American naval forces that would become known as the Great White Fleet, preparing to tour the world in an unprecedented, peaceful show of force. The top brass recommended that destroyers not be included in the flotilla. After meeting with several lieutenants TR was convinced that such vessels could make the cruise. He recognized the serious labor-relations problem lurking underneath the issue; enlisted men were threatening to leave the service unless their destroyers were included. "I accept[ed] the word of the men who were to do the job, . . . and within half an hour I sent out the order for the flotilla to be got ready." In a similar vein, after having inspected and gone underwater in a prototype submarine, the *Plunger,* TR ordered hazardous-duty pay for its crew.

Through his physical presence TR could remind his team that he was not asking them to do anything more than he would offer of himself; he could inspire them by reiterating the connection between their work as individuals and the broader enterprise; and he could personify their shared endeavor.

Continually convey gratitude and loyalty to your team, even after it has disbanded or leadership has been transferred. Roosevelt's heartfelt loyalty to his teams persisted for the remainder of his life. Understandably, given their shared experience, his relationship with the Rough Riders was a thing apart. Even as president TR would interrupt virtually anything he was doing to delightedly greet a comrade from the Cuban campaign. Almost no request from them could be too great.

A few erstwhile associates managed to explore his loyalty's outer limits. In correspondence in early 1901 Vice President Roosevelt related a recent request from a Rough Rider on trial for murder:

> "Dear Colonel: I write you because I am in trouble. I have shot a lady in the eye. But I did not mean to shoot that lady. It was all an accident, *for I was shooting at my wife*" [the italics are Roosevelt's] . . . Evidently he felt that the explanation was amply sufficient from one man of the world to another! However, I wrote him back that I drew the line at shooting at ladies and could not interfere.

TR's continuing concern won the lasting devotion of his past colleagues. A diverse group of individuals, representing each part of his varied career, constituted a network that would assist him in various, unforeseeable ways in his future endeavors.

Roosevelt was mindful of the gratitude he owed others for his opportunities to serve and for the success of their shared enterprises. A touching reminder is in a 1913 letter to his distant cousin Franklin Roosevelt, married to his niece Eleanor. President Wilson had recently appointed FDR assistant secretary of the navy. After congratulating the rising star and recounting the similarities in their early careers, TR gently reminded the ambitious younger man to do whatever he could to brighten the drab lives of naval wives: "[E]verything that can properly be done to make things pleasant for them should be done. When I see you and Eleanor I will speak to you more at length about this."

ROOSEVELT'S APPROACH to team leadership is consistent with Warren Bennis's maxim: "The leader finds greatness in the group. And he or she helps the members find it in themselves." TR recognized that any significant achievement requires the contributions of others. Much of the magic of Roosevelt's leadership arose from his high regard—at times approaching reverence—for those he served. He was manifestly willing to put himself in harm's way on their behalf. He delegated immense authority for the most important tasks, demonstrating as nothing else could his confidence—his faith—in his team.

Roosevelt was fond of an old military saying: "[T]here are few bad regiments but plenty of bad colonels." He need not have added that there are no extraordinary regiments without extraordinary colonels.

TR ON LEADERSHIP

- The welfare of your team is your overarching responsibility.
- A leader should develop leaders, not merely direct followers.
- Demonstrate faith in your team by delegation of authority.
- Back up and protect your team consistently.
- Delegation, though extensive, should be bounded by clear standards.
- Fortify delegation with selective intervention.

- Recognize strong performers.
- Acknowledge and forgive acceptable mistakes—including your own.
- Overlook minor differences.
- Create an "inner circle" of leadership.
- Manage by wandering around.
- Continually convey gratitude and loyalty to your team, even after it has disbanded or leadership has been transferred.

CHAPTER NINE

THE JOB ONLY YOU CAN DO

In my regiment nine-tenths of the men were better horsemen than I was, and probably two-thirds of them better shots than I was, while on the average they were certainly hardier and more enduring. Yet after I had had them a very short while they all knew, and I knew too, that nobody else could command them as well as I could.

—THEODORE ROOSEVELT

ROOSEVELT STUDIED and wrote about naval history over much of his life. Perhaps his palpable fascination with great commanders such as Nelson and Farragut reflected recognition that much of a captain's work is emblematic of the role of leaders generally.

A captain is unmistakably accountable for the safekeeping of his ship and crew. At the helm, he alone is accorded the means and responsibility to look into the distance. He visualizes how best to reach the ultimate destination. He discerns nascent risks—in the ocean waves, onshore, in the ship's crew or its machinery—unnoticed by those possessing less experience, knowledge, or intuition. To ensure safe passage, he nurtures relationships with captains of other ships and individuals controlling resources onshore. He translates his judgments into specific actions for which the crew can aim and be held accountable. He connects his team's work with his vision and links his vision to a broader narrative, so that every member of the crew comprehends the meaning and significance of his own actions.

An effective captain draws forth the best from his team by reposing his confidence in them. Their fates are intertwined. He is approachable, available to respond to the needs of others. Bridging the unavoidable distance, he demonstrates his devotion and respect by his willingness to share in the small sacrifices of daily life—perhaps uncomplainingly consuming the same watery gruel. Yet such conscious gestures of equality underscore rather than undermine his separate role and responsibility.

At times, amidst the bustle of daily life frazzling others, the captain may appear aloof, a mere observer. In fact, because to lead is to serve, his watch never ends. Every moment is occupied with thought; underneath, a flood of subconscious fragments continually courses through his mind. He is always in preparation: learning, improving, growing, evolving.

The captain's greatest value may be called on, without warning, in an instant of crisis. The entire team, on matters involving the highest stakes, may need to react as if by instinct, conditioned by painstaking preparation to apply virtuous and effective conduct without hesitation or reflection. In that moment of truth, though material resources are sufficient, traits of character may be decisive. As TR quoted approvingly from naval historian and theorist Alfred Thayer Mahan, "men fight, not ships."

Roosevelt's view of the contribution made by an effective leader includes the following aspects:

"The first duty of a leader is to lead." Early during his training of the Rough Riders, Roosevelt's eagerness to win the approval of his team caused him to blur the line between the commanding officer and the recruits. According to biographer

Henry Pringle, following a demanding day of drills in sweltering semitropical conditions, TR ordered his troops to dismount, announcing: "The men can go in and drink all the beer they want, which I will pay for!"

Roosevelt's commanding officer—and friend—Colonel Leonard Wood, summoned him to his headquarters that evening. Wood outlined the disciplinary problems that could result from an officer drinking with those under his command. TR departed, chastened, only to return a few minutes later: "Sir, I consider myself the damnedest ass within ten miles of this camp. Good night, sir."

That was strong language from Roosevelt. In *The Rough Riders* he explained that having exhibited his willingness to share privation with his troops, he then reestablished distance: "When things got easier I put up my tent and lived a little apart, for it is a mistake for an officer ever to grow too familiar with his men, no matter how good they are, and it is of course the greatest possible mistake to seek popularity either by showing weakness or mollycoddling the men. They will never respect a commander who does not enforce discipline, who does not know his duty, and who is not willing both himself to encounter and to make them encounter every species of danger and hardship when necessary."

TR found that his troops granted him respect while sustaining their affection. "After they had become convinced that I would share their hardships, they made it a point that I should not suffer any hardships at all; and I really had an extremely easy time. Whether I had any food or not myself made no difference, as there were sure to be certain troopers, and, indeed, certain troop messes, on the lookout for me. If they had any beans they would send me over a cupful, or I would suddenly receive a present of doughnuts from some ex-round-up cook who had succeeded in obtaining a little flour and sugar."

Roosevelt's aristocratic background and sense of leadership combined to make him approachable but not overly familiar. Anyone who overstepped the bounds did so at their peril—such as the bumptious corporate lawyer who addressed President Roosevelt as "Teddy," which TR immortalized in a letter as "outrageous impertinence." He doubtless would have appreciated British novelist E. M. Forster's observation of T. E. Lawrence (Lawrence of Arabia): "Though I was frank with him, he was never frank in return, nor did I resent his refusal to be so. This explains in part why he was a great leader of men: he was able to reject intimacy without impairing affection."

A leader must be self-contained. He must be, from the point of view of those he serves, constant. Amidst apparent chaos an exemplary leader may be the sole source of stability visible to his team. In some situations that very distance—and the leader's transformation from a personal presence into a symbolic one—may be a breeding ground for resentment. As TR wrote in 1911, when he was roundly criticized upon his return to the national political stage, "[O]ften men allow themselves the luxury of raving against a man and voting against him and exulting over it, and saying that he is a mighty poor creature, and yet down at the bottom, if a sufficient crisis arose, they would eagerly turn to him."

For a high-level leader, to whom others entrust their lives or livelihoods, the leadership role—and its distance—continues without respite. The burden may be lighter for an individual such as Roosevelt, whose life was never defined entirely by his work. In addition to a close family and network of trusted friends and advisers, he relied on the knowledge and perspective gained from his study of other leaders, past and present. Being "self-made," the author of his personality to an extraordinary extent, may have been significant. Since childhood TR was accustomed to envisioning and occupying a reality distinct from his immediate environs.

Craft and present a compelling vision. Roosevelt believed that the great histories—including Francis Parkman's studies of the American frontier and Mahan's *Life of Nelson*—were distinguished by the disciplined application and presentation of imagination and romance over a stolid foundation of fact. Paraphrasing Sir Walter Scott, perhaps unconsciously, he reserved highest praise for "the great master who can use the materials gathered, who has the gift of vision, the quality of the seer, the power himself to see what has happened and to make what he has seen clear to the vision of others. . . . [T]he extension of the activities of the most competent mason and most energetic contractor will [not] supply the lack of great architects."

Leadership, built on the hard ground of truth, also requires artistry to reach the summit. TR urged, "[W]e need leaders of inspired idealism, leaders to whom are granted great visions, who dream greatly and strive to make their dreams come true; who can kindle the people with the fire from their own burning souls." To achieve what he called "realizable ideals," it is essential that "men of action" be "men of vision."

It is not contradictory to maintain that "the greatest doer must also be a great dreamer." It is an uncommon achievement. As elsewhere, the first Republican president was Roosevelt's exemplar: "Lincoln saw into the future with the prophetic imagination usually vouchsafed only to the poet and the seer. He had in him all the lift toward greatness of the visionary, without any of the visionary's fanaticism or egoism, without any of the visionary's narrow jealousy of the practical man and inability to strive in practical fashion for the realization of an ideal. . . . No more practical man ever lived than this homely backwoods idealist."

Roosevelt's political creed was the "Square Deal." As he wrote in a letter in 1902: "If I stand for any principle whatever, it is for absolute fair play and square dealing as between creed and creed, class and class, section and section, man and man." It was an intergenerational pact placing obligations on the living. At the time he preached it—with the Civil War a living memory, the Gilded Age of industrial transformation abrading traditional values, and the unprecedented floodtide of immigration simultaneously invigorating and straining community structures—it was an inspiring vision to the vast majority of Americans.

Roosevelt's vision was not imposed by an immediate crisis. There was no calamitous war or economic depression to fill out the canvas, inevitably presenting a picture plain to most viewers. Moved by his sense of embryonic issues, TR culled colors from his imagination, mixed them on a palette, translated his vision onto a clean canvas—and by dint of personality compelled people to glance up from their demanding daily lives, if only for a moment, into the future. As James MacGregor Burns has written, "One of the arts of great leadership . . . is the capacity to convert latent crises into visible and dramatic ones. This was Theodore Roosevelt's central achievement."

TR added the power of personifying his vision. As he wrote in the robustly titled *Fear God and Take Your Own Part,* "The prime work for this nation at this moment is to rebuild its own character." The man who harnessed his romantic imagination to the down-to-earth tasks of recreating himself would now do the same for the nation. TR had overcome his own limitations: a feeble physical endowment; class- and geographic-based snobbery; presumptions of the wisdom, morality, and practicality of unchecked materialism and individualism; fear of accelerating change. When he beckoned the nation to aspire to greatness, his audience could see that Roosevelt was asking nothing more than he offered of himself.

Reframe the discussion in terms that advance your vision. In 1858 Lincoln declared, "[H]e who molds public sentiment, goes deeper than he who enacts statutes or pronounces decisions. He makes statutes and decisions possible or impossible to be executed." The leader who sets the terms of public discussion can predetermine the bounds of the resulting options for action.

Roosevelt's dexterity in defining the debate was evident in his advocacy of the cause that came to be known as "conservation." Within this rubric he unified issues and problems heretofore disparate: the closing of the frontier and the end of the pioneer life; the wastage of land and other natural resources; the uncertain outcome of the ferocious legal conflict between private and public assertions of property rights; the extinction of valued wildlife such as the bison; the necessity for water development and land reclamation to make the western states habitable; the increasing understanding of the international aspects of environmental issues; the updating of notions of the obligations of the present generation to posterity.

Rather than presenting and attempting to deal with such problems seriatim, TR fused them into a single story. He declared: "The conservation of our natural resources and their proper use constitute the fundamental problem which underlies almost every other problem in our national life."

Roosevelt's vision remains vital a century later. It met the criteria presented by Winston Churchill to his floundering political party in 1951: "It is not so much a program we require as a theme. We are concerned with a lighthouse, not a shop window." TR's vision of conservation, presented in moral terms, was large enough to encompass competing, evolving elements (such as John Muir's preservationist strand as well as Pinchot's utilitarian approach).

Set and enforce priorities for the achievement of the vision. A critical task of a leader is to discern, select, and implement priorities from the cacophony of options and demands besetting the enterprise he serves. This is especially urgent where a compelling, broad vision has energized many people into action.

President Roosevelt devoted considerable thought to what issues should receive priority. He held some in abeyance—such as comprehensive food and drug regulation—until he determined that public sentiment was ripe and the prospects of other priorities would not be damaged. He declined to take action where he divined scant prospect for progress, most notably reform of the tariff laws (where he also saw significant downside risk). Though he had long expressed private support for woman's suffrage, for most of his career he did "not regard it as a very important matter." (Later, seeking the presidency on the Bull Moose ticket in 1912, he offered public support.)

TR set forth his priorities with painstaking care in his presidential annual messages. After reviewing submissions from the various executive branch departments, he would draft the message with an eye toward multiple audiences: Congress, his administration, opinion leaders, and the general public. He consistently disciplined subsequent communications and policies to reflect and promote his priorities.

Implement the "theory of the next step." In a 1916 letter, Roosevelt cast aside the notion that he was "an astonishingly good politician [who] divined what the people were going to think. . . . I simply made up my mind what they *ought* to think, and then did my best to get them to think it." Without question, his expression of deeply held convictions was effective. He was manifestly willing, especially at the time he was writing, to sail against the winds of prevailing opinion.

Yet TR was not primarily a prophet; he was a leader who worked to achieve what he called "realizable ideals" with the tools at hand. Looking back on his presidency, Gifford Pinchot recalled that TR "was concerned with the fundamental truth that he who goes in advance of public opinion and expects it to follow him must move forward but one step at a time. If his advance is so rapid that the people cannot keep up with him; if they fail to see their way from one foothold to the next; if the gap becomes . . . too broad to be crossed in a single step—contact is broken and leadership fails."

Roosevelt understood that taking a step in the right direction—rather than holding out for nothing less than an ultimate, idealized goal—can have lasting consequences, particularly where it establishes a principle. A chief executive may establish policies and customs "which successors may follow even if they are unwilling to take the initiative themselves." It is often remarked that the administration of TR's successor, Taft, initiated a greater number of antitrust suits than his own. That was one of many situations where Roosevelt undertook the hard, pioneer work of breaking a path in uncertain terrain, making it possible for others to ride the rutted road with assurance.

The more you seek change, the more you should defer to tradition. President Kennedy once described TR as "that great destroyer of tradition." Though apt, it is incomplete.

As Roosevelt bestirred and responded to turbulent change, he consciously exhibited great respect for traditional values. Making the case for thoroughgoing reform at the conclusion of his 1912 Bull Moose campaign, TR tactfully admonished conservatives: "Again, friends, do not forget that we are proposing no new principles. The doctrines we preach reach back to the Golden Rule and the Sermon on the Mount. They reach back to the commandments delivered at Sinai. All that we are asking is to apply those doctrines in the shape necessary to make them available for meeting the living issues of our own day."

The power of his presentation rose from the sincerity of its expression. TR did not offer lengthy ruminations on his religious views (he said he preferred to show his faith by his works), but he was recognized as a regular churchgoer, an active member of congregations at Oyster Bay and in Washington.

Exhibit invincible optimism. Even now, seeing his faded photograph, one senses Roosevelt's vitalized optimism. Having declared that the future of the nation depended on the character of its citizens, TR said he was optimistic about both. He decried those early investigative journalists he termed "muckrakers," who focused almost entirely on what was wrong and dispiriting, rather than on what was good and inspiring. As he said of democracy, one should join those who "try to make the best of it," avoiding those who "always see the worst of it."

Though TR's leadership was suffused with optimism, those close to him were aware of what his daughter Alice called "a melancholic streak." Owen Wister discerned a "wistful conflict between his brain and his temperament over what he knew but did not wish to know: an optimist who saw things as they ought to be, wrestling with a realist who knew things as they were."

As with so much else, Roosevelt wrested his temperament into the service of his leadership.

Attend to important relationships outside the enterprise. As Peter Drucker points out, "[T]he higher the position an executive holds, the larger will the outside loom in his contribution." TR nurtured key outside relationships as a critical part of his leadership. He cultivated and worked alongside selected journalists throughout his career. He corresponded with an influential circle of intimates, as well as other opinion leaders and the general public. As president, he scheduled times each week to interact with the press, opinion leaders, and members of Congress. Roosevelt spent a surprisingly large amount of time maintaining cordial relations with individuals with whom he regularly fought—including some "reformers" on one side, some "conservatives" on the other—sharing information and laying the groundwork for future alliances.

Work by your own clock. Roosevelt strove to take the long view. He pondered the significance of dates, both for himself and for his enterprises. For example, he was moved by the coincidence that his first day in the White House as president was the anniversary of his late father's birthday. He thought that many contentious issues—such as conservation or the "sordid materialism" he deplored—would be properly comprehended and resolved only when people ceased being "shortsighted." Roosevelt's relentless focus on the future enabled him to craft a vision while creating urgency to accomplish short-term priorities. His attention to future generations also held within it an implicit, inspirational, energizing optimism.

TR comprehended the opportunity briefly open for decisive executive action when authority is newly granted or reconfirmed. At the Civil Service Commission, on the Police Board, and following his election as president in 1904, Roosevelt moved rapidly upon taking the reins to let everyone know that he was in the driver's seat, that the carriage would henceforth be going much faster, and in new directions.

As his presidential term moved to a close, TR did not go quietly, indulging in self-satisfying victory laps or obsequiously seeking the goodwill of the passing parade in Washington. The years 1907–09 were challenging: A major "panic" rattled confidence on Wall Street; many people were inevitably tiring of TR's hyperactive presence; he was sliding inexorably into lame-duck status. Unfazed, he grabbed hold of every weapon left in his dwindling armory. His political opponents kept coming, emerging more numerous and more brazen with each passing month. Intergovernmental relations became so strained that some executive branch communications were refused outright by a snarling legislative branch, reared back on its haunches.

Roosevelt's study of leadership made him aware that the course of history could be altered in an instant. The opportunity and necessity for heroic action—the defining moment, drawing together the experience and preparation of a lifetime—might arise with little or no time for reflection. For the remainder of his life, even after his successful presidency, the Nobel Peace Prize, and the rest, TR preferred to be addressed as "Colonel." All of his preparations to be worthy of leadership—beginning in his sickly childhood, when he was stirred by his mother's romantic stories of his swashbuckling Bulloch ancestors in battle—had been brought to bear during his "crowded hours" in Cuba.

Know when to break the rules. Roosevelt recognized that one person's insubordination might be another's gateway to heroism. Reviewing Mahan's *Life of Nelson,* he depicted the hero of Trafalgar with words that might have been applied to himself: "He was a self-willed man, not infrequently in trouble with his superiors, and sometimes guilty of flagrant disobedience which would have been fatal to a man of less genius. In this, as in other respects, he was a bad man to imitate. A great soldier may disregard rules which must be binding upon all save those of transcendent ability."

TR's bias for action allowed him to regard the absence of orders as a license to proceed according to his own judgment. As he wrote in an essay in praise of Admiral Dewey, wisdom dictates "the need of the naval officer's instantly accepting responsibility in a crisis, and doing what was best for the flag, even though it was probable that the action might be disavowed by his immediate superiors, and though it might result in his own personal inconvenience and detriment." An accountable officer, in or near the line of fire, must be willing to act without authority or even to disobey express or implied orders.

Roosevelt approached the presidency in the same way, asserting the "executive as subject only to the people, and, under the Constitution, bound to serve the people affirmatively in cases where the Constitution does not explicitly forbid him to render the service." TR granted that the adoption of an activist or passive style reflected the "temperamental lines" of the chief executive—he threw his lot with Andrew Jackson and Abraham Lincoln. As he wrote in 1913, with amusing understatement, he did not regard the Constitution as a "straight jacket." More to the point was a widely circulated bon mot that TR had no more use for the Constitution than a tomcat for a marriage license.

Roosevelt was not breaking laws or bending rules in pursuit of a lower moral standard. He questioned laws that were used to justify behavior that was plainly immoral, contravening shared ethical tenets. Thus he attacked "hired cunning" put to the service of "mere law honesty." Though the law to some extent reflects moral judgments, the amoral aspects of the legal process—such as the necessity that lawyers be able to argue for any side of a given question—mean that compliance with the law (or avoidance of violation) is no guarantee of moral conduct.

The dangers of Roosevelt's approach are evident. In a nation based on the rule of law, he provoked charges of Caesarism, megalomania, and the like. On the other hand, the personal risks he courted in disregarding the rules convinced many that he was motivated by a desire to serve others. TR took the long view. Future generations would not linger in consternation over customs or sensibilities he ignored or trampled—but they would long remember his accomplishments in building the Panama Canal, conserving environmental treasures, sending the Great White Fleet around the world, and so on. His historical perspective may also have restrained him from recklessness. As Julian Street noted in discussing TR's disregard of political niceties, Roosevelt was inclined toward "calculated indiscretions."

In crisis, a leader such as Washington or Lincoln—or those with more mundane responsibilities—may be called on to make judgments without guidance or restraint from law or custom. There may be circumstances where one person's power or judgment is, for the moment, unassailable. At such critical moments the character of the leader is determinative.

Strive to exemplify character. TR defined character in slightly different ways at different times, but generally stressed three components: honesty, courage, and common sense. A leader must display such traits in order to earn trust, to demonstrate that he is committed unreservedly to service. At the moment of truth—whether in holding power, facing attack, or sensing a prospective crisis over the horizon—habits of character are revealed. Having cultivated character one might achieve integrity—not merely the passive virtue of not lying or not making mistakes, but the active virtue of living one's life so as to meet one's duty, serving others. Only then can one attain the wholeness, the completion, that integrity denotes.

To some extent people might differ as to what character comprises—even in Roosevelt's time it was controversial, and his vociferous advocacy attracted some ridicule, along with charges of hypocrisy and self-idolatry. Yet if some sophisticated people found character difficult to define in the abstract, Roosevelt believed it would be conspicuous and prized when leadership was required. In his *Autobiography* he declared: "[N]o man can lead a public career really worth leading, no man can act with rugged independence in serious crises, nor afford to make powerful and unscrupulous foes, if he is himself vulnerable in his private character. . . . He must be clean of life, so that he can laugh when his public or his private record is searched."

Roosevelt was not suggesting that one avoid missteps by, as he might say, leaving one's talents undamaged in a napkin or finding amusement in the shortcomings of others from the comfort and safety of one's living room. ~~One must combine "blamelessness and the fighting edge~~." He underscored the seriousness of his point, quoting with approval a leading humorist of the late nineteenth century, Josh Billings: "~~[I]t is much easier to be a harmless dove than a wise serpent.~~"

TR ON LEADERSHIP

- "The first duty of a leader is to lead."
- Craft and present a compelling vision.
- Reframe the discussion in terms that advance your vision.
- Set and enforce priorities for the achievement of the vision.
- Implement the "theory of the next step."
- The more you seek change, the more you should defer to tradition.
- Exhibit invincible optimism.
- Attend to important relationships outside the enterprise.
- Work by your own clock.
- Know when to break the rules.
- Strive to exemplify character.

Part Three

BUILDING THE BULLY PULPIT

The word of command is useless in the fight
unless a reasonable number of those to whom it is uttered
not only listen to it but act upon it; and the man who utters it will not
find that the other men to whom he utters it will pay much heed to it
unless they know that he is prepared himself to show the way.

—Theodore Roosevelt

Chapter Ten

PUTTING ACTION INTO WORDS

[W]ords with me are instruments. I wish to impress upon the people to whom I talk the fact that I am sincere, that I mean exactly what I say, and that I stand for the things that are elemental in civilization.

—Theodore Roosevelt

Fully a century after he bounded onto the national political scene, Theodore Roosevelt speaks to us as if he were among us. When we examine the faces on Mt. Rushmore, we admire—from a distance—the austere Washington, the brilliant Jefferson, the sainted, melancholy Lincoln. Roosevelt is something different. Though he lived most of his life in the nineteenth century—he was born prior to Lincoln's election as president—TR's visage conveys vitality and approachability to twenty-first-century Americans.

Roosevelt's communication skills were central to his leadership. His heroism in the Spanish-American War became known to the general public through the dispatches of correspondents he cultivated (and to a lesser extent through his own book on the war, which one humorist said should have been titled *Alone in Cuba*). As president, his universally acknowledged capacity to rouse the people of the nation lay behind his extraordinary power to drive the machinery of government.

The experience of TR's post-presidential years brings to mind Winston Churchill's dictum: "Of all the talents bestowed upon men, none is so precious as the gift of oratory. . . . Abandoned by party, betrayed by his friends, stripped of his offices, whoever can command this power is still formidable." In his 1912 Bull Moose presidential campaign, bereft of institutional support, TR stood alone, reliant on his mastery of communication. In later years, when his causes—especially his demanding nationalism and clarion call for military "preparedness"—were out of fashion and he was shunned by the political establishment, his words kept the flame of his vision alive for the American people to rediscover.

Roosevelt was not naturally gifted as a public speaker. Charles Washburn recalled that as a young man TR had "a defect in his speech which made his utterance at times deliberate and even halting." His vocalization had an explosive aspect, as if disproportionate force was required to push the words forth—far from the mellifluous style we have come to expect on the public stage today. Yet his public speaking was unquestionably effective.

Roosevelt offers numerous lessons in communication, including the following:

Believe in your message. Roosevelt's manifest belief in his message more than overcame his limitations as a speaker. In his *Autobiography* he recalled that in college, "I had . . . no idea of going into public life, and I never studied elocution or practiced debating." Though he allowed that he might have benefited from elocution training, he had a low opinion of debate exercises in which a participant is taught to "talk glibly on the side to which he is assigned, without regard either to what his convictions are or to what they ought to be." By implication TR suggested that much of a speaker's power comes from "sincerity and intensity of conviction," which was certainly true in his case. A speaker who believes strongly in his cause can access the totality of his personality (including his knowledge, experience, and capabilities) in preparing and delivering a presentation.

Leaders compose their own speeches—in collaboration with the best available minds. Individuals holding high offices in important enterprises—government, corporations, nonprofit organizations—increasingly turn to professional writers to prepare speeches. When speakers present the words of others—no matter how well crafted—their messages often seem lifeless, disembodied.

TR generally spoke from prepared texts. His words were his own, though the composition did not come easily. As he told journalist O. K. Davis, "I am not a good writer. . . . I always compose with difficulty, and I have to work over everything I write, frequently several times, to get it to suit me."

Roosevelt's breadth of knowledge was extraordinary, but he was not so vain as to simply sit down shortly before an important presentation, dash out random thoughts on the spot, and assume that he had given birth to an excellent product. He understood that effective speeches—those that move listeners to action—tend to be written in collaboration with others.

TR followed an approach intended to bring to bear his ongoing thoughts and experiences—as well as the contributions of others—over an extended period. Gifford Pinchot recalled that several months prior to the date set for a major paper or speech, Roosevelt would draft, in consultation with others, an outline of his comments. He then would place the paper to one side, returning to it when his thoughts (including those rising from his subconscious or drawn from ongoing inspiration and experience) were further developed, or asking others to read all or part of the text. He would repeatedly alter and polish the product until the delivery date. Over the months prior to the Romanes lecture at Oxford in 1910—aware that he was following in the footsteps of the late, brilliant, eloquent British prime minister William Gladstone, among others—Roosevelt sought input from experts across the world. For less momentous speeches to be given in his later years as a private citizen, he would turn to others—for example, friends gathered for lunch at the Harvard Club of New York—for reaction, much like a prototype "focus group."

Compelling speakers communicate unreservedly with their audience. Leaders who communicate effectively see themselves in a *relationship* business, not a *transaction* business. The speech—in written or spoken form—should not be considered a product delivered *to* an audience on a single occasion. An effective speaker is creating, strengthening, or redefining an ongoing relationship *with* his audience. When an empathetic, well-informed speaker methodically takes the vantage point of the audience, he is most likely to discern and respond to its needs.

Seeking to communicate with a broad audience—the entirety of the American people—Roosevelt set out to understand their lives: "I was sometimes deliberate about it." His powers of observation were supplemented by what a shrewd and sympathetic contemporary called a "delicate intuition, . . . and the troubles or cares of others were never too small to arouse his human understanding."

Like numerous other skilled communicators, Roosevelt possessed a mental picture of the flesh and blood of his primary audience. In his *Autobiography,* he wrote about a cartoon he relished, entitled "His Favorite Author":

> It pictured an old fellow with chin whiskers, a farmer, in his shirt-sleeves, with his boots off, sitting before the fire, reading the President's Message [the annual presentation of administration goals and priorities]. On his feet were stockings of the kind I have seen hung up by the dozen in Joe Ferris' store at Medora, in the days when I used to come in to town and sleep in one of his rooms over the store. . . . *This was the old fellow whom I always used to keep in my mind.* He had probably been in the Civil War in his youth; he had worked hard ever since he left the army; he had been a good husband and father; he had brought up his boys and girls to work; he did not wish to do injustice to any one else, but he wanted justice done to himself and others like him; and I was bound to secure that justice for him if it lay in my power to do so.

In addition to the general audience he continually addressed as a national leader, Roosevelt was aware that numerous distinct audiences might be addressed in any given situation. When TR was a defendant in a libel trial brought by a New York political boss, the plaintiff's lawyer objected to his addressing the court in the manner of a public meeting. Such an objection was futile, since Roosevelt understood that his target audiences were the jury in the courtroom and the broader public that subsequently would read his statements in the press.

TR's approach to drafting speeches—they would "grow" through the addition of others' opinions and the application of his own expanding knowledge—included continuing refinement as he learned from audience reaction. Following his talks he often took questions, some of which inevitably suggested areas for clarification or adjusted emphasis in the future. Important concepts that would become staples of his speeches—such as the "Square Deal" rubric for his presidential programs—were in part the result of his methodical gauging of audience reaction.

An effective public speech is a poster, not an etching. Roosevelt wrote to Henry Cabot Lodge in 1916: "[T]he public cannot take in an etching. They want something along the lines of a circus poster. They do not wish fine details, and it is really not to be expected that they should see them. They want the broad strokes of the brush." With respect to the nation as a whole, Roosevelt told financier Otto Kahn: "If you want to wake up a hundred million people, you've got to make a big and resounding noise and you have got to keep that up for a while."

TR recognized that most people do not have the time or inclination to become sufficiently knowledgeable to follow the intricacies of a leader's thought. Most likely they would hear a leader's words as part of a large audience. As such, they would more likely respond to emotional appeals than to logical presentations.

That is not to say there is not a place for "etchings." Roosevelt's practiced capacity to take the perspective of his audience enabled him to give a nuanced lecture to the members of the American Historical Association on assuming its presidency, or to hold a group of children spellbound with an unforgettably vivid account of the lions of Africa.

Strive for clarity of expression. Viewing words as useful insofar as they motivated and guided useful action, Roosevelt strove for clarity of expression. He wrote to Lodge, "In order to succeed, I must use arguments that appeal to plain, rugged men, who are not subtle and who would simply be puzzled and repelled by what would strike our friends of the London *Nation* as 'originality' and 'distinction.' . . . I am not trying to be subtle or original." Elsewhere he told Lodge, "A public man is to be condemned if he fails to make his point clear."

He was painstaking in his choice of words. His ability to communicate with clarity was enhanced by his temperamental tendency toward directness. He advised one correspondent, a fellow writer, to use "die" rather than "pass on," preferring "[s]imple words, no euphemisms, for elemental facts!"

TR understood the wisdom within British author Virginia Woolf's observation: "The power of suggestion is one of the most mysterious properties of words. . . . English words, are full of echoes, memories, of associations—naturally. They have been out and about, on people's lips, in their houses, in the streets, in the fields, for so many centuries." In putting words to the service of one's cause, one's message is freighted or set to flight in part by their histories and associations. With respect to the Panama Canal, TR wrote: "I found many good people very much concerned over the separation of Panama from Colombia so long as it was called a secession, but not minding it at all as long as it was called a revolution! It took me a long time to realize that they identified secession with the action of the Southern Confederacy, and revolution with our action in 1776!"

Roosevelt's purposeful selection of words was reflected in the plethora of terms and phrases he coined or popularized—many of which remain familiar or apt a century later: Armageddon; bully!; captains of industry; clean as a hound's tooth; don't flinch, don't foul, and hit the line hard!; Good to the last drop! (which became the slogan for Maxwell House coffee); holes alone mean hits, and the shots that hit are the shots that count; hyphenated Americans; malefactors of great wealth; a man of hard mind and soft body; mollycoddles; muckrakers; my hat's in the ring!; no community can make much headway if it does not contain both a church and a school; outpatients of Bedlam; pussy-footed busybodies; puzzle-witted; the right stuff; small people, like small lies, love to contaminate great things; special interests; special privileges; the short and ugly word [lie]; [the wage worker] must never be looked upon as a mere cog in the industrial machine; when you play, play hard, and when you work, work hard.

TR honed descriptive phrases into shiny, lethal bayonets, emerging slippery with blood as they were pulled from stricken foes:

- "The man who loves other nations as much as he does his own country stands on a par with a man who loves other women as much as his own wife."
- "It is just as much a citizen's duty to defend his country as to pay his taxes. You can't conceive of it being left to citizens to 'volunteer' to pay their taxes. They must step to the desk and settle. Necessary military service is to the country a duty that should no more be left to volunteers than the payment of taxes."
- "What I have to say in the future [on military preparedness] will not be for sapheads or mollycoddles."
- "The policy of milk and water [of the Wilson administration] is an even worse policy than the policy of blood and iron [of the Kaiser's Germany]."
- "As for the professional pacifists and the poltroons and college sissies who organize peace-at-any-price societies, and the mere money getters and mere money spenders, they should be made to understand that they have got to render whatever service the country demands."

Some of his most colorful and oft-quoted comments were aimed at individuals who interposed themselves between TR and his goals:

- President McKinley had "no more backbone than a chocolate éclair."
- President Taft was "feebly well-meaning; but with plenty of small motive." He was a "fathead" with "brains less than a guinea pig."

- "I would like to break the neck of the feebly malicious angleworm who occupies the other seat as California's Senator; he is a milk-faced grub named Perkins."
- "[President] Wilson's conduct in international matters has been precisely that of a man whose wife's face is slapped by another man, who thinks it over and writes a note telling the other man he must not do it; and when the other man repeats the insult and slaps the wife's face again, writes him another note of protest, and then another and another and another; and lets it go on for a year. Technically that man may have 'kept the peace' and avoided trouble; but I cannot imagine any human being willing to be in his place."
- ~~TR was enraged by Wilson's refusal to avenge Germany's murder of American citizens lost on the high seas, and the loss of life and property in skirmishes along the Mexican border.~~ Roosevelt turned a visit by Wilson to his summer home, Shadow Lawn, into an occasion for merciless eloquence: "There should be shadows now at Shadow Lawn; the shadows of the men, women and children who have risen from the ooze of the ocean bottom and from graves in foreign lands; the shadows of the helpless whom Mr. Wilson did not dare protect lest he might have to face danger; the shadows of babies gasping pitifully as they sank under the waves; the shadows of women outraged and slain by bandits. . . . Those are the shadows proper for Shadow Lawn; the shadows of deeds that were never done; the shadows of lofty words that were followed by no action; the shadows of the tortured dead."

Roosevelt viewed Wilson as the archetypal leader of a type he abhorred, a "~~Byzantine logothete,~~" "a wonderful dialectician, with a remarkable command of language. But his language is admirably and intentionally designed not to reveal the truth but either to conceal his real purpose and persuade men of different views to think that theirs is his purpose or else to conceal the fact that he has no definite purpose at all."

In the course of a speech challenging Wilson's policies Roosevelt acknowledged that some of his characterizations might be criticized as "extreme" (though "my extremeness one year is another person's moderation later"). He added: "There will be one advantage in what I say. . . . You'll understand it and you won't need any key. You won't get a letter from me day after tomorrow explaining what I meant."

Clarity results not only from the crafting of the words, but from their methodical repetition. As TR told Otto Kahn, "[I]f you want any new notions and impressions to sink in and spread across a continent, you have got to iterate and reiterate and emphasize and drive home, until you are pretty well weary of the very sound of your own voice." Any communication to a large group—especially on a significant topic requiring thought, change of mind, or action—must be repeated and repeated and repeated in order to be persuasive and motivating.

Don't be dissuaded from restating "platitudes" representing the highest aspirations of your enterprise. Roosevelt was frequently taken to task for repeating platitudes. He was dismissed as an "apostle of the obvious," a bard of the banal, a tribune of the trite. The brilliant and caustic Thomas Reed, a legendary Speaker of the House of Representatives, observed: "If there is one thing more than another for which I admire you, Theodore, it is your original discovery of the Ten Commandments."

Roosevelt explained to Owen Wister, "I have to use bromides in my business." The more significant the action sought from an audience, the higher the stakes, the greater the complexity and controversy of the proposed solution, the more TR sought to justify his course on the tenets of basic morality. Appeals to action succeed by calling upon individuals' "character." Roosevelt explained, "[I]n making the appeal to a soldier, if you want to get out of him the stuff that is in him, you will have to use the phrases which the intellectual gentlemen who do not fight will say are platitudes." A leader must recognize when circumstances represent more than an occasion for reflection—they demand a summons to service.

The critics were right about Roosevelt and platitudes. Yet no one can deny that he heightened—or at least updated—public expectations of morality in American life, and he prepared citizens to accept their part in unprecedented national duties and responsibilities.

The language of TR that speaks to us a century later is not sophisticated, intellectual argument about the passing issues of the day (though he was capable of it). We hear and understand and are inspired by his "platitudes" asserting the significance of traditional notions of morality in times of turbulent change.

Use simple, down-to-earth stories to communicate complex issues. Roosevelt was a deft storyteller. At a campfire surrounded by attentive children or on the hustings campaigning for a candidate or a cause, he would weave stories or employ examples that infused a readily comprehensible immediacy into complex or distant issues.

Jacob Riis recalled how TR breathed life into the otherwise dull issue of civil service reform. Roosevelt described the consequences of public employees kicking back three percent of their salaries to their political patrons: to an average clerk it might mean "the difference between having and not having a winter coat for himself, a warm dress for his wife, or a Christmas tree for his children—a piece of cruel injustice and iniquity."

To rouse public opposition to proposed arbitration treaties empowering international bodies to adjudicate matters previously within the sole authority of the U.S. government, TR explained, "No such provision is made as among private individuals in any civilized community. No man is required to 'arbitrate' a slap in the face or an insult to his wife; no man is expected to 'arbitrate' with a burglar or a highwayman. If in private life one individual takes action which immediately jeopardizes the life or limb or even the bodily well-being and the comfort of another, the wronged party does not have to go into any arbitration with the wrong-doer."

As part of his campaign for preparedness for the First World War, Roosevelt sought to persuade the public that the U.S. naval fleet should undertake practice maneuvers:

> In spite of fleet maneuvering the navy may be unprepared. But it is an absolute certainty that without fleet maneuvering it cannot possibly be prepared. In the unimportant domain of sport there is not a man who goes to see the annual football game between Harvard and Yale who would not promptly cancel his ticket if either university should propose to put into the field a team which, no matter how good the players were individually, had not been practiced as a team during the preceding sixty days. If in such event the president of either university or the coach of the team should announce that in spite of never having had any team practice the team was nevertheless in first-class condition, there is literally no intelligent follower of the game who would regard the utterance as serious. Why should President Wilson and Secretary Daniels expect the American public to show less intelligence as regards the vital matter of our navy than they do as regards a mere sport . . . ?

Like a portraitist utilizing contrasts of darkness and light, Roosevelt's descriptions reflected and reinforced his tendency to cast issues in moral terms. He would urge that what is "moral" for the nation as a whole is what is moral in the case of an individual.

Characteristically, he detached conservation from its place within a larger, perpetual argument about contending property rights, exalting it as "a great moral issue." In a time when agricultural life was familiar to most Americans, TR compared the nation to a farmer. As such one could decide to be either "a poor creature who skins the land and leaves it worthless to his children" or "a good farmer who, having enabled the land to support himself and provide for his children, leaves it to them a little better than he found it himself."

On other occasions he made the case for preservation of natural resources in religious terms. California's Yosemite National Park, for example, was "a great solemn cathedral, far vaster and more beautiful than any built by the hand of man."

Adhere strictly to your message. TR took great care that his speeches and utterances would advance, not distract from, his intended message. Acting as a mentor in the 1908 presidential campaign, he warned his aspiring successor Taft to avoid "delicate subjects" where his meaning might be twisted by others. He urged him to keep his speeches "comparatively short" but aggressive, with "more elaborate discussion" to be reserved for more suitable formats and audiences, such as detailed letters to be distributed among opinion leaders. TR resisted publicly responding to hypothetical questions, which almost unavoidably beget purposeless mischief.

Don't exaggerate your case. A compelling speaker faces a seductive temptation to cross the sometimes indistinct line separating acceptable emphasis from unacceptable exaggeration. Roosevelt crossed the line from time to time. Nonetheless, he was aware that exaggeration could undermine the trust that is essential to effective leadership communication. He tended to step past this pitfall by relying on rigorously factual presentations. This is seen, for example, in TR's widely read annual presidential messages, in which he backed his sweeping policy recommendations with specificity and subtlety.

Remain attuned to the temper of your audience. Groups of people—including audiences—have identifiable moods and rhythms, just like individuals. Their composition or viewpoint may change over time. Skilled leaders are attuned to the disposition of their broader audiences, just as they pick up signals from live audiences and adjust in response while speaking.

Roosevelt was constantly in the public eye—he was never one to avoid the limelight—but he recognized the perils of too much exposure or exposure at an inopportune time. Leaving the White House in 1909 for a yearlong African safari, he curtailed his public communications; perhaps he sensed that the nation might be as tired of him as it was affectionate toward him. After a year of activity and controversy following his return home in 1910, TR wrote in a letter that his influence with the public would best be served by "silence and damned little of that." In 1916, in a comment that triggered ridicule from adversaries, Roosevelt expressed concern that the nation was not in a sufficiently "heroic mood" to be receptive to his leadership. Though his robust and self-regarding expression might fairly be questioned, his attention to the changing mood of the public was appropriate.

Master every available communications medium. Roosevelt lived in a time when communications technology was advancing rapidly. With periodicals newly able to reproduce photographs, TR made himself available as a subject in many settings. He was seen on horseback, in an airplane, at the helm of a bulldozer during construction of the Panama Canal, at work in the White House, at play at Sagamore Hill. Combined with the instantaneous communication made possible by the telegraph and long-distance telephony, Roosevelt's methods established the presidency as a regular presence touching the lives of ordinary Americans. He was among the first of the modern "celebrities" whose image was captured and disseminated by the new technologies of sound recording and the motion picture.

Roosevelt understood that the press itself constituted a communications medium with its own dynamics and rules. Perhaps his experience as a writer enhanced his sensitivity to the needs of reporters who faced inflexible deadlines and gnawing competitive pressures. Knowing that Sundays were not ordinarily occasions for breaking news—and that reporters understandably preferred to complete their work as early as possible on weekends—TR initiated the practice of providing news stories to be embargoed for use in the Monday papers, where they would face little competition on the front page. He generally treated journalists with respect; for example, he was the first president to reserve space in the White House for their use. TR took reporters into his confidence—but if they violated his trust he would deny everything publicly and induct the miscreants into the "Ananias Club" (named for the New Testament figure stricken dead for lying after Peter rebuked him).

"You are the message." Communications guru Roger Ailes has coached political and corporate leaders to outstanding performances on the theme: "*You* are the message." According to Ailes,

> [W]hen you communicate with someone, it's not just the words you choose to send to the other person that make up the message.

> You're also sending signals about what kind of person *you* are—by your eyes, your facial expression, your body movement, your vocal pitch, tone, volume, and intensity, your commitment to your message, your sense of humor, and many other factors. . . . Everything you do in relation to other people causes them to make judgments about what you stand for and what your message is. . . . [U]nless you identify yourself as a walking, talking message, you miss that critical point.

Roosevelt's force as a communicator ultimately rested on his personification of his message. His vision for America—vigorous, assertive, honest, gentle, generous—was based on traits of character. His own life story—presented as a parable of achievements by one not gifted by nature, but propelled by traits of character achievable by anyone—embodied his version of the national narrative. Lord Morley of Britain pithily said, "He is not an American, you know. He *is America*." In the words of Ezra Pound, "The age demanded an image"; TR's image became America's at the turn of the twentieth century.

Roosevelt fortified his verbal communications with nonverbal communications. He was surely the first and only New York police commissioner to sport a silk sash around his waist—combined with a pink shirt with knee-length tassels. In Cuba he was a ubiquitous presence on horseback, wearing a sombrero encircled by a polka dot handkerchief. At the Republican Convention in 1900, he was recognizable at any distance, branded by his trademark, broad-brimmed Rough Rider hat. During his presidency TR was constantly depicted, in photographs or cartoons, exhibiting boundless energy. He could be seen riding horses, chopping wood, walking purposefully on a hike or to an appointment—but he methodically avoided being photographed playing tennis or in any other activity that drew attention to the distance between his daily life and that of ordinary Americans.

His manner of speaking was as vigorous as his words. Arms waving, right fist slamming into left palm for a crack of emphasis, TR's heartfelt dedication to a cause could move a crowd far more than the melodious voices and cultivated but ambiguous phrases of others. Sometimes the force of his presentation overshadowed the words. More than once a reporter on the scene would report a Roosevelt speech to have been of great significance—only to run into a wall of resistance from an editor who, seeing the words unadorned by the performance, realized that nothing new had been said.

A leader who personifies his vision must always be "on" within his realm; at the highest levels his entire life becomes his stage. He is playwright, director, actor. In addition to his speeches and conspicuous actions, Roosevelt would communicate through subtle actions recognized by limited but intensely interested audiences. When, as president, he presented a speech in a private home, he consciously reinforced public understanding of his personal commitment to the subject at hand, conservation. On another occasion, he broke White House protocol, introducing a speaker to an audience. He stated that it was the only time he would do so while serving as president, underscoring his heartfelt agreement with the speaker's recent book on community morality. As ex-president en route to present a dinner speech in Chicago, TR was informed that a U.S. senator, tainted by a corrupt election, had been invited to attend. Roosevelt characteristically told the sponsors that he would not take part unless the senator's invitation was withdrawn. It was. There was at least one seat at the speakers' table not for sale.

TR's daughter Alice famously said, "Father always wanted to be the corpse at every funeral, the bride at every wedding and the baby at every christening." Wister added perspective: "He was his own limelight, and could not help it: a creature charged with such voltage as his, became the central presence at once, whether he stepped on a platform or entered a room—and in a room the other presences were likely to feel crowded, and sometimes displeased." His enthusiasm—the word's Greek roots refer to the spirit of God possessed by a man—rendered him and his causes almost irresistibly engaging.

TR ON LEADERSHIP

- Believe in your message.
- Leaders compose their own speeches—in collaboration with the best available minds.
- Compelling speakers communicate unreservedly with their audience.
- An effective public speech is a poster, not an etching.
- Strive for clarity of expression.
- Don't be dissuaded from restating "platitudes" representing the highest aspirations of your enterprise.
- Use simple, down-to-earth stories to communicate complex issues.
- Adhere strictly to your message.
- Don't exaggerate your case.
- Remain attuned to the temper of your audience.
- Master every available communications medium.
- "You are the message."

CHAPTER ELEVEN

FIGHTING WORDS—RESPONDING TO UNJUST CRITICISM

If a man has a very decided character,
has a strongly accentuated career, it is normally the case of course
that he makes ardent friends and bitter enemies.
—THEODORE ROOSEVELT

IN OCTOBER 1912, shortly before Roosevelt was shot in Milwaukee, a Philadelphia newspaper offered a sampler of recent characterizations of the former president:

> Shrieks his hostility, ridiculous, contemptible, eager to use fraud, unparalleled viciousness and dishonesty, insensate ambition, gnashing his teeth, dangerous demagogue, charlatan, plain aberration, bad faith, unworthy methods, dangerous, shocking, unscrupulous, horrible glibness, indecent performance, an Aaron Burr, shameless, crazy socialistic schemer, blatantly insincere, hypocritical, in favor of howling mobocracy, user of shabby tactics, hollow and untrustworthy, duplicitous, shrewd political trickster, a self-seeking autocrat, guilty of a squalid bandying of words, no respecter of truth, and full of unblushing effrontery.

In 1910 Mr. Rudolph M. Patterson of Chicago, a self-designated "Real Estate Expert," offered $1,000 "to an expert Sanity Commission and to the Associated Charities of Chicago and New York, if Col. T. Roosevelt, on examination, was not found to be insane, 'non compos mentis,' and a dangerous character at large among the peaceful citizens of the United States." In 1912, Patterson upped his offer to $5,000. Even placid President Taft described Roosevelt and his Bull Moose supporters as "political emotionalists or neurotics."

As the 1912 election neared, a respected periodical's signed editorial, melodramatically entitled "Roosevelt or the Republic," declared: "Roosevelt was the first President whose chief personal characteristic was mendacity, the first to glory in duplicity, the first braggart, the first bully, the first betrayer of a friend who ever occupied the White House." He was further condemned for "perpetual lying," his "shameless treatment of helpless women. . . . and the civil strife that would almost inevitably ensue from patriotic resistance to usurpation by a half mad genius at the head of the proletariat." One newspaper went the distance, calling him the "political anti-Christ."

Granting TR's acceptance of criticism as a "necessary incident" of public life, he inspired spitting, spiteful vituperation. A notably short-sighted thrust came from *Puck* magazine in May 1887, in the aftermath of his defeat in the New York mayoral race: "Be happy, Mr. Roosevelt, be happy while you may. You are young—yours is the time of roses—the time of illusions. . . . We wish you a gradual and gentle awakening. . . .You are not the timber of which Presidents are made." Some years later the president of his alma mater, outraged by his politics, termed him a "degenerated son of Harvard." Henry James called him "the mere monstrous embodiment of unprecedented and resounding Noise." A congressional opponent attacked him as the "bloody hero of Kettle Hill," "unreliable, a faker, and a humbug." Assorted cranks claimed that TR had not fought in the Spanish-American War—or, alternatively, that he had shot enemy soldiers in the back. During his governorship an unsympathetic New York newspaper managed to find fault even with his Thanksgiving Day proclamation: the "slap-dash governor" in "wretched taste" produced a "silly proclamation" giving "very much the impression of firing a revolver in the middle of a prayer." Robert Foran, who traveled with TR to Africa, recalled, "He was accused—and many people seem willing to believe it to be the fact—of shooting hand-fed lions, of killing rhinoceri which had been chained to a tree ready for the slaughter, and of massacre of elephants which were tamed."

Roosevelt preferred the actor to the critic. He "rank[ed] action far above criticism," dismissive of "the man who confines himself to talking about how [things] ought to be done." Nonetheless, he recognized constructive criticism as an important source of learning. As president, expressing appreciation for suggestions on how to improve the construction of the Panama Canal, he wrote, "Nothing is more helpful than criticism, provided the criticism is in good faith . . . that is, it is honest, intelligent, and meant to aid instead of hamper." He distinguished what he called "causes for criticism" from "occasions for diatribes."

Among the elements of Roosevelt's approach to unfair criticism are the following:

No matter how personal the attack, your response should be aimed entirely toward advancing the goals of those you serve. TR recommended that a leader continue to "fight his way forward" in the face of "unfair and ungenerous criticism," "paying only so much regard . . . as is necessary to enable him to win in spite of them." A leader, especially of a large enterprise, should not confuse his *symbolic* role with himself as a person. The fact that the criticism is personal does not necessarily indicate that the response should be along the same lines. Roosevelt was keenly aware that while people generally may not immediately draw conclusions from unfair criticisms, they tend to recoil if leaders appear to be attacking one another for reasons unrelated to serving others.

Identify your audience. As in any communication, a primary task is to identify the audience. This may range from the general public to opinion leaders, from competitors to the employees of one's own organization.

In the case of high-level leadership, in private and public life, one must consider future audiences. For major decisions with long-term impact, that might include preparation for questioning or criticism from competitors, critics, regulatory agencies, journalists, and others who might influence the verdict of history.

DIRECT, INDIRECT, OR HUMOROUS

Determine the appropriate response. Once the goals have been clarified and the audience identified, a leader should determine what response is appropriate.

Roosevelt's inclination was to be direct in all things. If an inaccurate or unfair criticism might gain credence because of the reputation or position of the critic, TR would act decisively. When a New York politician publicly charged that the construction of the Panama Canal was incompetently handled, President Roosevelt immediately responded in a public letter, "This is simple nonsense."

Early in his presidency, when TR was remodeling the White House, numerous articles tweaked him for alleged extravagance. Though the criticism was largely misplaced, Roosevelt understood that it might appear credible—and was especially dangerous in the early months of his administration, when public opinion was forming. The suggestion of profligacy was potent, because it was comprehensible to the mass of people from their own life experience. Left unanswered, it might open the door to unfounded accusations against much more significant spending matters (such as naval expansion) that most people otherwise would consider beyond their ken. Accordingly, President Roosevelt drafted and signed letters to key opinion leaders making his case for White House renovation with a blizzard of facts and figures.

When critics were predictably negative in their comments, TR often dismissed them out of hand. He sometimes employed humor. In one speech he gently brushed aside former secretary of state William Jennings Bryan and automobile magnate Henry Ford, prominent opponents of Roosevelt's "preparedness" campaign urging American entrance into the First World War: "I don't have to deal with Mr. Bryan and Mr. Ford. I regard them both as nice, amiable men, and I like them in private life; but I decline to take part in any such wild mental joy rides as would be necessary if I had to discuss seriously their attitude." In another context, referring to a political opponent, Roosevelt said with a smile: "Don't speak of him as my enemy. I like him. He is interesting. It is pleasant to see how many ways he has of not doing the thing he has exactly promised to do."

Some criticisms are best ignored altogether. Not only will some critics ignore facts, making a direct response pointless, but their constant carping, left uninterrupted, may enable others to see them as they are. As TR said, "There are many occasions when the highest praise one can receive is the attack of some given scoundrel."

As far as possible, plan the timing and content of your response on your own terms. An unfair critic may have the advantage of the initiative. Roosevelt took care not to respond reflexively or in the terms of the attacker—unless, of course, he determined that would advance his larger aims. Late in the

1904 election campaign, he was pelted with criticism arising from his campaign's fundraising from corporations the federal government regulated. Over the course of several weeks, the Democratic candidate and his supporters escalated their attacks. Some of the charges were accurate (though now and again misleading in context); others were demonstrably false. TR remained silent until the final days before the election. With his opponents precluded, as a practical matter, from a timely rejoinder, TR responded selectively to those charges that he could persuasively label as "wicked falsehoods."

One of the more vexing—and inaccurate—slurs hurled at Roosevelt was that he was an alcoholic. Perhaps in reaction to the self-destruction of his brother Elliott, TR's drinking was quite moderate—generally limited to Apollonaris water, sometimes mixed with champagne or wine, often in a metallic chalice whose level could not be observed from the outside. Nonetheless his uncommon exuberance—conveyed through unusually emphatic gesticulation and a near-explosive manner of speech—left many people predisposed to believe the worst.

TR understood that such allegations could not be credibly refuted through repeated denials. He awaited an opportunity to correct the record while not interfering with ongoing leadership responsibilities. Such an opportunity arose in 1913. Roosevelt sued the proprietor of a small Michigan publication, the *Iron Ore,* for its October 12, 1912, assertion: "Roosevelt lies and curses in a most disgusting way; he gets drunk too, and that not infrequently, and all his intimate friends know about it." TR won the case, received a public apology from the publisher, and asked the court to assess damages of six cents—the minimum allowed under Michigan law.

Carefully consider to whom the response should be addressed. In 1908 correspondence with Mark Sullivan, editor of the influential *Collier's* magazine, Roosevelt took umbrage at an article by novelist Jack London. London criticized the president's views on various scientific issues, fanning a controversy in which Roosevelt, backed by leading naturalists, attacked "nature fakers" who mixed fiction into purportedly factual presentations.

In writing Sullivan, TR sought to affix accountability for London's article on the publication rather than the author: "I want to speak to *Collier's* rather than to Jack London, altho[ugh] of course you are perfectly welcome to show him this letter, with the distinct understanding, however, that I am not entering into a controversy with him but with *Collier's;* and that of a purely private, not public, nature." In one stroke he protected the dignity of the presidency, avoided having the controversy dismissed as a mere personality fight, and communicated that London lacked the stature to justify a direct response.

Similarly, Roosevelt asked Lincoln Steffens not to mention a particularly nettlesome "reformer" by name in a forthcoming book: "He is not of sufficient importance and I do not wish him dignified." In his 1913 *Autobiography* TR chose to ignore a series of overwrought criticisms by his erstwhile ally, Senator Robert LaFollette. He made his case on disputed points without reference to LaFollette—but included, as an appendix, earlier, rather effusive words of praise from the Wisconsin progressive.

If a powerful, symbolic individual or institution stood behind an individual making the criticism, TR might ignore the accuser and publicly excoriate the backers. Challenged by an agent of John D. Rockefeller, TR publicly responded to Rockefeller himself. Running for governor of New York, he overlooked charges from his nominal opponent Augustus Van Wyck, targeting his public responses toward the Democratic Party leader, an unsavory man of ill repute with a conveniently Dickensian name: Boss Croker.

Carefully consider from whom the response should come. Once an appropriate response is prepared, the question arises as to who should present it. Roosevelt understood that in some cases a direct response from the leader would be the preferred course, though to do so indiscriminately would be a mistake. Even if he "wins," a chief executive errs if he enters fights that do not advance the goals of his enterprise.

A chief executive's decision not to deliver the public response personally does not necessarily suggest that he not be involved in crafting the response and deciding from whom it should come. Whether to publicly disclose his involvement or otherwise associate himself with the response is another decision.

In 1900, while governor of New York, Roosevelt corresponded with individuals pressing his case for the Medal of Honor. After supplying facts that might be used in his behalf against critics, TR added: "I ask you not to quote this letter or to say that I have written to you. I do not wish to appear in any newspaper as answering these attacks myself. If you choose to use the facts you are welcome to use them."

One of the consequences of the practice of elevating disputes to matters of principle, as TR did with London over "nature fakers," is that third-party experts may be more likely to wade in and help resolve a controversy on its merits. To the extent that the response relies on declarations of good faith of an individual, it is more credible coming from third parties.

Remember the two most powerful words in response to general charges: Be specific. In some cases unfair criticism may be concealed within a general attack that has surface plausibility. President Roosevelt faced this when the financier and railroad magnate E. H. Harriman charged that a federal government bureau had falsified material information and committed statistical errors relating to railroad regulation. Rather than respond in a general way to the charge of governmental incompetence, Roosevelt focused with precision on the relevant matters. He wrote the agency in question, acknowledging that they would not be able to respond to "indefinite charges; but I should like you to take the definite charges I have quoted, and any other specific instances contained in this letter or any specific instances which Mr. Harriman gives which you think of importance, and report to me thereon, so that I might know, as to these specific instances, whether [the government] has done anything that is wrong in form or anything that is wrong in substance."

After the bureau completed its review, Roosevelt wrote to one of Harriman's associates, reporting, "The examination has been made and the charges of Mr. Harriman are found to be without any foundation whatever. Under the circumstances it would be simply folly for me to pay any further heed to any allegations whatever made in regard to the work of the [agency] by Mr. Harriman or you." TR made his letter public, sending a copy to the office in question.

Anticipate truth-twisters. Owen Wister's description of the presidency also applies to other chief executives in the twenty-first century: They must operate "with organized misrepresentation listening at the door and peeping through the key-hole to catch and distort and send flying to the four points of the compass every gesture that he makes and every syllable that he speaks." As Roosevelt wrote in an essay on reform, "There is always a danger of being misunderstood when one writes about a subject such as this, because there are on each side unhealthy extremists who like to take half of any statement and twist it into an argument in favor of themselves or against their opponents." He followed Lincoln's lead, as he explained in a letter in 1912, "consistently declin[ing] to make statements which, though true, would give opportunities for misrepresentation."

Almost any significant communication from a leader is susceptible to misrepresentation. To the extent this is foreseeable, one should work to ensure that any such communication is self-contained, that it includes elements sufficient for a fair-minded person of reasonable intelligence to understand the context and discern the distortions of critics.

Roosevelt was remarkably disciplined in this regard. His sentences were sometimes ungainly and unintentionally humorous in their regimented application of balanced phrasing: labor and capital, the "plain people" and the "rich," "Our purpose is to shackle greedy cunning as we shackle brutal force," and so on. His rather spectacular lapse was a speech proposing popular recall of judicial decisions. Though couched in conservative terms, harking back to the tradition of Lincoln, it was readily—and predictably—twisted to credibly characterize TR as a reckless radical.

Create and maintain contemporaneous records for future use. Roosevelt created and maintained a vast collection of records intended for future reference. He constantly wrote letters laying forth his views on issues or interpretations of events. Though estimates vary, TR told a friend that he had written 150,000 letters in the White House alone.

In another context, in an editorial entitled "What's the Use?" the *New York Times* vented frustration from its inability to pierce Roosevelt's defenses. Journalist O. K. Davis recalled, "The *Times* complained that if a committee of the Colonel's most distinguished and reliable neighbors were to visit Sagamore and find the dismembered remains of his grandmother, boiled in oil, in the cellar, it would be no use assailing him about it, for he would come out with a letter to some friend, written long before, that would show the whole thing to have been entirely innocent."

This practice also helped Roosevelt and his close advisers maintain discipline in the substance of their internal communications. In 1915, William Barnes, a New York Republican political boss who objected to being characterized as such, sued Roosevelt for libel. TR's complete correspondence was trawled by lawyers seeking to embarrass him. When the New York trial, like the earlier Michigan suit, concluded with Roosevelt's vindication, he told a friend with pride, "There was not a single thing in all these old letters of mine that I am ashamed to have my children read." (His children, well aware that much of their father's correspondence to them was also aimed at a broader audience, joked about his "posterity letters.")

Contemporaneous records can constitute a "rough draft" for historians. TR's experience as an author likely motivated him to tend to the unavoidably tedious task of record keeping. He left written accounts and interpretations discussing his service in various posts, as well as contemporary views on people, places, and ideas. His writings included factual responses to criticisms on issues that Roosevelt decided not to engage directly, at least at the time of the charges, but on which he wished to bequeath an accurate account. In numerous situations—such as the encounter with J. P. Morgan at the White House shortly after the filing of the Northern Securities suit—TR's contemporaneous account stands unchallenged, the only one known to have survived.

Like Winston Churchill, Roosevelt would not fear the verdict of history—especially since he would help write it.

Remind unfair critics that if they start shooting, they are going to be shot at. In dealing with critics for whom the truth is no object, to whom slander and libel are tools of the trade, TR stood prepared to respond with direct—at times ferocious—

counterattack. Roosevelt's temperament and capacity as a fighter requires no elaboration. One point worth reemphasizing is his ability to maintain his composure and affability in the heat of combat. Though there were notable exceptions (for example, as president he once engaged in a rather embarrassing shouting match with an annoying senator before a large crowd at the annual Gridiron Club dinner), he generally acted in line with Churchill's dictum: "When you have to kill a man it costs nothing to be polite."

"Don't attempt to change to suit the notions of critics." During the 1900 campaign for governor of New York, Roosevelt's longtime friend Billy O'Neill was dispatched to accompany the novice candidate. It was intended that O'Neill would tactfully nudge TR toward campaigning in a more traditional manner, with less use of the personal pronoun.

After several days of observation O'Neill wrote to Roosevelt: "For the most part men are as nearly alike as peas—once in a while Nature produces a new type which she never duplicates—an original which sets at naught all our previous standards—These are the fellows who win the world, who can say and do things when and how they please. You belong to this order. Don't attempt to change to suit the notions of critics."

It is often fruitless to attempt to change to satisfy critics in any event. As Roosevelt later noted: "There are only two elevators in this building [*Outlook* magazine, where he worked for a time after the presidency], and I must use one or the other of them. If I go down by the side elevator, that is evidence of furtiveness. If I go down in front, that is proof of ostentation."

Become thick-skinned. It is one thing to assert that a leader should not take malicious attacks personally; it is something else to handle them with equanimity in the event. It was not natural, even for Roosevelt, to have the thick skin he considered necessary to weather unfair, misguided, sometimes malicious criticism.

In September 1898, TR was exhausted by a stream of political attacks on the eve of the state party convention that would ultimately nominate him for governor. The national hero, who exhibited no fear amidst deadly bullets in Cuba, was visibly shaken by the rhetorical fusillades of New York politics. According to historian Wallace Chessman, a contemporary found the Rough Rider "hardly able to eat or sleep." At one time he "cried like a baby—I don't mean in a babyish way," as he confronted charges of double-dealing by a group of independents who thought they had his support, as well as accusations of perjury and tax dodging arising from his abandoning his New York state residency for tax purposes while working in Washington.

Roosevelt recovered his composure. Over the years he developed an ability to "take a punch" and stay on his feet, all the while hewing to his plan of action. At the same time a thick skin should not be impervious to disagreeable but essential information; a resourceful executive should filter what might be useful from what is not. As in other areas of leadership, this is made more likely when one focuses on the needs and goals of those one would serve, rather than on oneself.

Always adhere to the truth. In the thick of a fight, when counterpunching against malicious critics habitually dealing in falsehood, there is a risk of lowering one's own standards of honesty. That can have serious consequences. Though it may take time and persistence, the truth can emerge and will always be the ultimate defense against mendacity.

Roosevelt understood that where essentially virtuous leaders cut ethical corners, even for worthy ends, the benefits attained are evanescent. Individuals of lesser character gain the upper hand whenever the boundaries of honesty and character are breached. TR wrote, "Incessant falsehood inevitably produces in the public mind a certain disbelief in good men and a considerable disbelief in the charges against bad men; so that there results the belief that there are no men entirely good or any men entirely bad, and that they are all about alike and colored gray."

~~Most significantly, the bonds of trust unifying the leader and those he would serve are attenuated if not broken whenever the truth is compromised. At the highest level of leadership, a hard-earned, lifelong reputation for veracity can be imperiled by a single lapse~~.

TR ON LEADERSHIP

- No matter how personal the attack, your response should be aimed entirely toward advancing the goals of those you serve.
- Identify the audience for your response.
- Determine the appropriate response—direct, indirect, humorous—to convey your message to your intended audience.
- As far as possible, plan the timing and content of your response on your own terms.
- Carefully consider to whom the response should be addressed.
- Carefully consider from whom the response should come.
- Remember the two most powerful words in response to general charges: Be specific.
- Anticipate truth-twisters.
- Create and maintain contemporaneous records for future use.

- Remind unfair critics that if they start shooting, they are going to be shot at.
- "Don't attempt to change to suit the notions of critics."
- Become thick-skinned.
- Always adhere to the truth.

Chapter Twelve

PUTTING WORDS INTO ACTION

Example is the most potent of all things.

—Theodore Roosevelt

[Roosevelt's] . . . instinct was always to say "come" rather than "go."

—Henry Cabot Lodge

In an interview shortly before his death, Roosevelt related a transformative incident from his early adolescence. One day, reading a volume of one of his favorite poets, Robert Browning, he happened upon "The Flight of the Duchess." His attention was irresistibly drawn to a description of an unprepossessing young duke, "the pertest little ape / That ever affronted human shape." Young "Teedie"—the self-conscious, timid, diffident, delicate scion of a distinguished lineage—read further, with rising unease: "All that the old Dukes had been without knowing it / This Duke would fain know he was, without being it."

Roosevelt never forgot how he was jolted into action by those words. He resolved at a stroke to move aggressively from passive appreciation to active emulation of his heroes' accomplishments. The interviewer, Hermann Hagedorn, concluded: "The story of Theodore Roosevelt is the story of a small boy who read about great men and decided that he wanted to be like them . . . and he succeeded."

TR's life experience afforded him a profound appreciation of the potential effect—for good or ill—of the power of example. Always focused on character, believing it to be composed of choices made by individuals in their daily lives, Roosevelt strove to make his own life a compelling example for others. As he once instructed a group of young people, "Example is the most potent of all things. . . . You must feel that the most effective way in which you can preach is by your practice."

In Roosevelt's romantic vision, history was a cavalcade of heroic leaders. In their preface to *Hero Tales from American History,* TR and co-author Henry Cabot Lodge expressed their goal: "to tell . . . the story of some Americans who showed that they knew how to live and how to die; who proved their truth by their endeavor." Elsewhere he wrote admiringly of General Ulysses Grant and the magnificent generation that fought the Civil War and reunited the nation, expressing gratitude for "the great memory of their great deeds, to serve forever as an example and inspiration, to spur us on so that we may not fall below the level reached by our fathers." Characteristically, he added a caveat: "[M]ere lip-loyalty is not loyalty at all . . . , the only homage that counts is the homage of deeds, not of words."

In opposition to the false sophistication of the cynical, Roosevelt openly emulated those he considered heroes—most notably his father, Washington, and Lincoln. They were constantly in his thoughts. Their portraits adorned his offices and home. He treasured a lock of Lincoln's hair, in a ring given to him by John Hay. TR regularly invoked his heroes' example in framing or understanding the circumstances of his own time. Acknowledging that the limitations of his own abilities and circumstances made it unlikely he would reach their level of service, he nonetheless honored their example by his endeavor. His ideal was reflected in one of his favorite verses from the Bible: "Be ye doers of the word, not hearers only."

When the Spanish-American War erupted in 1898, Roosevelt had no doubt what his role must be: "[I]f I am to be of any use in politics it is because I am supposed to be a man who does not preach what he fears to practice, and who will carry out himself what he advocates others carrying out. . . . I should feel distinctly ashamed, and I should feel that my possibilities of usefulness were largely at an end if I now failed to practice what I have preached." He later said that he "would have turned from my wife's deathbed to have answered that call."

In Cuba, TR seized his opportunity to exhibit the virtues of the martial heroes he had long revered, studied, and written about. On horseback in the midst of spraying gunfire, he was a conspicuous presence, at once vulnerable and commanding. He urged the troops on the ground forward toward him—in many cases, to their deaths. Even in the unfamiliar and inhospitable Cuban terrain, Roosevelt likely experienced a sense of déjà vu in the chaos of battle. In one sense he had been there many times before, from hearing his mother tell of the exploits of the Bulloch men to being transported by books to the side of such great military commanders as Marlborough and Lord Nelson, Robert E. Lee and David Farragut.

As president, in his role as commander in chief of the armed forces, he set an example for officers being considered for promotion, rousting indolent generals from the comfort of their sinking armchairs to join him for vigorous hikes in Rock Creek Park or other outdoor venues near Washington. In 1909 he went further, ordering that high officers demonstrate their ability to ride ninety miles on horseback in three days. Uproar inevitably ensued, occasioning familiar charges that Roosevelt was a tyrant. Unperturbed, he responded by mounting a horse and riding nearly 100 miles in a single day—partly in a snowstorm.

As president he disregarded personal safety, going underwater for more than an hour in a submarine (then a new and largely untested vessel). TR explained his descent on the *Plunger* in a letter to a friend: "I went down in it chiefly because I did not like to have the officers and enlisted men think I wanted them to try things I was reluctant to try myself."

In 1917, as America at long last entered the Great War raging in Europe for three years, Roosevelt stepped forward to lead one of the volunteer divisions authorized by Congress. The longtime prophet of preparedness was visibly infirm.

In TR's mind, perhaps more daunting than the prospect of death in the industrialized slaughter damping the cold ground of France was the necessity that he obtain President Wilson's permission to serve. Many others intervened in his behalf. The great French leader Georges Clemenceau importuned Wilson: "It is possible that your own mind, enclosed in its austere legal frontiers, which has been the source of so many noble actions, has failed to be impressed by the vital hold which personalities like Roosevelt have on the popular imagination. . . . [T]he influence on the people of great leaders of men often exceeded their personal merits, thanks to the legendary halo surrounding them. The name of Roosevelt has this legendary force in our country at this time."

Wilson rejected Roosevelt's offer. Reliably described as brokenhearted, TR soldiered on in every way open to him. He campaigned across the nation in support of the war effort. He and Edith saw their four sons off to Europe, where each earned recognition for valor. Their daughter Ethel served in France as a nurse. One son would not return.

The leader most identified with the ideal of universal national service led by example to the end.

ROOSEVELT FAMOUSLY SAID, "[M]y problems are moral problems, and my teaching has been plain morality." Owen Wister was right: "If they treated Theodore as they deal with certain composite substances in chemistry, and put him in a crucible, and melted him down and down until nothing of him remained . . . but this ultimate, central, indestructible stuff, it's not statesman that they'd find, or a hunter, or a historian, or a naturalist—they'd find a preacher militant."

TR would have agreed with the British essayist Matthew Arnold that example is not a "little thing." Roosevelt believed that "the immense and indefinable moral influence" of example would be felt not only in the aftermath of the heroic acts of heroic figures, but also from the everyday choices of everyday people.

As president, he personally intervened to make certain that the government he led would set a beneficent example on matters ranging from binding reports inexpensively to setting wage and hour guidelines for contractors.

Throughout his career—as a leader who sought to raise the moral tone (and morale) of the enterprises he led—TR understood that his own life would constantly be observed and evaluated by others. He did not lead two lives, one "private," another "public." Leadership is built on trust; extraordinary leadership is built on extraordinary trust; extraordinary trust is built on a leader's adherence to shared tenets of personal morality. In the aftermath of his victory in the 1904 campaign, President Roosevelt wrote:

> It is a peculiar gratification to me to have owed my election . . . above all to Abraham Lincoln's "plain people"; to the folk who worked hard on farm, in shop, or on the railroads, or who owned little stores, little businesses which they managed themselves. I would literally, not figuratively, rather cut off my right hand than forfeit by any improper act of mine the trust and re-

gard of these people. . . . I shall endeavor not to merit their disapproval by any act inconsistent with the ideal they have formed with me.

Through all the controversies he created or courted, Roosevelt's character was never credibly attacked. John Hay, who served Lincoln as aide-de-camp and Roosevelt as secretary of state, said in 1904: "Each [of his political opponents] knows very well that he could wish no happier lot to his boy in the cradle than that he might grow up to be such a man as Theodore Roosevelt."

Some people, then and now, have found this a bit hard to take. TR's proclivity to define morality in poster-like terms, which might be appropriate for the general public, could appear callous in personal situations calling for the more nuanced rendering of an etching. He acknowledged he could at times be fairly labeled a "prig." When his drive for action, ruthlessly applied, coexisted uneasily with his moral compass—as in his "taking" of Panama—Roosevelt might respond to critics with disproportionate vehemence.

His saving graces were his evident sincerity of belief, his ability to forgive others, and his humor. An example of the latter was supplied by Edward Wagenknecht. John Reed, an American journalist who joined the Bolshevik cause in the Revolution of 1917, was about as far as one could be from TR in political and cultural views. Perhaps thinking he would rattle the aging ex-president, Reed declared his belief in free love. Roosevelt replied drolly, "A young man should believe in something."

THE CAPACITY TO forgive or find humor in the infractions of his own family did not come as easily. Though he protected them from journalistic intrusions he considered inappropriate (at the same time as he established the modern trend of presenting presidential families to the public), Roosevelt believed that their actions inevitably set an example as well. His children attended public schools in their early years. He generally backed their teachers' decisions to administer discipline, particularly as the prominence of his career—and teachers' likely discomfiture—grew. When his spirited daughter Alice came of age during the White House years, gaining notoriety from smoking in public and other conspicuous challenges to convention, TR upbraided her: "In your present position your example might be one for good; at least you need not make it one for evil."

One wonders to what extent his loved ones suffered, as well as benefited, from the strictures imposed by TR's quest for his family—as well as himself—to serve as exemplars. There is evidence on both sides, sometimes with respect to the same person. His eldest son, Ted, apparently collapsed under the strain at one point in his youth; as an adult he exhibited singular courage in battle, culminating in his earning the Medal of Honor for service in the Second World War (achieving a distinction denied his father until 2001). Roosevelt recognized that the benefits of his example, which he considered his greatest legacy to his family, were accompanied by burdens.

As the United States was demobilizing in the aftermath of World War I, Ted's wife visited TR, bedridden in a hospital. According to Joan Paterson Kerr in *A Bully Father,* the daughter-in-law confided that Ted was dogged by fear that he would not be worthy of his illustrious father's name. Roosevelt answered, "Worthy of me? Darling, I'm so proud of him. He has won high honor not only for his children but, like the Chinese, he has ennobled his ancestors. I walk with my head higher because of him. I have always taken satisfaction from the fact that when there was a war in 1898 I fought in it and did my best to get into this one. But my war was a bow-and-arrow affair compared with Ted's, and no one knows this better than I do."

His daughter-in-law recorded TR's sentiments in writing. One expects that, from his family's point of view, it may have been among the most important of the "posterity letters" he left behind.

ON WEDNESDAY, October 30, 1912, six days before the historic election pitting him against Taft and Wilson, Roosevelt spoke at Madison Square Garden in New York City. Just over two weeks had passed since he electrified supporters—and exacted respect from detractors—with his indomitable courage and sangfroid after taking a bullet in the chest in Milwaukee.

From the beginning of his 1912 campaign, Roosevelt had been dogged by charges of opportunism and self-seeking. Such charges were not new; this time they were harder to rebut. Having bolted and split his ancestral party, TR ensured the election of Woodrow Wilson, the first Democrat to win the White House in twenty years.

In closing his Madison Square Garden address, Roosevelt said:

> Seven months ago in this city, almost at the beginning of the present campaign, I spoke as follows:
>
> The leader for the time being, whoever he may be, is but an instrument, to be used until broken and then to be cast aside; and if he is worth his salt he will care no more when he is broken than a soldier cares when he is sent where his life is forfeit in order that the victory may be won. In the long fight for righteousness the watchword for all of us is spend and be spent. It is of little matter whether any one man fails or succeeds; but the cause shall not fail, for it is the cause of mankind.

One is reminded of what was once written about the British statesman William Pitt the Elder: "It is not merely the thing that is said, but the man that says it that counts, the character which breathes through the sentences." Roosevelt's example bestowed an eloquence that words alone could not have achieved: the eloquence of action.

TR ON LEADERSHIP

- "Example is the most potent of all things."
- Leaders can rise to the level of events by honoring and applying examples of heroic lives to new circumstances.
- Though a worthy example can be a priceless legacy, others may feel it to be a burden. Leaders should strive to lighten that burden, especially on loved ones.
- Words, no matter how well chosen and crafted, approach the heights of eloquence only when recognized as aligned with actions.
- A leader's example can have an almost infinite reach across space and time.

PART FOUR

ACHIEVING INTEGRITY

Effective leaders—and effective people—. . . understand that there is no difference between becoming an effective leader and becoming a fully integrated human being.

—WARREN BENNIS

CHAPTER THIRTEEN

THE VIGOR OF LIFE

I wish to preach, not the doctrine of ignoble ease, but the doctrine of the strenuous life, the life of toil and effort, of labor and strife; to preach that highest form of success which comes, not to the man who desires mere easy peace, but to the man who does not shrink from danger, from hardship, or from bitter toil, and who out of these wins the splendid ultimate triumph.

—THEODORE ROOSEVELT

How good is man's life, the mere living.

—ROBERT BROWNING, QUOTED BY ROOSEVELT IN THE EPIGRAPH TO *RANCH LIFE AND THE HUNTING TRAIL*

AS ROOSEVELT PREPARED for graduation from college in the spring of 1880 he would have been justified in a degree of satisfaction, along with celebration and anticipation. Though he had lost his father in his sophomore year, Alice Lee had entered his life. TR could look forward—despite intermittent anxieties that he might lose her—to their wedding in the autumn, on his twenty-second birthday. Though he was not the dominant personality of the Harvard class of 1880—that distinction was held by Robert Bacon, who would eventually enter TR's cabinet—he earned high marks and vigorously participated in campus life.

On March 26, Roosevelt visited the college physician, Dr. Dudley A. Sargeant, for a comprehensive physical examination. The outcome was anything but routine. Though Roosevelt appeared strong—beginning to exhibit the pronounced musculature from his years of increasing physical exertion—he was diagnosed as having a weak heart. The doctor warned him that his life, including his choice of an occupation, must henceforth be one of limited physical exertion. He should not even run up flights of stairs. His ambitious project of remaking his body would have to be limited severely if not abandoned. To do otherwise, Dr. Sargeant said, would be to risk death.

Roosevelt's response was immediate, unconditional, and decisive. "Doctor, I am going to do all the things you tell me not to do. If I've got to live the sort of life you have described, I don't care how short it is." Rather than acknowledge defeat in his campaign of self-transformation, he silently vowed to "live my life to the hilt until I was sixty."

IN A LETTER to a British acquaintance in 1900, Roosevelt referred to his book *The Strenuous Life* as presenting "my philosophy of life." In his *Autobiography* he referred to it as "my philosophy—of bodily vigor as a method for getting that vigor of soul without which vigor of the body counts for nothing." He was particularly pleased with an Italian translation, *Vigor di Vita,* "and have always wished that I had myself used 'The Vigor of Life' as a heading to indicate what I was trying to preach, instead of the heading I actually did use."

The keystone of the "strenuous life" is the possibility—and necessity—of choice. Roosevelt viewed himself as a self-made man, in the sense that he "made" his body, simultaneously fortifying his mind and spirit. Looking back on his youth, TR felt "as if that child were not the present he, individually, but an ancestor; just as much an ancestor as either of his parents." He added, "The child is the father to the man in the sense that his individuality is separate from the individuality of the grown-up into which he turns." In contrast, Charles Washburn, a friend from college days forward, said, "The qualities I knew in the boy are the qualities most observed in the man, and that of all the men I have known for as long a time he has changed the least."

The views of Roosevelt and Washburn can be reconciled. Warren Bennis writes of "once-borns" and "twice-borns." The latter "generally suffer as they grow up; they feel different, even isolated. Unsatisfied with life as it is, they write new lives for themselves." Anticipating the objection that such self-creation is contrived or inauthentic, Bennis continues: "To be authentic is literally to be your own author (the words derive from the same Greek root), to discover your native energies and desires, and then to find your own way of acting on them. . . . When you write your own life, you have played the game that was natural for you to play. You have kept your covenant with your own promise."

Rousing himself to achieve his potential, TR followed his father's guidance: "You must *make* your body." The little boy wracked with asthma so enervating he could not summon the breath to extinguish his bedside candle understood that he had to fight for life, one day at a time. One did not have the option of standing still; idleness left one vulnerable in the ongoing struggle for mastery. His intermittent asthma attacks intimated that life could never be taken for granted; as he saw with his father, his mother, and his first wife, Alice, death might arrive without warning, far too soon.

These experiences likely underscored the injunctions Roosevelt heard from his father and passed along to his own children. "Get action; do things," "carpe diem!", "don't fritter away your time; create; act; take a place wherever you are and be somebody!" He squeezed every ounce of living from his experience, day to day. From a young age, he accounted for his time with the exactitude of an accountant scouring the books to bolster the bottom line. This was not living defensively, the equivalent of the miser's delusion of control against a dark, unknowable future. It was a way to ensure that he could do more, learn more, live more.

As TR's friend George Haven Putnam wrote, "He believed that life was worthwhile; that the years and days were given to a man in trust, and that it was a crime to waste even an hour." If there was a lull in conversation, he might pick up a book, transporting himself to another time and place. At the end of an exhausting day in the outdoors, he would put pen to paper, writing an article or working on a book that would simultaneously immerse him further into his experience and afford him greater perspective. Roosevelt would eventually go to bed, generally obtaining the five hours of sleep he said he found sufficient—and then arising and beginning anew, customarily stimulated by large amounts of coffee, sweetened with heaping spoonfuls of sugar or saccharine.

Owen Wister recalled TR thinking aloud, "I wish I knew how Washington managed to do his work." Wister, along with other close observers such as Jacob Riis, concluded that Roosevelt had, through some mixture of gifts and grit, "the power to organize and concentrate [himself] wholly upon a given matter, in an instant, leaving nothing of [himself] out; and then, when this is dispatched, drop it as if it had never existed, and go on to the next matter." Washburn found that throughout his life Roosevelt "was intense in everything he did."

One of TR's more amusing critics was author James Gilmore, who publicly charged that it was "impossible" for the future president to have written *The Winning of the West*, because of the short amount of time involved. In a letter dated October 10, 1889, Roosevelt responded:

> As a matter of fact I began the actual writing somewhere about the first of May, and finished the second volume about the first of

> April following, when much of the first volume was already in press; two months or over were taken out, while I was away on my ranch, or on the stump in the political campaign; so that the actual writing occupied a scant nine months—and a good part of that time I reproached myself for idleness. Of course my rough notes and manuscripts were already carefully arranged when I began and I had been for years saturating myself with the subject.

Roosevelt was a master of what we now call "multitasking." He combined activities that did not draw on his full powers—talking while reviewing and signing letters, granting interviews while being shaved, and so on. He tended, as Riis and others noted, to begin work well in advance of its projected due date, so as to bring to bear his onrushing subconscious thought, as well as his intervening experiences and the advice of others.

Like the wealthy, generous individual whose frugality in small things helps make his large gifts possible, TR safeguarded his time ruthlessly so as to have time for the most important things. Doubtless many Washingtonians smiled indulgently when they heard that President Roosevelt set appointments with his sisters and other family members. Yet this discipline enhanced his capacity to get the most from every moment, to give more of himself to more people, and to be at his best when an emergency arose. He strove to make his schedule serve his priorities. Hermann Hagedorn recounted a telling incident at Sagamore Hill. A ragged gaggle, including some of TR's children and their cousins, appeared at the door of the library as the president conferred with a dignitary on a pressing political matter.

"Cousin Theodore, it's after four."

Roosevelt expressed surprise and turned to his visitor: "I must ask you to excuse me. We'll finish this talk some other time. I promised the boys I'd go shooting with them at four o'clock, and I never keep boys waiting. It's a hard trial for a boy to wait."

EVEN IN THE White House, Roosevelt "always tried to get a couple of hours' exercise in the afternoons—sometimes tennis, more often riding, or else a rough cross-country walk." Characteristic was his description of New Year's Day, 1908, in a letter to an English friend: "This morning I shook hands with six thousand people at the White House reception. This afternoon I took a two hours good hard ride with four of my children and a dozen of their cousins and friends; jumping fences, scrambling over the wooded hills, galloping on the level; and it was the kind of fun to fit a public man for work."

One of TR's boxing partners rightly characterized him as a "manufactured" rather than natural athlete. Beginning as a youth, he undertook increasingly daring feats. He sought more than bodily exercise, expressing admiration for "the sports which develop such qualities as courage, resolution, and endurance." Injuries were unavoidable. At the White House, losing the sight in his left eye from a trainer's punch (but thankful that it was not the right eye, in which case he would no longer have been able to fire guns), he "thought it better to acknowledge that I had become an elderly man and would have to stop boxing. I then took up jujitsu for a year or two."

Roosevelt was inclined to be a participant rather than a spectator. Declining an invitation to attend a baseball game, he explained: "I will not sit for two hours and a half, and watch someone else do something." (Nonetheless he could not resist watching an occasional boxing match and dismissed critics of the sport: "Most certainly prize-fighting is not half as brutalizing or demoralizing as many forms of big business and the legal work carried on in connection with big business.") In the same vein, TR believed that people who used motor boats "missed a great deal" in comparison with those who made their own way in rowboats and canoes.

If Roosevelt displayed formidable force of character in developing his body and becoming a sportsman, he soon chose to find fun in his health-enhancing habits. As he wrote in his *Autobiography,* "the joy of life is a very good thing, and while work is the essential in it, play also has its place." In 1902 he wrote to a German diplomat of long acquaintance:

> You and I have owed a great deal to our fondness for sport, for riding, shooting and walking; but we have made everything secondary to our respective works. It is an excellent thing for me to go on a mountain lion hunt and to ride a bloody hunter who can take me over fences; but it would be a very bad thing indeed if I treated either exercise as anything but a diversion and as a means of refreshing me for doing double work in serious government business. Of course I think that there is danger that the mere office man—the mere drudge who does not take part in rough game and rough play outside—will become a wretched routine creature, adept only in the pedantry of his profession and apt to come to an unexpected disaster.

AS A YOUNG MAN Roosevelt determined to shape his life to find the joy of living. While a freshman in college he wrote to his mother: "It seems perfectly wonderful, in looking back over my eighteen years of existence, to see how I have literally never spent an unhappy day, unless by my own fault!" Years later he famously urged: "The joy of living is his who has the heart to demand it." Rather humorously—as if there were an Olympic medal for delight—each decade of Roosevelt's correspondence is marked by declarations such as: "I have had the best time of any man of my age in all the world. . . . I have enjoyed myself in the White House more than I have ever known any other President to enjoy himself."

Journalist Lincoln Steffens was partly right: "The gift of the gods to Theodore Roosevelt was joy . . . joy in life." More discerning contemporaries sensed the self-mastery beneath the surface. Historian Elting Morison observed, "There is apparent throughout his life a surprising determination. The energies and talents he possessed were not placed at birth in some natural harmony; they were through the passing years organized and directed by a sustained and splendid act of will."

Owen Wister believed his friend was fleeing melancholy. Like Winston Churchill, Roosevelt sought the company of those who brought zest to the table—eschewing the "timid good" or "that enormous proportion of sentient beings who are respectable but dull"—even at the foreseeable cost of occasionally misjudging character. Perhaps he viewed it as one more among the risks one took to find the joy of life.

TR's physical power, his zest, his intense living in the moment, his unquenchable curiosity, his evident interest in others, his aura of destiny and adventure enhanced by others' awareness of his life history—all these were fused by his manifest joy into a charismatic force that was remembered with awe and affection by many who came within its magnetic field. As one friend, William Hard, recalled, "He was the prism through which the light of day took on more colors than could be seen in anyone else's company."

ROOSEVELT'S WORLDLY accomplishments did not distract him from what he considered most important in life. He wrote in his *Autobiography:*

> There are many kinds of success worth having. It is exceedingly interesting and attractive to be a successful business man, or railroad man, or farmer, or a successful lawyer or doctor; or a writer, or a President, or a ranchman, or the colonel of a fight-

> ing regiment, or to kill grizzly bears and lions. But for unflagging interest and enjoyment, a household of children, if things go reasonably well, certainly makes all other forms of success and achievement lose their importance by comparison.

He added what he may have considered the ultimate tribute: "children are better than books."

The woman who bore five of his six children, Roosevelt's second wife, Edith, was an exceptional individual in her own right. Her strong personality brought TR down to earth. It often fell to her to balance the family's strained finances or to appraise, shrewdly and unsentimentally, the character of one of her husband's colleagues. Sophisticated and knowledgeable observers, from journalist Mark Sullivan to young Franklin Roosevelt, detected her hand in many of TR's better judgments—and sensed its absence elsewhere. Edith doubtless shared her husband's belief that "the simple life is normally the healthy life." Whether with their family at Sagamore Hill, or alone as husband and wife at Pine Knot, their Spartan cabin outside Washington, Edith and Theodore Roosevelt created a life that was unapologetically middle class in its attitudes, avoiding without regret many of the temptations that their social and economic status might have occasioned. As his father had done earlier, his wife created a safe harbor from which Roosevelt could confidently venture into the hazards of the broader world.

TR was a legendary father. As David McCullough has written: "The youngest of our presidents in fact, he remained the youngest in spirit as well. He was exuberantly fond of any number and variety of household pets. He joined in pillow fights, picnics, relished ghost stories in the dark, bedtime stories, stories of any kind. . . . He was the kind of father who, at the dinner table, would serve the youngest child first, or who, when their mother was not looking, would cut the icing off his own cake and slip it to the nearest child. A baby's hand, he thought, was the most beautiful of God's creations." No matter how busy he was, Roosevelt made time to write letters to his children, covering every conceivable topic. McCullough explains: "Full of news, advice, opinion, always full of affection, the letters can be seen now as child support of another kind from another era."

In his *Autobiography*, Roosevelt proudly related an incident in which he and his friend Leonard Wood were leading their children on a vigorous walk through Rock Creek Park in Washington. TR, walking across a fallen log, "[made] a clutch at one peculiarly active and heedless child" and lost his footing. Wood's young son exclaimed: "Oh! Oh! The father of all the children fell into the creek!"

His friend Jacob Riis believed that the secret of Roosevelt's success as a father was his ability to become a child when among children. TR's boyish streak was no less apparent outside the home. Wister explained, "It can hardly be repeated too often that in Roosevelt's nature from his beginning to his end there lived what Shakespeare calls the 'boy eternal.'" This was essential to his leadership. TR found wonder all around him; he believed in his power to remake himself or his circumstances, and to achieve large things. Apparently undiscouraged by past disappointments or what his vivid imagination might conjure for the future, he could live unreservedly in the moment.

AT A HIGH point of his career, shortly after his second inauguration, having become president in his own right, Roosevelt wrote to a British friend: "Life is a long campaign where every victory merely leaves the ground free for another battle, and sooner or later defeat comes to every man, unless death forestalls it. But the final defeat does not and should not cancel the triumphs, if the latter have been substantial and for a cause worth championing."

TR lived for a decade after leaving the White House. Having so often known triumph, he would now encounter, to use the characterization of his friend Rudyard Kipling, that other "impostor," defeat. In 1912, just three years after voluntarily relinquishing the presidency, he set about to get it back. Roosevelt may have taken false comfort in the example of Grover Cleveland, his predecessor as governor of New York and president, who returned to the White House for a nonconsecutive term. In fact, TR's personality, combined with the circumstances he faced, made his situation entirely unprecedented. He rent his political party asunder, paving the way for the election of Woodrow Wilson, whom he came to regard with contempt verging on hatred. Though Roosevelt took solace from the fact that much of his Bull Moose platform would be adopted and enacted in the Wilson administration (and still more in subsequent years), his political project lay in ruins. TR was cast out by many longtime allies who believed him more the wrongdoer than the wronged in his bitter struggle with his handpicked successor, Taft.

After the summer of 1914, with Europe ineluctably engulfed in the First World War, TR emerged as the prophet of American "preparedness." Inevitably, he incited vehement criticism, including open questioning of his motives as well as his objectives. Rather than retreat, he redoubled his efforts, fanning the flames of controversy by advocating universal national service for young Americans. In 1916 Roosevelt wrote a friend that he had become "one of Abraham Lincoln's 'splashed and battered pioneers.'" He was breaking new ground, with the understanding that in so doing he was making it less likely he would be chosen to lead later.

Roosevelt's post-presidential years continue to occasion controversy among historians. He may well have been, as John Milton Cooper argues, "America's greatest ex-president." Remarkably, TR, private citizen, set the terms for much of the national dialogue. Some of his less attractive qualities also came to the fore—arguably putting himself before those he would serve, directing the full force of his ferocious fighting energy ruthlessly against political opponents, displaying self-righteousness in the guise of "righteousness." Poignancy as well as instruction emerge from his 1916 letter to the poet Edwin Arlington Robinson: "There is not one among us in whom a devil does not dwell; at some time, on some point, that devil masters each of us; he who has never failed has never been tempted; but the man who does in the end conquer, who does painfully retrace the steps of his slipping, why he shows that he has been tried in the fire and not found wanting. It is not having been in the Dark House, but having left it, that counts." Though TR found it difficult to acknowledge—perhaps even to himself—his own deviations from his demanding moral tenets, he recognized that failures and shortcomings were as much a part of leadership as successes and achievements. As he said at the Sorbonne in 1910: "It is warworn Hotspur, spent with hard fighting, he of the many errors and the valiant end, over whose memory we love to linger, not over the memory of the young lord who 'but for the vile guns would have been a soldier.'"

Roosevelt's philosophy of the "strenuous life" decreed that his pursuit of self-mastery continue long after he had achieved many of the greatest prizes the world offered. Journalist Henry Luther Stoddard recalled a conversation with TR in 1916: "[P]eople talk much of my battles in life! . . . The hardest battle I have had to fight, however, is one that no one knows about. It was a battle to control my own temper. That battle I never won until recent years. I now have won that fight and I consider it to be the hardest struggle—it certainly was the longest—of my career."

ROOSEVELT TURNED SIXTY on Sunday, October 27, 1918. His years in the political wilderness appeared to be coming to an end. With America's entry into the First World War in the spring of 1917, Roosevelt's virtues again found an appreciative public. His lonely calls to service had been prophetic. In Kaiser Wilhelm's German regime, TR—and the nation—found a target worthy of Roosevelt's fighting spirit. With the passage of time, many concluded that TR's adherence to unpopular stands made plain that service, not personal ambition, was his primary motivation. This was underscored by his wartime efforts—and those of his family. In a striking indication of the new mood, the November 5 election returned Republican majorities to both houses of Congress for the first time in a decade. Roosevelt was widely viewed as the inevitable Republican nominee for the presidency in 1920, and as the prohibitive favorite in the general election.

Roosevelt's body, which he had pushed so hard for so many years, was failing. He was dangerously overweight. His vision and hearing were impaired. He was debilitated, apparently in significant part from the lingering effects of parasitic disease from his 1914 Amazon expedition. Perhaps most important, TR was spiritually exhausted. When America finally entered the war he had seen as inevitable so long before, his offer of service in the field was rejected. Instead, he would be at home with Edith when their son, Quentin, whom many saw as remarkably like his father, died in a dogfight over France in the summer of 1918. Observing Roosevelt's inconsolable grief at the loss of his youngest son—who met his end, at least in part, endeavoring to follow his father's example of courage in combat—Hermann Hagedorn reported that the boy in TR finally died.

On Armistice Day, Monday, November 11, 1918, as the guns fell silent across Europe, Roosevelt was hospitalized in New York City. Doctors said he was suffering from inflammatory rheumatism. There were questions of whether he would become an invalid. Nonetheless, from his hospital bed, there were occasional flashes of the old fire. At one point, weighing his prospective race for the presidency, he set his sights on the party leaders he had always fought: "[B]y George, if they take me, they will take me without a single reservation or modification of the things I have always stood for!"

On Christmas day, a physically faltering TR emerged from six weeks of hospital confinement. Making his way to a waiting automobile, he pointedly declined a doctor's solicitous offer of a steadying arm. Though recovery was hoped for, it would not come soon. Back at Sagamore Hill, TR was reduced to little more than riding as a passenger in a motor car or brief walking respites from his medically supervised—and entirely uncongenial—sedentary lifestyle.

Several months earlier, following Quentin's death, Roosevelt wrote movingly of the "Great Adventure": "Only those are fit to live who do not fear to die; and none are fit to die who have shrunk from the joy of life and the duty of life." Facing his own mortality, perhaps TR recalled the sentiments he expressed in a letter following the death of Secretary of State John Hay in 1905: "[I]t is a good thing to die in the harness at the zenith of one's fame, with the consciousness of having lived a long, honorable and useful life. After we are dead it will make not the slightest difference whether men speak well or ill of us. But in the days or hours before dying it must be pleasant to feel that you have done your part as a man . . . and that your children and children's children, in short all those that are dearest to you, have just cause for pride in your actions."

The early days of the New Year brought signs of renewed vitality. On Sunday, January 5, 1919, Roosevelt put in a full day of work, including writing and touching up several articles for publication. In the evening, sitting with Edith before a fire, he closed his book and mused, "I wonder if you will ever know how much I love Sagamore Hill."

Having "warmed both hands before the fire of life," Roosevelt died in his sleep shortly after 4 A.M. on the following morning. His son Archie cabled his brothers Kermit and Ted, who remained encamped in Europe: "The old lion is dead." A political opponent, Vice President Thomas Marshall, said, "Death had to take him sleeping, for if Roosevelt had been awake there would have been a fight." A New York City police captain remarked, "It was not only that he was a great man, but, oh, there was so much fun in being led by him." Journalist Irvin S. Cobb concluded, "You had to hate the Colonel a whole lot to keep from loving him."

On Wednesday, January 8, memorial services were held at Oyster Bay. As Roosevelt had wished, they were austere. There was no music and no eulogy. Most of the guests were family and friends and schoolchildren; the eminence of the relatively small proportion of dignitaries was the sole indication that it was a funeral of a former president of the United States. His oak coffin, draped by an American flag, was carried to nearby Youngs Cemetery.

IN "THE CHOICE," Yeats wrote hauntingly of the conflict between "[p]erfection of the life, or of the work." Roosevelt's example of the "strenuous life" stands in joyous defiance. His personality was not divided against itself. TR combined his extraordinary leadership with a full family life; indeed, his conspicuously integrated personality appears to have been the mainspring of his capacity as a leader. To a remarkable extent, he achieved what Stephen Covey has termed "an integrated character, a oneness, primarily with self but also with life." The common element binding his life and work was service. TR believed, "In the long run no man or woman can really be happy unless he or she is doing service. Happiness springing exclusively from some other cause crumbles in your hands, amounts to nothing." As Roosevelt intended, those who continue to learn from his leadership find inspiration not only in what he did, but even more from what he was.

THEODORE ROOSEVELT CHRONOLOGY

October 27, 1858	TR born in New York City, 28 East Twentieth Street, eldest son of Theodore Roosevelt, Sr., and Martha ("Mittie") Bulloch Roosevelt.
April 25, 1865	Watches President Lincoln's funeral procession through New York City.
1876–1880	Attends Harvard College, Cambridge, Massachusetts.
February 9, 1878	Theodore Roosevelt, Sr., dies in New York City.
February 14, 1880	Announcement of engagement to Alice Hathaway Lee of Chestnut Hill, Massachusetts.
June 30, 1880	Graduates from Harvard College, *magna cum laude,* Phi Beta Kappa honors.
October 27, 1880	Marries Alice Lee.
1880–1882	Attends Columbia Law School but does not complete course.
November 8, 1881	Wins New York Assembly election, representing Manhattan; serves three one-year terms, ending in 1884.
August 1, 1882	Commissioned second lieutenant in New York National Guard.
1882	Publishes *The Naval War of 1812.*
February 3, 1883	Promoted to captain in the New York National Guard.
February 1883	Travels to the West and purchases share in ranch, near what is now Medora, North Dakota.

November 6, 1883	Overwhelmingly reelected to the assembly; becomes minority leader.
February 12, 1884	Daughter Alice Lee Roosevelt born.
February 14, 1884	Death of wife Alice; death of mother, Mittie.
February 16, 1884	Funeral services for Alice and Mittie.
June 1884	Delegate to Republican National Convention in Chicago; emerges as national leader in unsuccessful opposition to nomination of James G. Blaine.
1884	Travels to Badlands, Dakota Territory, to become cattle rancher (intermittently until 1886).
1885	Publishes *Hunting Trips of a Ranchman.*
November 2, 1886	Defeated as Republican candidate for mayor of New York City, placing third in three-way race with Democratic victor Abram Hewitt and Labor candidate Henry George.
December 2, 1886	Marries Edith Kermit Carow in London.
September 13, 1887	Son Theodore born.
1887	Edith and Theodore Roosevelt establish residence at Sagamore Hill, their home at Oyster Bay, Long Island, New York.
	Publishes *Life of Thomas Hart Benton.*
1888	Publishes *Life of Gouverneur Morris; Ranch Life and the Hunting Trail; Essays in Practical Politics.*
May 7, 1889	Becomes one of three U.S. civil service commissioners, Washington, D.C. (appointed initially by Republican president Benjamin Harrison; reappointed by Democrat Grover Cleveland; serves until 1895).
October 10, 1889	Son Kermit born.
1889	Publishes two volumes of *The Winning of the West* (four total would be published, the last in 1896).
August 13, 1891	Daughter Ethel born.

1891	Publishes *History of New York.*
1893	Publishes *The Wilderness Hunter;* also *American Big Game* (co-editor, contributor, with George Bird Grinnell).
April 10, 1894	Son Archibald born.
August 14, 1894	Death of brother Elliott, an alcoholic.
May 5, 1895	Effective date of resignation as U.S. civil service commissioner.
May 6, 1895	Appointed by Mayor Strong to Board of Police Commissioners, New York City; elected president (until 1897).
1895	Publishes *Hero Tales of American History,* co-authored with Henry Cabot Lodge.
April 19, 1897	Begins duties as assistant secretary of the navy; appointed by President McKinley; confirmed by U.S. Senate (until 1898).
November 19, 1897	Son Quentin born.
1897	Publishes *American Ideals.*
March 25, 1898	Recommends study of "flying machine" for potential military application.
April 24, 1898	Spain declares war against the United States.
April 25, 1898	Appointed lieutenant colonel of the First U.S. Volunteer Cavalry Regiment, soon known as the "Rough Riders."
May 6, 1898	Resigns post as assistant secretary of the navy.
May 15, 1898	Begins service with Rough Riders in San Antonio, Texas; promoted to colonel before Battle of San Juan.
July 1, 1898	Distinguishes self for heroism, leading charges at Kettle Hill and San Juan Hill.
August 15–September 16, 1898	Stationed at Camp Wikoff, Montauk, Long Island.
September 27, 1898	Receives Republican nomination for governor of New York.

November 8, 1898	Elected governor of New York, with 661,715 votes, against 643,921 for Democrat Augustus Van Wyck.
December 31, 1898	Sworn in as governor (term to end on December 31, 1900).
November 21, 1899	Vice President Garret Hobart dies unexpectedly.
1899	Publishes *The Rough Riders.*
June 21, 1900	Nominated for vice presidency on Republican ticket with incumbent President McKinley.
November 6, 1900	McKinley-Roosevelt ticket elected with 7,219,530 votes against the 6,358,071 for the William Jennings Bryan–Adlai Stevenson Democratic ticket.
1900	Publishes *Oliver Cromwell; The Strenuous Life.*
March 4, 1901	McKinley-Roosevelt inaugural, Washington, D.C.
September 6, 1901	McKinley shot at Pan-American Exposition in Buffalo, New York.
September 14, 1901	McKinley dies; Roosevelt sworn into office as twenty-sixth president of the United States at Wilcox Mansion, Buffalo, New York.
February 19, 1902	Orders federal antitrust suit against Northern Securities Company.
May 22, 1902	Establishes Crater Lake National Park, Oregon. Would also establish Wind Cave National Park (1903); Sullys Hill, North Dakota (1904); Platt National Park, Oklahoma (1906); Mesa Verde National Park (1906).
June 17, 1902	Signs Newlands Reclamation Act, spurring federal irrigation projects to develop western United States.
June 28, 1902	Signs Isthmian Canal Act.
October 1902	Successfully mediates Anthracite Coal Strike.
December 31, 1902	Settles dispute involving Germany and Venezuela.
1902	Publishes *The Deer Family* (coauthor).

February 14, 1903	Establishes Department of Commerce and Labor.
February 20, 1903	Signs Elkins Anti-Rebate Act (railroad regulation).
March 14, 1903	Proclaims Pelican Island, Louisiana, as first federal bird reservation; fifty-one total would be established during TR administration.
November 18, 1903	Treaty signed with new nation of Panama for building Panama Canal, which would be completed in 1914 during Wilson administration.
June 23, 1904	Receives Republican presidential nomination at Chicago convention.
November 8, 1904	Elected president with 7,628,834 votes, against 5,084,491 for Democrat Alton B. Parker of New York.
December 6, 1904	Declares "Roosevelt Corollary" to Monroe Doctrine (asserting right to intervene to reestablish order in Americas).
February 1, 1905	National Forest Service established, to be led by Gifford Pinchot. Under Roosevelt administration forest reserves would increase from approximately 43 million acres to nearly 200 million acres.
March 4, 1905	Roosevelt–Charles W. Fairbanks inaugural.
March 17, 1905	Standing in for deceased brother Elliott, gives away niece Eleanor Roosevelt to distant cousin Franklin Roosevelt in New York City wedding.
June 2, 1905	Declares Wichita Forest, Oklahoma, as first federal game preserve. Would also establish federal game preserves at the Grand Canyon (1908), Fire Island, Alaska (1909), and National Bison Range, Montana (1909).
August 25, 1905	Goes into ocean off Long Island in prototype navy submarine, *Plunger;* subsequently orders hazardous-duty pay for submarine crews.
September 5, 1905	Signing of Portsmouth Treaty ending Russo-Japanese War, following mediation by Roosevelt.
1905	Publishes *Outdoor Pastimes of an American Hunter.*

January 1906	Mediates dispute between France and Germany over Moroccan claims.
February 17, 1906	Presides at White House wedding of daughter Alice to Ohio congressman Nicholas Longworth.
June 8, 1906	Signs Antiquities Act. Under this authority Roosevelt would establish first eighteen national monuments, including Devil's Tower (1906), Muir Woods (1908), and Grand Canyon (1908).
June 29, 1906	Signs Hepburn Act, establishing federal regulation of railroad rates.
June 30, 1906	Signs Pure Food and Drug Act and federal meat inspection statute.
November 8–26, 1906	Visits Panama Canal Zone to review progress of construction—first time sitting president leaves continental United States.
December 10, 1906	Awarded Nobel Peace Prize for his mediation of Russo-Japanese War in 1905.
December 16, 1906	Great White Fleet launches off for the first circumnavigation of the globe by a national navy.
January 1, 1907	Shakes 8,150 hands, setting Guinness world record.
June 15, 1907	Second Hague Peace Conference opens, following Roosevelt's urging.
October–November 1907	"Panic of 1907" roils Wall Street and bank depositors across nation.
1907	Publishes *Good Hunting.*
May 13–15, 1908	Convenes first conference of governors at the White House, to discuss conservation.
June 8, 1908	Appoints National Conservation Commission to prepare inventory of natural resources.
November 3, 1908	William Howard Taft, Roosevelt's handpicked successor, elected president with 7,675,320 votes, against 6,412,294 for Democrat William Jennings Bryan.

January 13, 1909	Rides horseback 100 miles from Washington, D.C., to Warrenton, Virginia, setting example of fitness for military brass.
February 18, 1909	Convenes North American Conservation Conference at the White House.
February 22, 1909	Greets Great White Fleet as it returns from successful goodwill tour.
March 4, 1909	Taft inaugurated.
March 23, 1909	Leads expedition to Africa for Smithsonian Institution, accompanied by son Kermit.
1909	Becomes contributing editor of *Outlook* magazine, New York (until 1914).
	Publishes *Outlook Editorials.*
March 30, 1910	Departs Africa; begins European tour.
April 23, 1910	Delivers classic speech, "Citizenship in a Republic," at the Sorbonne, Paris.
May 5, 1910	Accepts Nobel Peace Prize, gives address at Oslo, Norway.
June 7, 1910	Delivers Romanes lecture at Oxford.
June 18, 1910	Returns to triumphal reception in New York City.
August 31, 1910	Delivers "New Nationalism" address, presenting progressive vision, at Osawatomie, Kansas.
September 27, 1910	Elected temporary chairman of New York State Republican Convention.
October 11, 1910	Flies in airplane near St. Louis, Missouri.
November 8, 1910	Republicans sustain significant losses in midterm elections, including campaigns assisted by TR. Democrats control U.S. House for first time since 1894.
1910	Publishes *African and European Addresses; African Game Trails; American Problems; The New Nationalism; Presidential Addresses and State Papers and European Addresses.*

February 21, 1912	Declaring "My hat is in the ring," Roosevelt announces he will seek Republican nomination against President Taft.
June 18–22, 1912	Defeated by Taft at Republican National Convention in Chicago, Roosevelt backers bolt convention, charging that the nomination had been "stolen" in a series of procedural votes.
June 30, 1912	Governor Woodrow Wilson of New Jersey receives Democratic nomination, running as a progressive. With the Republicans split between Taft and Roosevelt, it is generally assumed that Wilson is the likely winner in November.
August 5–7, 1912	National Progressive ("Bull Moose") Party convenes in Chicago, adopts reform platform ("Contract with the People"), nominates Roosevelt for president, California Governor Hiram W. Johnson for vice president.
October 14, 1912	TR shot in chest while campaigning in Milwaukee, Wisconsin. Delivers ninety-minute speech before accepting medical assistance. Hospitalized until October 21; resumes campaigning on October 30.
November 5, 1912	Democrat Woodrow Wilson elected president with 6,301,254 votes; Roosevelt places second with 4,127,788; Taft struggles to a third with 3,485,831. Wilson elected as minority president, garnering fewer votes than the Democrats received in defeat in 1908; Roosevelt earns the highest percentage of votes of any third party candidate in American history.
1912	Publishes *The Conservation of Womanhood and Childhood*.
May 26–31, 1913	Prevails as plaintiff in libel suit against Michigan editor who accused him of alcohol abuse.
October 4, 1913	Departs for South America to lecture and explore jungles.

1913	Publishes *Autobiography;* also *History as Literature and Other Essays; Progressive Principles.*
February 27–April 27, 1914	Roosevelt-Rondon Expedition, sponsored by American Museum of Natural History and Brazilian government, successfully explores Brazil's River of Doubt. The river is renamed "Rio Teodoro." Roosevelt narrowly escapes death in a harrowing journey.
May 7, 1914	Returns to the United States.
May 30–June 24, 1914	Travels to Europe for son Kermit's wedding in Spain and to lecture to the Royal Geographic Society, London.
August 1914	The First World War breaks out across Europe, in a chain of events following the assassination of Archduke Ferdinand on June 28.
November 3, 1914	Progressive Party defeated in federal and state elections.
December 1914	Signs contract to write for *Metropolitan* magazine, New York.
1914	Publishes *Through the Brazilian Wilderness;* also, with Edmund Heller, *Life Histories of African Game Animals.*
April 19–May 22, 1915	Roosevelt is defendant, primary witness, and victor in libel suit filed against him by New York Republican leader William Barnes, who objected to TR's characterization of his machine politics.
1915	Publishes *America and the World War.* Increasingly identified with "preparedness" as goal of U.S. policy toward European war.
June 7–10, 1916	Republican and Progressive Parties meet simultaneously in Chicago in effort to combine nominations. Charles Evans Hughes nominated by Republicans; Roosevelt nominated by Progressives. TR declines Progressive nomination, backs Hughes.
November 7, 1916	Running on platform "He Kept Us Out of War," Wilson narrowly defeats Hughes.

1916	Publishes *Fear God and Take Your Own Part;* and *A Booklover's Holidays in the Open.*
April 6, 1917	United States declares war on Germany, entering the First World War.
May 19, 1917	Wilson refuses Roosevelt's offer to raise and lead a volunteer division on the western front in the First World War.
July 14, 1917	Quentin Roosevelt, TR's beloved youngest son, killed as pilot in action over France.
July 17, 1917	TR receives official notice of Quentin's death.
July 18, 1917	Speaks at Republican State Convention at Saratoga; declines requests that he run for governor.
1917	Members of Roosevelt family throw themselves into war effort. TR speaks across nation; all four sons enlist; daughter Ethel serves as Red Cross nurse in France.
	Publishes *The Foes of Our Own Household; National Strength and International Duty.*
October 28, 1918	Speaks at Carnegie Hall, New York, attacks Wilson's plea for a Democratic Congress.
November 5, 1918	Republicans sweep midterm elections, winning both houses of Congress for first time since 1908.
1918	Roosevelt odds-on favorite for Republican nomination for 1920.
	Publishes *The Great Adventure.*
January 6, 1919	Roosevelt, age sixty, dies in his sleep, about 4:15 A.M., at Sagamore Hill.
January 8, 1919	Funeral service at Christ Church, Oyster Bay, New York; burial at Youngs Memorial Cemetery, Oyster Bay.

NOTES ON SOURCES

By far the best source of information on Theodore Roosevelt's leadership approach—and the most important source for this book—is the public record of his writings and utterances. Specific references are included in these notes only for Roosevelt quotations that appear to require explanation or context. *The Works of Theodore Roosevelt: National Edition* (used by the author for this book) includes almost all of his books, as well as selected articles and public papers. *The Letters of Theodore Roosevelt,* ably edited by Elting Morison with the assistance of a top-flight team including historian John Morton Blum, is an incomparable source of TR's views on many topics. Taken together, the *Works* and the *Letters* present Roosevelt as he wished to be viewed by his contemporaries and in history. His *Autobiography,* included in the *Works,* has been dismissed by some observers. Nonetheless, it includes useful insights on Roosevelt, and a few of the chapters are beautifully written.

There are several fine biographies introducing Roosevelt to a general readership. TR scholars tend to agree that William Harbaugh's *Power and Responsibility: The Life and Times of Theodore Roosevelt* is the best one-volume rendering. Edmund Morris's Pulitzer Prize–winning *The Rise of Theodore Roosevelt* is the first of a projected trilogy. John Milton Cooper's *The Warrior and the Priest,* which examines the careers of Roosevelt and Woodrow Wilson, is outstanding. David McCullough's *Mornings on Horseback* is an elegantly written, solidly researched account of TR's youth and the remarkable family of which he was a part. Henry Pringle's one-volume biography, though marred by the author's inflexible skepticism toward his subject, remains useful after several generations.

Several earlier books, now regrettably neglected, are worthy of rediscovery. Diplomat Lewis Einstein's *Roosevelt: His Mind in Action* offers an admiring contemporary's view of TR's approach to life, leadership, and politics. Sylvia Jukes Morris reports that Edith Roosevelt considered it an accurate portrait of her husband. Owen Wister's *Roosevelt: The Story of a Friendship* has an intimate, authentic sensibility, likely arising from the author's shared experience of an aristocratic, Eastern background combined with a love of the West; he and TR shared aspirations to combine the life of action and the life of thought. Carleton Putnam's *Theodore Roosevelt: The Formative Years* was intended to be the first of three volumes. Though the trilogy was not completed, this volume provides the best single account of TR's early years, including well-crafted foreshadowing of events in his later life. Edward Wagenknecht's *The Seven Worlds of Theodore Roosevelt* is a scholarly compendium of observations concerning various aspects of Roosevelt's protean personality. Frederick S. Wood's *Roosevelt As We Knew Him* is a delightful period piece, including personal accounts of TR as known by his contemporaries.

In this volume, the quotations from the period occasionally have been updated where the meaning is clear and the change unambiguous: For example, "especial" has been changed to "special." The text bows to the traditional, universal usage of the masculine: "he" meaning "he and she" and so on. To do otherwise in writing about the world of 1900 might seem contrived and could create distracting complications in crafting the writing. Roosevelt's "virile virtues" include qualities that later generations would not view as entirely or primarily achievable by the male gender. Though less than most, Roosevelt was nonetheless a creature of his time. In this regard, as in others, we may wish to accord the same understanding that we would seek from generations succeeding our own.

PROLOGUE

Among the sources for general information on American life at the turn of the twentieth century are Cooper (*Pivotal Decades*), Crichton, and Sullivan. Additional statistics were gleaned from "The Greatest Century That Ever Was: Twenty-five Miraculous Trends of the Past One Hundred Years," by Stephen Moore and Julian L. Simon, *Policy Analysis*, No. 364, December 15, 1999, published by the Cato Institute, Washington, D.C. Measurements of the world's population in 1900 are necessarily less exact than today; the number offered is within the lower and upper boundary estimates from the U.S. Bureau of the Census, http/www.census.gov/ipc/www/worldhis.html. The reference to

Morgan and the formation of the United States Steel Corporation is from Strouse. The recollection that McKinley had attended a luncheon of the Vermont Fish and Game League on Lake Champlain like that attended by Roosevelt on September 6, 1901, is from Vermont newspaperman and politician Frank Lester Greene, in Wood.

CHAPTER ONE

The quotation in the epigraph of this chapter was one of TR's favorites; the version used here is from the *Autobiography,* where it is offered as "a bit of homely philosophy, quoted by Squire Bill Widener, of Widener's Valley, Virginia." It is also found, in various permutations, throughout TR's writings over the course of his life. The quoted material on character is from an address at Redlands, California, on May 7, 1903, included in Roosevelt, *California Addresses.* Character is a continuing theme of that collection, and the quotation chosen is representative. Emphasis is added to the quotations from the letter to the British journalist, to TR's spring 1884 letter regarding adhering to his "own terms," and to his letter to Wister dated November 19, 1904. The quotation on Roosevelt's defeat in the 1886 New York mayoralty race is from Robert Adamson, quoted by Julian Street in his introduction to Volume X of Roosevelt's *Works.* The Shaw quotation is from his introduction to Volume XIV of Roosevelt's *Works.* Secretary Long's admonition to Roosevelt from February 25, 1898, is from Bishop.

CHAPTER TWO

Among the best sources for information on the shooting in Milwaukee are Bishop, Davis, Lorant, and Roosevelt's *Autobiography.* The quotation "brass monkey's nerve" is from James F. Vivian, "Badlands Bricolage," Naylor et al.

CHAPTER THREE

The best overall source concerning TR's habits of learning is his *Autobiography.* The datum concerning college attendance is from Putnam. Also useful was TR's essay "The Pigskin Library," from the *Works,* Volume XII. John Milton Cooper shared his judgment that Roosevelt's writings sometimes appeared limited by his lack of real sympathy with others.

CHAPTER FOUR

Various sources were used for the account of the death of Alice Lee Roosevelt, including Felsenthal, McCullough, Miller, Edmund Morris, Pringle, Putnam, and Teague. The most meticulous sources, on which subsequent historians appear to have placed the greatest reliance, are Pringle and Putnam. The quotation from Roosevelt's telegram that his wife was "only fairly well" is from his telegram to Dora Watkins, in Volume 1 of the *Letters.* The diary entries quoted are from the Theodore Roosevelt Papers of the Library of Congress and are reproduced in facsimile on the Internet at http://lcweb2.loc.gov/ammem/trhtml/trl.html. Putnam is the source for Assemblyman Lucas Van Allen's urging that TR "work bravely in the darkness," convincingly deducing its significance. The quotation from TR's letter to Alice, wondering whether his happiness had become "too great," is from Miller. With respect to not speaking of Alice Lee again, some writers have suggested that he may have spoken of her to a limited extent in the Badlands. This was likely inevitable since he would have needed to explain his presence and he wrote his valedictory to her there. As such, this would not detract from the broader point. "Live for the living" is from Caroli. Roosevelt's excessive severity in the aftermath of the Brownsville riot has been a source of continuing criticism. Some critics today offer it as part of a pattern of racial and ethnic insensitivity. Others defend Roosevelt's record in this regard, especially citing his appointments of African-Americans and Jews to significant offices. TR's record, though better than those of many other leaders of his era, is nonetheless reflective of the prejudices that were widespread in the United States at the turn of the twentieth century; it is difficult if not fruitless to attempt to place his views into today's categories. The discussion on simplified spelling relies primarily on Sullivan.

CHAPTER FIVE

The reference to the offer from Post is from the correspondence reprinted in the *Letters,* Volume 7, from June 27, 1910. This offer, with a salary of $100,000 (likely over $1 million in today's dollars) may have been prompted in part by TR's Nobel Prize committee acceptance address, on May 5, 1910, in which he announced his intention to donate the proceeds to serve as "a nucleus for a foundation to forward the cause of industrial peace." Ultimately those funds were donated for relief in the First World War. With respect to the Bull Moose campaign, Elihu Root observed in a letter, "He is essentially a fighter and when he gets into a fight he is completely dominated by the desire to destroy his adversary. He instinctively lays hold of every weapon which can be used for that end. Accordingly he is saying a lot of things and taking a lot of positions which are inspired by the desire to win. I have no doubt he thinks he believes what he says, but he doesn't. He has merely picked up certain popular ideas which were at hand as one might pick up a poker or chair with which to strike." John Allen Gable provided valuable information and perspectives on Roosevelt's international diplomacy, both in interviews and in his essay "The Historiography of Theodore Roosevelt," in Naylor et al. Also useful on TR's foreign policy is the essay in Naylor et al. by Frederick W. Marks III. The quotation on force without violence is from Rear-Admiral Colby M. Chester, in Wood. The reference to the quarreling and fighting is from Judge John Carter Rose, in Wood, quoting Roosevelt as civil service commissioner speaking of a colleague: "I can't stop him quarreling with Congressmen, and I can't make him fight them." The quotation "as sweet a man as ever scuttled a ship" is from Edmund Morris. The quotation concerning TR's tact at the Russo-Japanese mediation is from Professor Frederic Frommhold De Martens, in Bishop. The issue of maintaining open negotiations is clearly based on the context in which one is working. In foreign affairs, for example, Roosevelt of necessity engaged in closed, sometimes secret negotiations. The ultimate criterion for judgment is, as always in a negotiation, what will best advance the interests of the party one represents.

CHAPTER SIX

Strouse is the main source of this chapter's references to J. P. Morgan. Sullivan is a good general source on Morgan, as well as the Northern Securities suit. Other sources on Northern Securities are Bishop, Brands, Cooper, Harbaugh, and Pringle. The Sims quotation is from his recollections in Wood. The Root quotation on TR's temperament is from a letter dated February 12, 1912, quoted in the *Letters,* Volume 7, in a footnote relating to Roosevelt's subsequent letter of February 14, 1912. Given Root's apparent understanding of Roosevelt, and the latter's penchant for observing the significance of dates, one wonders if Root intended a veiled suggestion in dating his letter on the anniversary of the birthday of TR's hero, Lincoln. The reference to Roosevelt's shooting of a dog is from Putnam. Though Foraker got the best of Hanna in the 1904 nomination dustup referred to, he later challenged TR and earned his undisguised enmity. When evidence of corruption was subsequently uncovered with respect to Foraker's relationship with the oil industry, Roosevelt helped ensure the Ohioan's defeat. After Foraker's return to private life, perhaps reflecting TR's magnanimity in victory, they resumed a cordial correspondence.

CHAPTER SEVEN

The references to TR's correspondence on personnel shortly after assuming office are from the *Letters*, Volume 3. The information regarding William Moody is from William Tyler Page, in Wood. Surprisingly, given his accession by assassination, TR not only failed to establish a comprehensive process for succession, but acceded to the selection of a weak vice president for whom he had scant regard, Charles Fairbanks.

CHAPTER EIGHT

The paragraph of observations about the challenges of constructing the Panama Canal is from Alfred D. Chandler, Jr., "Theodore Roosevelt and the Panama Canal: A Study in Administration," Appendix I to Volume 6 of the *Letters.* Among the sources of information on the Brazilian expedition are Roosevelt's account in Volume V of the *Works* and the introduction to this volume by Frank M. Chapman. TR's personal interest in the Navy Department may have presented challenges for the secretaries who "ran" the department during his administration. Given the relatively high turnover, and the movement of several naval secretaries to higher cabinet positions, one advantage of the position may have been the familiarity and confidence developed from working closely with the president. It may also have been the case that Roosevelt's personal experience in the department caused him to assign special value to others who served there. The use of the terms "moralize" and "First Reader" is from the author, not Roosevelt. For a discussion of the Pinchot-Roosevelt relationship, including the former's service as a "lightning rod," see Char Miller, "Keeper of His Conscience? Pinchot, Roosevelt, and the Politics of Conservation," in Naylor et al. Late in the writing of this section, the author became aware of the work of Colonel David Hackworth, whose views on team leadership are uncannily similar to Roosevelt's.

CHAPTER NINE

A useful discussion of the development of the vision of conservation is found in Pinchot, *Breaking New Ground*. Roosevelt's positions on women's issues remain controversial among some historians attempting to place his views into the context of our time. He was the first major presidential candidate to advocate a constitutional amendment for woman's suffrage; more remarkably, as he wrote in a letter after the 1912 election, he intended to appoint a woman to his cabinet, had he been elected (this would have created the peculiar situation of having one of the nation's top governmental offices led by an individual who was not legally entitled to vote for president!). At the same time, Roosevelt strongly supported what we would call the "traditional" female role in the family, honoring mothers, along with soldiers, as playing an indispensable role in ensuring the nation's greatness. The definition of character is from Roosevelt's address at Ventura, California, May 9, 1903, reprinted in *California Addresses*. Roosevelt's view of "mere law honesty" was turned on its head in an unprecedented legal filing by President William Clinton, seeking to avoid disbarment in Arkansas. Clinton's legal brief, filed in May 2000, attempted to defend his apparent lies in legal proceedings: "Many categories of responses which are misleading, evasive, nonresponsive or frustrating are nevertheless not legally 'false.'"

CHAPTER TEN

The Pinchot reference relating to TR's speech composition is from his introduction to Volume XV of *Works*. The italicization of the sentence in the quotation concerning "His Favorite Author" is added. The quotations about "deliberately" seeking to learn about others' lives, as well as those from TR to Otto Kahn, are from Wood. The intuition quotation is from Viscount Lee of Fareham, introductory essay to *Oliver Cromwell,* in Volume X, *Works.* John Allen Gable shared his observations about Roosevelt's development of the "Square Deal" over a series of speeches. Good lists of phrases coined or popularized by TR are found in Drinker & Mowbray, and Street.

CHAPTER ELEVEN

Abbott, Bishop, Chessman, Harbaugh, Lorant, and Mowry are the main sources of critical comments about Roosevelt. The discussion relating to the timing and content of the response to the 1904 campaign charges relies primarily on Pringle. The quotation from Billy O'Neill is from Chessman.

CHAPTER TWELVE

The recounting of the incident involving young TR's reaction to the Browning lines, including the Hagedorn quotation, is from Hagedorn, *The Boy's Life of Theodore Roosevelt.* The quotation from John Hay concerning TR's political opponents was the basis for a Homer Davenport cartoon, ca. 1904, reprinted in Hagedorn & Wallach, *A Theodore Roosevelt Round-Up.*

CHAPTER THIRTEEN

The incident involving Dr. Sargeant is discussed in Hagedorn (*Boy's Life*), Edmund Morris, Putnam, and Wood. The quotation concerning TR's "living to the hilt" is from Will Hays in Wood. The philosophy expressed in Roosevelt's essay "The Strenuous Life" is elaborated in his *Autobiography,* especially Chapter II ("The Vigor of Life") and Chapter IX ("Outdoors and Indoors"). The reference to TR's sleeping habits is from Edgar Erastus Clark, in Wood. The incident concerning TR's leaving a meeting to keep a date with children is from Hagedorn (*The Roosevelt Family of Sagamore Hill*). The Roosevelt quotation concerning TR's unwillingness to sit as a mere spectator of sports is from Henry Litchfield West, in Wood. The McCullough quotations are from Kerr. John Milton Cooper's views on Roosevelt as ex-president are discussed extensively in his perceptive essay "If TR Had Gone Down with the Titanic: A Look at His Last Decade," in Naylor et al. The quotation from Henry Luther Stoddard is from Wood. Among the sources consulted on Roosevelt's last months: Abbott, Bishop, Brands, Harbaugh, Lorant, Renehan, Ward, and Wood.

SELECT BIBLIOGRAPHY

Abbott, Lawrence. 1920. *Impressions of Theodore Roosevelt.* Garden City (New York): Doubleday, Page.

Abshire, David. 1998. "The Character of George Washington and the Challenges of the Modern Presidency." 2nd printing. Washington: Center for the Study of the Presidency.

Adams, Henry. 1918. *The Education of Henry Adams.* Boston: Houghton Mifflin.

Ailes, Roger, with Jon Kraushar. 1995. *You Are the Message: Getting What You Want by Being Who You Are.* New York: Currency/Doubleday.

Amos, James E. 1927. *Theodore Roosevelt: Hero to His Valet.* New York: John Day.

Auchincloss, Louis. 2000. *Woodrow Wilson.* New York: Penguin Putnam.

Augustine, Norman, and Kenneth Adelman. 1999. *Shakespeare in Charge: The Bard's Guide to Leading and Succeeding on the Business Stage.* New York: Hyperion.

Bate, Walter Jackson. 1977. *Samuel Johnson.* New York: Harcourt Brace Jovanovich.

Bennis, Warren. 2000. *Managing the Dream: Reflections on Leadership and Change.* Cambridge (Massachusetts): Perseus Publishing.

———. 1989. *On Becoming a Leader.* Reading (Massachusetts): Addison-Wesley.

Bennis, Warren, and Patricia Ward Biederman. 1997. *Organizing Genius: The Secrets of Creative Collaboration.* Reading (Massachusetts): Addison-Wesley.

Bennis, Warren, and Burt Nanus. 1997. *Leaders: Strategies for Taking Charge.* 2nd ed. New York: HarperBusiness.

Beveridge, Albert J. 1928. *Abraham Lincoln: 1809–1858*. 4 vols. New York: Houghton Mifflin.

Bishop, Joseph Bucklin. 1920. *Theodore Roosevelt and His Time—Shown in His Own Letters*. 2 vols. New York: Charles Scribner's Sons.

Blum, John Morton. 1993. *The Republican Roosevelt*. 2nd ed. Cambridge (Massachusetts): Harvard University Press.

Brands, H. W. 1997. *T.R.: The Last Romantic*. New York: Basic Books.

Bryce, James. 1995 reprint [1888]. *The American Commonwealth*. 2 vols. Indianapolis (Indiana): Liberty Fund.

Bull, Bartle. 1988. *Safari: A Chronicle of Adventure*. New York: Viking.

Burns, James MacGregor. 1979. *Leadership*. New York: HarperTorchbooks.

Caroli, Betty Boyd. 1998. *The Roosevelt Women*. New York: Basic Books.

Charnwood, Lord. 1924. *Theodore Roosevelt*. Boston: Atlantic Monthly Press.

Chessman, G. Wallace. 1965. *Governor Theodore Roosevelt: The Albany Apprenticeship, 1898–1900*. Cambridge (Massachusetts): Harvard University Press.

Churchill, Winston S. 1968 reprint [1933]. *Marlborough: His Life and Times*. Henry Steele Commager, ed. New York: Charles Scribner's Sons.

Cooper, John Milton. 1990. *Pivotal Decades: The United States, 1900–1920*. New York: W. W. Norton.

———. 1983. *The Warrior and the Priest: Woodrow Wilson and Theodore Roosevelt*. Cambridge (Massachusetts): Harvard University Press.

Covey, Stephen R. 1990. *The Seven Habits of Highly Effective People*. New York: Fireside.

Crichton, Judy. 1998. *America 1900: The Turning Point*. New York: Henry Holt.

Crocker, H. W., III. 1999. *Robert E. Lee on Leadership*. Rocklin (California): Prima.

Croly, Herbert. 1965 [1909]. *The Promise of American Life*. Cambridge (Massachusetts): Harvard University Press.

Davis, Oscar King. 1925. *Released for Publication: Some Inside Political History of Theodore Roosevelt and His Times, 1898–1918*. Boston: Houghton Mifflin.

Drinker, Frederick E., and Jay Henry Mowbray. 1919. *Theodore Roosevelt: His Life and Work*. National Publishing.

Drucker, Peter F. 1993 reprint [1966]. *The Effective Executive*. New York: HarperBusiness.

Einstein, Lewis. 1930. *Roosevelt: His Mind in Action*. Cambridge (Massachusetts): Riverside.

Felsenthal, Carol. 1988. *Princess Alice: The Life and Times of Alice Roosevelt Longworth*. New York: St. Martin's Press.

Fisher, Roger, William Ury, and Bruce Patton. 1991. *Getting to Yes*. 2nd ed. New York: Penguin Books.

Franklin, Benjamin. 1990. *The Art of Virtue*. George L. Rogers, ed. Eden Prairie (Minnesota): Acorn Publishing.

Gable, John Allen. 1978. *The Bull Moose Years*. Port Washington (New York): Kennikat Press.

Gardner, John W. 1993. *On Leadership*. New York: Free Press.

Gatewood, Willard B., Jr. 1970. *Theodore Roosevelt and the Art of Controversy: Episodes of the White House Years*. Baton Rouge: Louisiana State University Press.

Hackworth, Col. David H., and Julie Sherman. 1990. *About Face: The Odyssey of an American Warrior*. New York: Touchstone Books.

Hagedorn, Hermann. 1950 reprint [1919]. *The Boys' Life of Theodore Roosevelt*. New York: Harper & Brothers.

———. 1954. *The Roosevelt Family of Sagamore Hill*. New York: Macmillan.

Harbaugh, William H. 1997 reprint [1961]. *Power and Responsibility: The Life and Times of Theodore Roosevelt*. Newtown (Connecticut): American Political Biography Press.

Hard, William. 1954 reprint [1919]. "Theodore Roosevelt: A Tribute." New York: Theodore Roosevelt Association.

Harlow, Alvin F. 1943. *Theodore Roosevelt: Strenuous American*. New York: Julian Messner.

Henderson, Daniel. 1919. *"Great-Heart"—The Life Story of Theodore Roosevelt*. 2nd ed. New York: William Edwin Rudge.

Hunter, James C. 1998. *Servant Leadership*. Rocklin (California): Prima.

Isaacs, Stanley M. 1962. "An Interview on Theodore Roosevelt." New York: Theodore Roosevelt Association.

Jessup, Philip C. 1938. *Elihu Root*. 2 vols. New York: Dodd, Mead.

Johnson, Paul. 1997. *A History of the American People*. New York: HarperCollins.

Johnston, William Davison. 1981 reprint [1958]. *TR: Champion of the Strenuous Life*. New York: Theodore Roosevelt Association.

Kipling, Rudyard. 1944 reprint [1939]. *Verse: Definitive Edition*. Garden City: Doubleday, Doran.

Leary, Thomas, and Elizabeth Sholes. 1998. *Buffalo's Pan-American Exposition*. Charleston (South Carolina): Arcadia.

Liddell-Hart, Basil H. 1960 reprint [1954]. *Strategy*. New York: Praeger.

Lorant, Stefan. 1959. *The Life and Times of Theodore Roosevelt*. Garden City (New York): Doubleday.

Maxwell, John C. 1999. *The Twenty-one Indispensable Qualities of a Leader*. Nashville: Thomas Nelson Publishers.

———. 1998. *The Twenty-one Irrefutable Laws of Leadership*. Nashville: Thomas Nelson Publishers.

McCullough, David. 1981. *Mornings on Horseback*. New York: Simon and Schuster.

Miller, Nathan. 1992. *Theodore Roosevelt: A Life*. New York: Quill.

Morgan, John J. B., and Ewing T. Webb. 1932. *Making the Most of Your Life*. New York: Ray Long & Richard R. Smith.

Morison, Elting E. 1960. *Turmoil and Tradition: A Study of the Life and Times of Henry L. Stimson*. Boston: Houghton Mifflin.

Morris, Charles. 1910. *The Marvelous Career of Theodore Roosevelt*. W. E. Scull.

Morris, Edmund. 1979. *The Rise of Theodore Roosevelt*. New York: Coward, McCann & Geoghegan.

Morris, Sylvia Jukes. 1980. *Edith Kermit Roosevelt: Portrait of a First Lady*. New York: Coward, McCann & Geoghegan.

Mowry, George E. 1946. *Theodore Roosevelt and the Progressive Movement*. Madison: University of Wisconsin Press.

Naylor, Natalie A., Douglas Brinkley, and John Allen Gable (eds.). 1992. *Theodore Roosevelt: Many-Sided American*. Interlaken (New York): Heart of the Lakes Publishing.

Neilson, Winthrop. 1953. *The Story of Theodore Roosevelt*. New York: Grosset & Dunlap.

Pinchot, Gifford. 1974 reprint [1947]. *Breaking New Ground*. Washington, D.C.: Island Press.

Pringle, Henry F. 1931. *Theodore Roosevelt*. New York: Blue Ribbon.

Putnam, Carleton. 1958. *Theodore Roosevelt: The Formative Years, 1858–1886*. New York: Charles Scribner's Sons.

Renehan, Edward J. 1998. *The Lion's Pride: Theodore Roosevelt and His Family in Peace and War*. New York: Oxford University Press.

Reynolds, Michael. 1999. *Hemingway: The Final Years*. New York: W. W. Norton.

Riis, Jacob A. 1904. *Theodore Roosevelt the Citizen*. New York: Outlook.

Roberts, J. M. 1999. *The Twentieth Century: The History of the World, 1901 to 2000*. New York: Viking.

Robinson, Corinne Roosevelt. 1921. *My Brother, Theodore Roosevelt*. New York: Charles Scribner's Sons.

Roosevelt, Theodore. 1956. *The Free Citizen: A Summons to the Service of the Democratic Ideal*. Hermann Hagedorn, ed. New York: Macmillan.

———. 1995. *A Bully Father: Theodore Roosevelt's Letters to His Children*. Kerr, Joan Paterson (ed.). New York: Random House.

———. 1903. *California Addresses by President Roosevelt*. San Francisco: California Promotion Committee.

———. 1923. The Americanism of Theodore Roosevelt. Hermann Hagedorn, ed. Boston: Houghton Mifflin.

———. 1951–54. *The Letters of Theodore Roosevelt*. 8 vols. Elting E. Morison, ed. Cambridge (Massachusetts): Harvard University Press.

———. 1989. *Theodore Roosevelt Cyclopedia*. Hart, Albert Bushnell, Herbert Ronald Ferleger, and John Allen Gable (eds.). 2nd ed. Westport (Connecticut): Meckler.

———. 1958. *A Theodore Roosevelt Round-Up.* Hagedorn, Hermann, and Sidney Wallach (eds.). New York: Theodore Roosevelt Association.

———. 1926. *The Works of Theodore Roosevelt: National Edition.* New York: Charles Scribner's Sons.

Simonton, Dean Keith. 1994. *Greatness: Who Makes History and Why.* New York: Guilford Press.

State of New York (Authorized by the Legislature). 1919. *A Memorial to Theodore Roosevelt.* New York: J. B. Lyon.

Steffens, Lincoln. 1931. *The Autobiography of Lincoln Steffens.* New York: Harcourt, Brace & Co.

Street, Julian. 1915. *The Most Interesting American.* New York: Century.

Strouse, Jean. 2000. *Morgan: American Financier.* New York: Perennial.

Sullivan, Mark. 1934 reprint [1925]. *Our Times: The United States, 1900–1925.* 6 vols. New York: Charles Scribner's Sons.

Teague, Michael. 1981. *Mrs. L: Conversations with Alice Roosevelt Longworth.* Garden City (New York): Doubleday.

Thayer, William Roscoe. 1919. *Theodore Roosevelt: An Intimate Biography.* Boston: Houghton Mifflin.

Wagenknecht, Edward. 1958. *The Seven Worlds of Theodore Roosevelt.* New York: Longmans, Green.

Ward, Geoffrey C. 1989. *A First-Class Temperament: The Emergence of Franklin Roosevelt.* New York: Harper & Row.

Washburn, Charles G. 1916. *Theodore Roosevelt: The Logic of His Career.* London: William Heinemann.

White, William Allen. 1946. *The Autobiography of William Allen White.* New York: Macmillan.

Wister, Owen. 1930. *Roosevelt: The Story of a Friendship, 1880–1919.* New York: Macmillan.

Wood, Frederick S. 1927. *Roosevelt As We Knew Him.* Philadelphia: John C. Winston.

Yeats, William Butler. 1996. *The Collected Poems of W. B. Yeats.* 2nd ed. Richard J. Finneran, ed. New York: Scribner Paperback Poetry.

ACKNOWLEDGMENTS

DR. JOHN ALLEN GABLE, executive director of the Theodore Roosevelt Association, based at Sagamore Hill, Oyster Bay, New York, helped make this project possible. Dr. Gable provided guidance from its genesis and reviewed the manuscript with precision. His knowledge of Roosevelt is so extensive—and presented with such enthusiasm and informed immediacy—that in his company one feels TR and his time come alive.

Professor John Milton Cooper was generous in reviewing numerous chapters, applying his formidable skills as a writer and historian—and gracefully but firmly disputing points with which he disagreed, particularly concerning Woodrow Wilson.

Wallace Dailey, curator of the Theodore Roosevelt Collection at Harvard, consented to the use of the photograph on the jacket of this book. Lawrence F. Abbott, who worked with TR at the *Outlook,* believed it to be Roosevelt's favorite photograph of himself.

Among others to whom thanks is owed for their influence or assistance on this work: Dave Anderson, Stephen Anderson, Rachel and Charles Bernheim, Rosaleen Bertolino, Edita Bodner, Andi Reese Brady, Andrew Esposto, Ann Fishman, Elizabeth Fowler, Jay Lee, Kenneth S. MacKenzie, John C. Maxwell, Linda E. Milano, James D. Mullins, Patrick Mullins, Bret Muse, Bo Price, Courtney Price, Juergen Resch,

Brian Runkel, Richard Norton Smith, Yaroslav Sochynsky, Jon Wells, F. Bradford Westerfield, and Michael Young. Special thanks are owed to the Forum publisher Steven K. Martin for his dedication, enthusiasm, and perseverance.

The impetus for this project was supplied by my mother, Augusta Mullins. Her lovingly calculated gift, long ago, of Winthrop Neilson's children's biography of TR sparked my lifelong interest. To paraphrase Henry Adams, the influence of a teacher is infinite.

INDEX

ABOUT THE AUTHOR

James M. Strock is an award-winning writer and speaker. He is the author of *Reagan on Leadership* (Prima, 1998). His San Francisco firm, James Strock & Co. (www.jamesstrock.com), provides management consulting, communications, and dispute resolution services. Educated at Harvard, he has served as the first secretary for environmental protection for the state of California, chief law enforcement officer of the U.S. Environmental Protection Agency, special counsel to the U.S. Senate Environment and Public Works Committee, and general counsel for the U.S. Office of Personnel Management. Strock is a director on corporate and nonprofit boards, a senior fellow at the Pacific Research Institute, and a member of the Council of Foreign Relations.

ABOUT THE THEODORE ROOSEVELT ASSOCIATION

The Theodore Roosevelt Association (TRA), chartered by an act of Congress in 1920, undertakes numerous activities to maintain the memory of the nation's twenty-sixth president. For membership and other information, please contact TRA, Box 719, Oyster Bay, New York 11771. Web address: www.theodoreroosevelt.org.